Praise for *Fundamentals of Software Architecture*

Neal and Mark aren't just outstanding software architects; they are also exceptional teachers. With *Fundamentals of Software Architecture*, they have managed to condense the sprawling topic of architecture into a concise work that reflects their decades of experience. Whether you're new to the role or you've been a practicing architect for many years, this book will help you be better at your job. I only wish they'd written this earlier in my career.

—*Nathaniel Schutta, Architect as a Service, ntschutta.io*

Mark and Neal set out to achieve a formidable goal—to elucidate the many, layered fundamentals required to excel in software architecture—and they completed their quest. The software architecture field continuously evolves, and the role requires a daunting breadth and depth of knowledge and skills. This book will serve as a guide for many as they navigate their journey to software architecture mastery.

—*Rebecca J. Parsons, CTO, ThoughtWorks*

Mark and Neal truly capture real world advice for technologists to drive architecture excellence. They achieve this by identifying common architecture characteristics and the trade-offs that are necessary to drive success.

—*Cassie Shum, Technical Director, ThoughtWorks*

Fundamentals of Software Architecture

An Engineering Approach

Mark Richards and Neal Ford

Beijing · Boston · Farnham · Sebastopol · Tokyo

Fundamentals of Software Architecture

by Mark Richards and Neal Ford

Published by O'Reilly Media, Inc., 1005 Gravenstein Highway North, Sebastopol, CA 95472.

O'Reilly books may be purchased for educational, business, or sales promotional use. Online editions are also available for most titles (*http://oreilly.com*). For more information, contact our corporate/institutional sales department: 800-998-9938 or *corporate@oreilly.com*.

Acquisitions Editor: Chris Guzikowski
Development Editors: Alicia Young and Virginia Wilson
Production Editor: Christopher Faucher
Copyeditor: Sonia Saruba

Proofreader: Amanda Kersey
Indexer: Ellen Troutman-Zaig
Interior Designer: David Futato
Cover Designer: Karen Montgomery
Illustrator: Rebecca Demarest

February 2020:   First Edition

Revision History for the First Edition

2020-01-27:   First Release
2020-06-12:   Second Release
2020-11-06:   Third Release
2021-02-12:   Fourth Release

See *http://oreilly.com/catalog/errata.csp?isbn=9781492043454* for release details.

978-1-492-04345-4

[LSI]

Table of Contents

Preface: Invalidating Axioms

Axiom
> A statement or proposition which is regarded as being established, accepted, or self-evidently true.

Mathematicians create theories based on axioms, assumptions for things indisputably true. Software architects also build theories atop axioms, but the software world is, well, *softer* than mathematics: fundamental things continue to change at a rapid pace, including the axioms we base our theories upon.

The software development ecosystem exists in a constant state of dynamic equilibrium: while it exists in a balanced state at any given point in time, it exhibits *dynamic* behavior over the long term. A great modern example of the nature of this ecosystem follows the ascension of containerization and the attendant changes: tools like Kubernetes (*https://kubernetes.io*) didn't exist a decade ago, yet now entire software conferences exist to service its users. The software ecosystem changes chaotically: one small change causes another small change; when repeated hundreds of times, it generates a new ecosystem.

Architects have an important responsibility to question assumptions and axioms left over from previous eras. Many of the books about software architecture were written in an era that only barely resembles the current world. In fact, the authors believe that we must question fundamental axioms on a regular basis, in light of improved engineering practices, operational ecosystems, software development processes—everything that makes up the messy, dynamic equilibrium where architects and developers work each day.

Careful observers of software architecture over time witnessed an evolution of capabilities. Starting with the engineering practices of Extreme Programming (*http://www.extremeprogramming.org*), continuing with Continuous Delivery, the DevOps revolution, microservices, containerization, and now cloud-based resources, all of these innovations led to new capabilities and trade-offs. As capabilities changed, so did architects' perspectives on the industry. For many years, the tongue-in-cheek definition of software architecture was "the stuff that's hard to change later." Later, the microservices architecture style appeared, where *change* is a first-class design consideration.

Each new era requires new practices, tools, measurements, patterns, and a host of other changes. This book looks at software architecture in modern light, taking into account all the innovations from the last decade, along with some new metrics and measures suited to today's new structures and perspectives.

The subtitle of our book is "An Engineering Approach." Developers have long wished to change software development from a *craft*, where skilled artisans can create one-off works, to an *engineering* discipline, which implies repeatability, rigor, and effective analysis. While software engineering still lags behind other types of engineering disciplines by many orders of magnitude (to be fair, software is a very young discipline compared to most other types of engineering), architects have made huge improvements, which we'll discuss. In particular, modern Agile engineering practices have allowed great strides in the types of systems that architects design.

We also address the critically important issue of *trade-off analysis*. As a software developer, it's easy to become enamored with a particular technology or approach. But architects must always soberly assess the good, bad, and ugly of every choice, and virtually nothing in the real world offers convenient binary choices—everything is a trade-off. Given this pragmatic perspective, we strive to eliminate value judgments about technology and instead focus on analyzing trade-offs to equip our readers with an analytic eye toward technology choices.

This book won't make someone a software architect overnight—it's a nuanced field with many facets. We want to provide existing and burgeoning architects a good modern overview of software architecture and its many aspects, from structure to soft skills. While this book covers well-known patterns, we take a new approach, leaning on lessons learned, tools, engineering practices, and other input. We take many existing axioms in software architecture and rethink them in light of the current ecosystem, and design architectures, taking the modern landscape into account.

Conventions Used in This Book

The following typographical conventions are used in this book:

Italic
> Indicates new terms, URLs, email addresses, filenames, and file extensions.

`Constant width`
> Used for program listings, as well as within paragraphs to refer to program elements such as variable or function names, databases, data types, environment variables, statements, and keywords.

Constant width bold

Shows commands or other text that should be typed literally by the user.

Constant width italic

Shows text that should be replaced with user-supplied values or by values determined by context.

 This element signifies a tip or suggestion.

Using Code Examples

Supplemental material (code examples, exercises, etc.) is available for download at *http://fundamentalsofsoftwarearchitecture.com*.

If you have a technical question or a problem using the code examples, please send email to *bookquestions@oreilly.com*.

This book is here to help you get your job done. In general, if example code is offered with this book, you may use it in your programs and documentation. You do not need to contact us for permission unless you're reproducing a significant portion of the code. For example, writing a program that uses several chunks of code from this book does not require permission. Selling or distributing examples from O'Reilly books does require permission. Answering a question by citing this book and quoting example code does not require permission. Incorporating a significant amount of example code from this book into your product's documentation does require permission.

We appreciate, but generally do not require, attribution. An attribution usually includes the title, author, publisher, and ISBN. For example: "*Fundamentals of Software Architecture* by Mark Richards and Neal Ford (O'Reilly). Copyright 2020 Mark Richards, Neal Ford, 978-1-492-04345-4."

If you feel your use of code examples falls outside fair use or the permission given above, feel free to contact us at *permissions@oreilly.com*.

O'Reilly Online Learning

 For more than 40 years, *O'Reilly Media* has provided technology and business training, knowledge, and insight to help companies succeed.

Our unique network of experts and innovators share their knowledge and expertise through books, articles, and our online learning platform. O'Reilly's online learning platform gives you on-demand access to live training courses, in-depth learning paths, interactive coding environments, and a vast collection of text and video from O'Reilly and 200+ other publishers. For more information, please visit *http:// oreilly.com*.

How to Contact Us

Please address comments and questions concerning this book to the publisher:

O'Reilly Media, Inc.
1005 Gravenstein Highway North
Sebastopol, CA 95472
800-998-9938 (in the United States or Canada)
707-829-0515 (international or local)
707-829-0104 (fax)

We have a web page for this book, where we list errata, examples, and any additional information. You can access this page at *https://oreil.ly/fundamentals-of-software-architecture*.

Email *bookquestions@oreilly.com* to comment or ask technical questions about this book.

For news and information about our books and courses, visit *http://oreilly.com*.

Find us on Facebook: *http://facebook.com/oreilly*

Follow us on Twitter: *http://twitter.com/oreillymedia*

Watch us on YouTube: *http://www.youtube.com/oreillymedia*

Acknowledgments

Mark and Neal would like to thank all the people who attended our classes, workshops, conference sessions, user group meetings, as well as all the other people who listened to versions of this material and provided invaluable feedback. We would also like to thank the publishing team at O'Reilly, who made this as painless an experience as writing a book can be. We would also like to thank No Stuff Just Fluff director Jay Zimmerman for creating a conference series that allows good technical content to grow and spread, and all the other speakers whose feedback and tear-soaked shoulders we appreciate. We would also like to thank a few random oases of sanity-preserving and idea-sparking groups that have names like Pasty Geeks and the Hacker B&B.

Acknowledgments from Mark Richards

In addition to the preceding acknowledgments, I would like to thank my lovely wife, Rebecca. Taking everything else on at home and sacrificing the opportunity to work on your own book allowed me to do additional consulting gigs and speak at more conferences and training classes, giving me the opportunity to practice and hone the material for this book. You are the best.

Acknowledgments from Neal Ford

Neal would like to thank his extended family, ThoughtWorks as a collective, and Rebecca Parsons and Martin Fowler as individual parts of it. ThoughtWorks is an extraordinary group who manage to produce value for customers while keeping a keen eye toward why things work so that that we can improve them. ThoughtWorks supported this book in many myriad ways and continues to grow ThoughtWorkers who challenge and inspire every day. Neal would also like to thank our neighborhood cocktail club for a regular escape from routine. Lastly, Neal would like to thank his wife, Candy, whose tolerance for things like book writing and conference speaking apparently knows no bounds. For decades she's kept me grounded and sane enough to function, and I hope she will for decades more as the love of my life.

CHAPTER 1

Introduction

The job "software architect" appears near the top of numerous lists of best jobs across the world. Yet when readers look at the *other* jobs on those lists (like nurse practitioner or finance manager), there's a clear career path for them. Why is there no path for software architects?

First, the industry doesn't have a good definition of software architecture itself. When we teach foundational classes, students often ask for a concise definition of what a software architect does, and we have adamantly refused to give one. And we're not the only ones. In his famous whitepaper "Who Needs an Architect?" (*https://oreil.ly/-Dbzs*) Martin Fowler famously refused to try to define it, instead falling back on the famous quote:

> Architecture is about the important stuff…whatever that is.
>
> —Ralph Johnson

When pressed, we created the mindmap shown in Figure 1-1, which is woefully incomplete but indicative of the scope of software architecture. We will, in fact, offer our definition of software architecture shortly.

Second, as illustrated in the mindmap, the role of software architect embodies a massive amount and scope of responsibility that continues to expand. A decade ago, software architects dealt only with the purely technical aspects of architecture, like modularity, components, and patterns. Since then, because of new architectural styles that leverage a wider swath of capabilities (like microservices), the role of software architect has expanded. We cover the many intersections of architecture and the remainder of the organization in "Intersection of Architecture and…" on page 13.

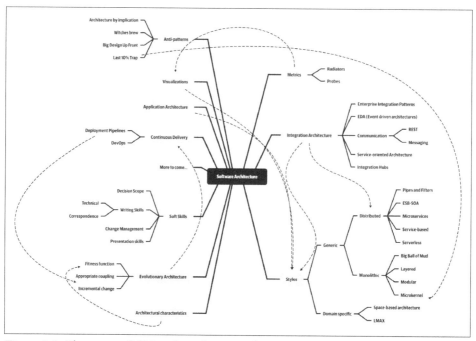

Figure 1-1. The responsibilities of a software architect encompass technical abilities, soft skills, operational awareness, and a host of others

Third, software architecture is a constantly moving target because of the rapidly evolving software development ecosystem. Any definition cast today will be hopelessly outdated in a few years. The Wikipedia definition of software architecture (*https://oreil.ly/YLsY2*) provides a reasonable overview, but many statements are outdated, such as "Software architecture is about making fundamental structural choices which are costly to change once implemented." Yet architects designed modern architectural styles like microservices with the idea of incremental built in—it is no longer expensive to make structural changes in microservices. Of course, that capability means trade-offs with other concerns, such as coupling. Many books on software architecture treat it as a static problem; once solved, we can safely ignore it. However, we recognize the inherent dynamic nature of software architecture, including the definition itself, throughout the book.

Fourth, much of the material about software architecture has only historical relevance. Readers of the Wikipedia page won't fail to notice the bewildering array of acronyms and cross-references to an entire universe of knowledge. Yet, many of these acronyms represent outdated or failed attempts. Even solutions that were perfectly valid a few years ago cannot work now because the context has changed. The history of software architecture is littered with things architects have tried, only to realize the damaging side effects. We cover many of those lessons in this book.

Why a book on software architecture fundamentals now? The scope of software architecture isn't the only part of the development world that constantly changes. New technologies, techniques, capabilities…in fact, it's easier to find things that haven't changed over the last decade than to list all the changes. Software architects must make decisions within this constantly changing ecosystem. Because everything changes, including foundations upon which we make decisions, architects should reexamine some core axioms that informed earlier writing about software architecture. For example, earlier books about software architecture don't consider the impact of DevOps because it didn't exist when these books were written.

When studying architecture, readers must keep in mind that, like much art, it can only be understood in context. Many of the decisions architects made were based on realities of the environment they found themselves in. For example, one of the major goals of late 20th-century architecture included making the most efficient use of shared resources, because all the infrastructure at the time was expensive and commercial: operating systems, application servers, database servers, and so on. Imagine strolling into a 2002 data center and telling the head of operations "Hey, I have a great idea for a revolutionary style of architecture, where each service runs on its own isolated machinery, with its own dedicated database (describing what we now know as microservices). So, that means I'll need 50 licenses for Windows, another 30 application server licenses, and at least 50 database server licenses." In 2002, trying to build an architecture like microservices would be inconceivably expensive. Yet, with the advent of open source during the intervening years, coupled with updated engineering practices via the DevOps revolution, we can reasonably build an architecture as described. Readers should keep in mind that all architectures are a product of their context.

Defining Software Architecture

The industry as a whole has struggled to precisely define "software architecture." Some architects refer to software architecture as the *blueprint* of the system, while others define it as the *roadmap* for developing a system. The issue with these common definitions is understanding what the blueprint or roadmap actually contains. For example, what is analyzed when an architect *analyzes* an architecture?

Figure 1-2 illustrates a way to think about software architecture. In this definition, software architecture consists of the *structure* of the system (denoted as the heavy black lines supporting the architecture), combined with *architecture characteristics* ("-ilities") the system must support, *architecture decisions*, and finally *design principles*.

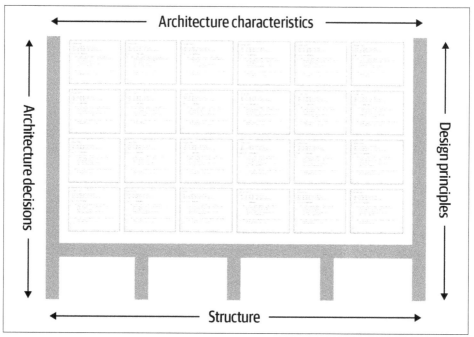

Figure 1-2. Architecture consists of the structure combined with architecture characteristics ("-ilities"), architecture decisions, and design principles

The *structure* of the system, as illustrated in Figure 1-3, refers to the type of architecture style (or styles) the system is implemented in (such as microservices, layered, or microkernel). Describing an architecture solely by the structure does not wholly elucidate an architecture. For example, suppose an architect is asked to describe an architecture, and that architect responds "it's a microservices architecture." Here, the architect is only talking about the *structure* of the system, but not the *architecture* of the system. Knowledge of the architecture characteristics, architecture decisions, and design principles is also needed to fully understand the architecture of the system.

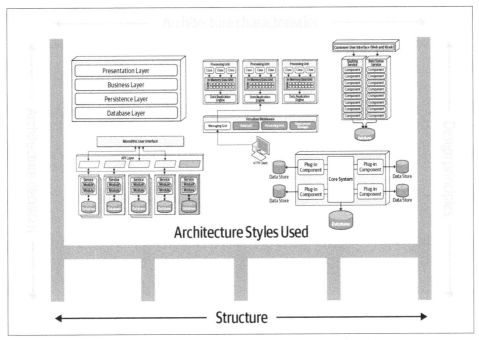

Figure 1-3. Structure refers to the type of architecture styles used in the system

Architecture characteristics are another dimension of defining software architecture (see Figure 1-4). The architecture characteristics define the success criteria of a system, which is generally orthogonal to the functionality of the system. Notice that all of the characteristics listed do not require knowledge of the functionality of the system, yet they are required in order for the system to function properly. Architecture characteristics are so important that we've devoted several chapters in this book to understanding and defining them.

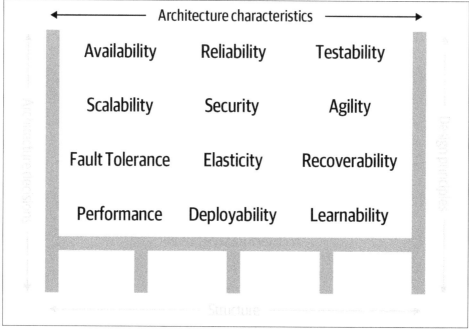

Figure 1-4. Architecture characteristics refers to the "-ilities" that the system must support

The next factor that defines software architecture is *architecture decisions*. Architecture decisions define the rules for how a system should be constructed. For example, an architect might make an architecture decision that only the business and services layers within a layered architecture can access the database (see Figure 1-5), restricting the presentation layer from making direct database calls. Architecture decisions form the constraints of the system and direct the development teams on what is and what isn't allowed.

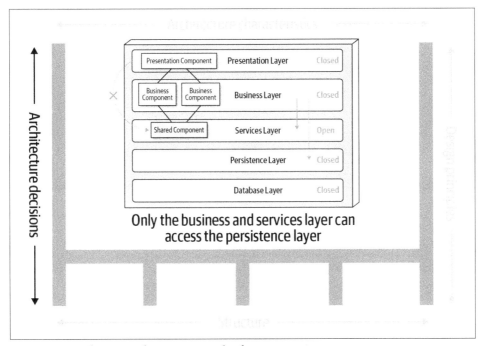

Figure 1-5. Architecture decisions are rules for constructing systems

If a particular architecture decision cannot be implemented in one part of the system due to some condition or other constraint, that decision (or rule) can be broken through something called a *variance*. Most organizations have variance models that are used by an architecture review board (ARB) or chief architect. Those models formalize the process for seeking a variance to a particular standard or architecture decision. An exception to a particular architecture decision is analyzed by the ARB (or chief architect if no ARB exists) and is either approved or denied based on justifications and trade-offs.

The last factor in the definition of architecture is *design principles*. A design principle differs from an architecture decision in that a design principle is a *guideline* rather than a hard-and-fast *rule*. For example, the design principle illustrated in Figure 1-6 states that the development teams should leverage asynchronous messaging between services within a microservices architecture to increase performance. An architecture decision (rule) could never cover every condition and option for communication between services, so a design principle can be used to provide guidance for the preferred method (in this case, asynchronous messaging) to allow the developer to choose a more appropriate communication protocol (such as REST or gRPC) given a specific circumstance.

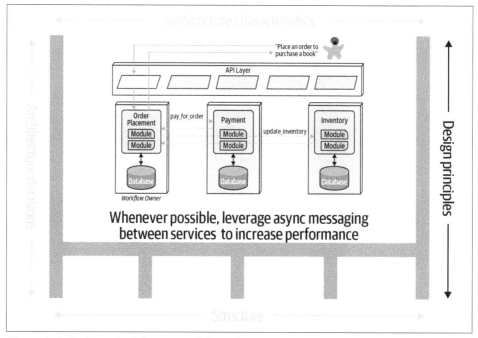

Figure 1-6. Design principles are guidelines for constructing systems

Expectations of an Architect

Defining the role of a software architect presents as much difficulty as defining software architecture. It can range from expert programmer up to defining the strategic technical direction for the company. Rather than waste time on the fool's errand of defining the role, we recommend focusing on the *expectations* of an architect.

There are eight core expectations placed on a software architect, irrespective of any given role, title, or job description:

- Make architecture decisions
- Continually analyze the architecture
- Keep current with latest trends
- Ensure compliance with decisions
- Diverse exposure and experience
- Have business domain knowledge
- Possess interpersonal skills
- Understand and navigate politics

The first key to effectiveness and success in the software architect role depends on understanding and practicing each of these expectations.

Make Architecture Decisions

An architect is expected to define the architecture decisions and design principles used to guide technology decisions within the team, the department, or across the enterprise.

Guide is the key operative word in this first expectation. An architect should *guide* rather than *specify* technology choices. For example, an architect might make a decision to use React.js for frontend development. In this case, the architect is making a technical decision rather than an architectural decision or design principle that will help the development team make choices. An architect should instead instruct development teams to use a *reactive-based framework for frontend web development*, hence guiding the development team in making the choice between Angular, Elm, React.js, Vue, or any of the other reactive-based web frameworks.

Guiding technology choices through architecture decisions and design principles is difficult. The key to making effective architectural decisions is asking whether the architecture decision is helping to *guide* teams in making the right technical choice or whether the architecture decision *makes* the technical choice for them. That said, an architect on occasion might need to make specific technology decisions in order to preserve a particular architectural characteristic such as scalability, performance, or availability. In this case it would be still considered an architectural decision, even though it specifies a particular technology. Architects often struggle with finding the correct line, so Chapter 19 is entirely about architecture decisions.

Continually Analyze the Architecture

An architect is expected to continually analyze the architecture and current technology environment and then recommend solutions for improvement.

This expectation of an architect refers to *architecture vitality*, which assesses how viable the architecture that was defined three or more years ago is *today*, given changes in both business and technology. In our experience, not enough architects focus their energies on continually analyzing existing architectures. As a result, most architectures experience elements of structural decay, which occurs when developers make coding or design changes that impact the required architectural characteristics, such as performance, availability, and scalability.

Other forgotten aspects of this expectation that architects frequently forget are testing and release environments. Agility for code modification has obvious benefits, but if it takes teams weeks to test changes and months for releases, then architects cannot achieve agility in the overall architecture.

An architect must holistically analyze changes in technology and problem domains to determine the soundness of the architecture. While this kind of consideration rarely appears in a job posting, architects must meet this expectation to keep applications relevant.

Keep Current with Latest Trends

An architect is expected to keep current with the latest technology and industry trends.

Developers must keep up to date on the latest technologies they use on a daily basis to remain relevant (and to retain a job!). An architect has an even more critical requirement to keep current on the latest technical and industry trends. The decisions an architect makes tend to be long-lasting and difficult to change. Understanding and following key trends helps the architect prepare for the future and make the correct decision.

Tracking trends and keeping current with those trends is hard, particularly for a software architect. In Chapter 24 we discuss various techniques and resources on how to do this.

Ensure Compliance with Decisions

An architect is expected to ensure compliance with architecture decisions and design principles.

Ensuring compliance means that the architect is continually verifying that development teams are following the architecture decisions and design principles defined, documented, and communicated by the architect. Consider the scenario where an architect makes a decision to restrict access to the database in a layered architecture to only the business and services layers (and not the presentation layer). This means that the presentation layer must go through all layers of the architecture to make even the simplest of database calls. A user interface developer might disagree with this decision and access the database (or the persistence layer) directly for performance reasons. However, the architect made that architecture decision for a specific reason: to control change. By closing the layers, database changes can be made without impacting the presentation layer. By not ensuring compliance with architecture decisions, violations like this can occur, the architecture will not meet the required architectural characteristics ("-ilities"), and the application or system will not work as expected.

In Chapter 6 we talk more about measuring compliance using automated fitness functions and automated tools.

Diverse Exposure and Experience

An architect is expected to have exposure to multiple and diverse technologies, frameworks, platforms, and environments.

This expectation does not mean an architect must be an expert in every framework, platform, and language, but rather that an architect must at least be familiar with a variety of technologies. Most environments these days are heterogeneous, and at a minimum an architect should know how to interface with multiple systems and services, irrespective of the language, platform, and technology those systems or services are written in.

One of the best ways of mastering this expectation is for the architect to stretch their comfort zone. Focusing only on a single technology or platform is a safe haven. An effective software architect should be aggressive in seeking out opportunities to gain experience in multiple languages, platforms, and technologies. A good way of mastering this expectation is to focus on technical breadth rather than technical depth. Technical breadth includes the stuff you know about, but not at a detailed level, combined with the stuff you know a lot about. For example, it is far more valuable for an architect to be familiar with 10 different caching products and the associated pros and cons of each rather than to be an expert in only one of them.

Have Business Domain Knowledge

An architect is expected to have a certain level of business domain expertise.

Effective software architects understand not only technology but also the business domain of a problem space. Without business domain knowledge, it is difficult to understand the business problem, goals, and requirements, making it difficult to design an effective architecture to meet the requirements of the business. Imagine being an architect at a large financial institution and not understanding common financial terms such as an average directional index, aleatory contracts, rates rally, or even nonpriority debt. Without this knowledge, an architect cannot communicate with stakeholders and business users and will quickly lose credibility.

The most successful architects we know are those who have broad, hands-on technical knowledge coupled with a strong knowledge of a particular domain. These software architects are able to effectively communicate with C-level executives and business users using the domain knowledge and language that these stakeholders know and understand. This in turn creates a strong level of confidence that the software architect knows what they are doing and is competent to create an effective and correct architecture.

Possess Interpersonal Skills

An architect is expected to possess exceptional interpersonal skills, including teamwork, facilitation, and leadership.

Having exceptional leadership and interpersonal skills is a difficult expectation for most developers and architects. As technologists, developers and architects like to solve technical problems, not people problems. However, as Gerald Weinberg (*https://oreil.ly/wyDB8*) was famous for saying, "no matter what they tell you, it's always a people problem." An architect is not only expected to provide technical guidance to the team, but is also expected to lead the development teams through the implementation of the architecture. Leadership skills are at least half of what it takes to become an effective software architect, regardless of the role or title the architect has.

The industry is flooded with software architects, all competing for a limited number of architecture positions. Having strong leadership and interpersonal skills is a good way for an architect to differentiate themselves from other architects and stand out from the crowd. We've known many software architects who are excellent technologists but are ineffective architects due to the inability to lead teams, coach and mentor developers, and effectively communicate ideas and architecture decisions and principles. Needless to say, those architects have difficulties holding a position or job.

Understand and Navigate Politics

An architect is expected to understand the political climate of the enterprise and be able to navigate the politics.

It might seem rather strange talk about negotiation and navigating office politics in a book about software architecture. To illustrate how important and necessary negotiation skills are, consider the scenario where a developer makes the decision to leverage the strategy pattern (*https://oreil.ly/QG3RQ*) to reduce the overall cyclomatic complexity of a particular piece of complex code. Who really cares? One might applaud the developer for using such a pattern, but in almost all cases the developer does not need to seek approval for such a decision.

Now consider the scenario where an architect, responsible for a large customer relationship management system, is having issues controlling database access from other systems, securing certain customer data, and making any database schema change because too many other systems are using the CRM database. The architect therefore makes the decision to create what are called *application silos*, where each application database is only accessible from the application owning that database. Making this decision will give the architect better control over the customer data, security, and change control. However, unlike the previous developer scenario, this decision will also be challenged by almost everyone in the company (with the possible exception of the CRM application team, of course). Other applications need the customer management data. If those applications are no longer able to access the database directly, they must now ask the CRM system for the data, requiring remote access calls through REST, SOAP, or some other remote access protocol.

The main point is that *almost every decision an architect makes will be challenged*. Architectural decisions will be challenged by product owners, project managers, and business stakeholders due to increased costs or increased effort (time) involved. Architectural decisions will also be challenged by developers who feel their approach is better. In either case, the architect must navigate the politics of the company and apply basic negotiation skills to get most decisions approved. This fact can be very frustrating to a software architect, because most decisions made as a developer did not require approval or even a review. Programming aspects such as code structure, class design, design pattern selection, and sometimes even language choice are all part of the art of programming. However, an architect, now able to finally be able to make broad and important decisions, must justify and fight for almost every one of those decisions. Negotiation skills, like leadership skills, are so critical and necessary that we've dedicated an entire chapter in the book to understanding them (see Chapter 23).

Intersection of Architecture and…

The scope of software architecture has grown over the last decade to encompass more and more responsibility and perspective. A decade ago, the typical relationship between architecture and operations was contractual and formal, with lots of bureaucracy. Most companies, trying to avoid the complexity of hosting their own operations, frequently outsourced operations to a third-party company, with contractual obligations for service-level agreements, such as uptime, scale, responsiveness, and a host of other important architectural characteristics. Now, architectures such as microservices freely leverage former solely operational concerns. For example, elastic scale was once painfully built into architectures (see Chapter 15), while microservices handled it less painfully via a liaison between architects and DevOps.

History: Pets.com and Why We Have Elastic Scale

The history of software development contains rich lessons, both good and bad. We assume that current capabilities (like elastic scale) just appeared one day because of some clever developer, but those ideas were often born of hard lessons. Pets.com represents an early example of hard lessons learned. Pets.com appeared in the early days of the internet, hoping to become the Amazon.com of pet supplies. Fortunately, they had a brilliant marketing department, which invented a compelling mascot: a sock puppet with a microphone that said irreverent things. The mascot became a superstar, appearing in public at parades and national sporting events.

Unfortunately, management at Pets.com apparently spent all the money on the mascot, not on infrastructure. Once orders started pouring in, they weren't prepared. The website was slow, transactions were lost, deliveries delayed, and so on…pretty much the worst-case scenario. So bad, in fact, that the business closed shortly after its disastrous Christmas rush, selling the only remaining valuable asset (the mascot) to a competitor.

What the company needed was elastic scale: the ability to spin up more instances of resources, as needed. Cloud providers offer this feature as a commodity, but in the early days of the internet, companies had to manage their own infrastructure, and many fell victim to a previously unheard of phenomenon: too much success can kill the business. Pets.com and other similar horror stories led engineers to develop the frameworks that architects enjoy now.

The following sections delve into some of the newer intersections between the role of architect and other parts of an organization, highlighting new capabilities and responsibilities for architects.

Engineering Practices

Traditionally, software architecture was separate from the development process used to create software. Dozens of popular methodologies exist to build software, including Waterfall and many flavors of Agile (such as Scrum, Extreme Programming, Lean, and Crystal), which mostly don't impact software architecture.

However, over the last few years, engineering advances have thrust process concerns upon software architecture. It is useful to separate software development *process* from *engineering practices*. By *process*, we mean how teams are formed and managed, how meetings are conducted, and workflow organization; it refers to the mechanics of how people organize and interact. Software *engineering* practices, on the other hand, refer to process-agnostic practices that have illustrated, repeatable benefit. For example, continuous integration is a proven engineering practice that doesn't rely on a particular process.

The Path from Extreme Programming to Continuous Delivery

The origins of Extreme Programming (XP) (*http://www.extremeprogramming.org*) nicely illustrate the difference between *process* and *engineering*. In the early 1990s, a group of experienced software developers, led by Kent Beck, started questioning the dozens of different development processes popular at the time. In their experience, it seemed that none of them created repeatably good outcomes. One of the XP founders said that choosing one of the extant processes was "no more guarantee of project success than flipping a coin." They decided to rethink how to build software, and they started the XP project in March of 1996. To inform their process, they rejected the conventional wisdom and focused on the *practices* that led to project success in the past, pushed to the extreme. Their reasoning was that they'd seen a correlation on previous projects between more tests and higher quality. Thus, the XP approach to testing took the practice to the extreme: do test-first development, ensuring that all code is tested before it enters the code base.

XP was lumped into other popular Agile processes that shared similar perspectives, but it was one of the few methodologies that included engineering practices such as automation, testing, continuous integration, and other concrete, experienced-based techniques. The efforts to continue advancing the engineering side of software development continued with the book *Continuous Delivery* (Addison-Wesley Professional)—an updated version of many XP practices—and came to fruition in the DevOps movement. In many ways, the DevOps revolution occurred when operations adopted engineering practices originally espoused by XP: automation, testing, declarative single source of truth, and others.

We strongly support these advances, which form the incremental steps that will eventually graduate software development into a proper engineering discipline.

Focusing on engineering practices is important. First, software development lacks many of the features of more mature engineering disciplines. For example, civil engineers can predict structural change with much more accuracy than similarly important aspects of software structure. Second, one of the Achilles heels of software development is estimation—how much time, how many resources, how much money? Part of this difficulty lies with antiquated accounting practices that cannot accommodate the exploratory nature of software development, but another part is because we're traditionally bad at estimation, at least in part because of *unknown unknowns*.

> …because as we know, there are known knowns; there are things we know we know. We also know there are known unknowns; that is to say we know there are some things we do not know. But there are also unknown unknowns—the ones we don't know we don't know.
>
> —Former United States Secretary of Defense Donald Rumsfeld

Unknown unknowns are the nemesis of software systems. Many projects start with a list of *known unknowns*: things developers must learn about the domain and technology they know are upcoming. However, projects also fall victim to *unknown unknowns*: things no one knew were going to crop up yet have appeared unexpectedly. This is why all "Big Design Up Front" software efforts suffer: architects cannot design for unknown unknowns. To quote Mark (one of your authors):

> All architectures become iterative because of *unknown unknowns*, Agile just recognizes this and does it sooner.

Thus, while process is mostly separate from architecture, an iterative process fits the nature of software architecture better. Teams trying to build a modern system such as microservices using an antiquated process like Waterfall will find a great deal of friction from an antiquated process that ignores the reality of how software comes together.

Often, the architect is also the technical leader on projects and therefore determines the engineering practices the team uses. Just as architects must carefully consider the problem domain before choosing an architecture, they must also ensure that the architectural style and engineering practices form a symbiotic mesh. For example, a microservices architecture assumes automated machine provisioning, automated testing and deployment, and a raft of other assumptions. Trying to build one of these architectures with an antiquated operations group, manual processes, and little testing creates tremendous friction and challenges to success. Just as different problem domains lend themselves toward certain architectural styles, engineering practices have the same kind of symbiotic relationship.

The evolution of thought leading from Extreme Programming to Continuous Delivery continues. Recent advances in engineering practices allow new capabilities within architecture. Neal's most recent book, *Building Evolutionary Architectures* (O'Reilly), highlights new ways to think about the intersection of engineering practices and architecture, allowing better automation of architectural governance. While we won't summarize that book here, it gives an important new nomenclature and way of thinking about architectural characteristics that will infuse much of the remainder of this book. Neal's book covers techniques for building architectures that change gracefully over time. In Chapter 4, we describe architecture as the combination of requirements and additional concerns, as illustrated in Figure 1-7.

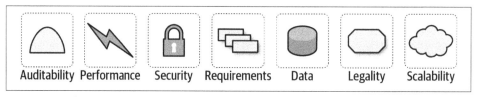

Figure 1-7. The architecture for a software system consists of both requirements and all the other architectural characteristics

As any experience in the software development world illustrates, nothing remains static. Thus, architects may design a system to meet certain criteria, but that design must survive both implementation (how can architects make sure that their design is implemented correctly) and the inevitable change driven by the software development ecosystem. What we need is an *evolutionary architecture*.

Building Evolutionary Architectures introduces the concept of using *fitness functions* to protect (and govern) architectural characteristics as change occurs over time. The concept comes from evolutionary computing. When designing a genetic algorithm, developers have a variety of techniques to mutate the solution, evolving new solutions iteratively. When designing such an algorithm for a specific goal, developers must measure the outcome to see if it is closer or further away from an optimal solution; that measure is a fitness function. For example, if developers designed a genetic algorithm to solve the traveling salesperson problem (whose goal is the shortest route between various cities), the fitness function would look at the path length.

Building Evolutionary Architectures co-opts this idea to create *architectural fitness functions*: an objective integrity assessment of some architectural characteristic(s). This assessment may include a variety of mechanisms, such as metrics, unit tests, monitors, and chaos engineering. For example, an architect may identify page load time as an importance characteristic of the architecture. To allow the system to change without degrading performance, the architecture builds a fitness function as a test that measures page load time for each page and then runs the test as part of the continuous integration for the project. Thus, architects always know the status of critical parts of the architecture because they have a verification mechanism in the form of fitness functions for each part.

We won't go into the full details of fitness functions here. However, we will point out opportunities and examples of the approach where applicable. Note the correlation between how often fitness functions execute and the feedback they provide. You'll see that adopting Agile engineering practices such as continuous integration, automated machine provisioning, and similar practices makes building resilient architectures easier. It also illustrates how intertwined architecture has become with engineering practices.

Operations/DevOps

The most obvious recent intersection between architecture and related fields occurred with the advent of DevOps, driven by some rethinking of architectural axioms. For many years, many companies considered operations as a separate function from software development; they often outsource operations to another company as a cost-saving measure. Many architectures designed during the 1990s and 2000s assumed that architects couldn't control operations and were built defensively around that restriction (for a good example of this, see Space-Based Architecture in Chapter 15).

However, a few years ago, several companies started experimenting with new forms of architecture that combine many operational concerns with the architecture. For example, in older-style architectures, such as ESB-driven SOA, the architecture was designed to handle things like elastic scale, greatly complicating the architecture in the process. Basically, architects were forced to defensively design around the limitations introduced because of the cost-saving measure of outsourcing operations. Thus, they built architectures that could handle scale, performance, elasticity, and a host of other capabilities internally. The side effect of that design was vastly more complex architecture.

The builders of the microservices style of architecture realized that these operational concerns are better handled by operations. By creating a liaison between architecture and operations, the architects can simplify the design and rely on operations for the things they handle best. Thus, realizing a misappropriation of resources led to accidental complexity, and architects and operations teamed up to create microservices, the details of which we cover in Chapter 17.

Process

Another axiom is that software architecture is mostly orthogonal to the software development process; the way that you build software (*process*) has little impact on the software architecture (*structure*). Thus, while the software development process a team uses has some impact on software architecture (especially around engineering practices), historically they have been thought of as mostly separate. Most books on software architecture ignore the software development process, making specious assumptions about things like predictability. However, the process by which teams develop software has an impact on many facets of software architecture. For example, many companies over the last few decades have adopted Agile development methodologies because of the nature of software. Architects in Agile projects can assume iterative development and therefore a faster feedback loop for decisions. That in turn allows architects to be more aggressive about experimentation and other knowledge that relies on feedback.

As the previous quote from Mark observes, all architecture becomes iterative; it's only a matter of time. Toward that end, we're going assume a baseline of Agile methodologies throughout and call out exceptions where appropriate. For example, it is still common for many monolithic architectures to use older processes because of their age, politics, or other mitigating factors unrelated to software.

One critical aspect of architecture where Agile methodologies shine is restructuring. Teams often find that they need to migrate their architecture from one pattern to another. For example, a team started with a monolithic architecture because it was easy and fast to bootstrap, but now they need to move it to a more modern architecture. Agile methodologies support these kinds of changes better than planning-heavy processes because of the tight feedback loop and encouragement of techniques like the Strangler Pattern (*https://oreil.ly/ZRpCc*) and feature toggles (*https://trunkbasedde velopment.com*).

Data

A large percentage of serious application development includes external data storage, often in the form of a relational (or, increasingly, NoSQL) database. However, many books about software architecture include only a light treatment of this important aspect of architecture. Code and data have a symbiotic relationship: one isn't useful without the other.

Database administrators often work alongside architects to build data architecture for complex systems, analyzing how relationships and reuse will affect a portfolio of applications. We won't delve into that level of specialized detail in this book. At the same time, we won't ignore the existence and dependence on external storage. In particular, when we talk about the operational aspects of architecture and *architectural quantum* (see "Architectural Quanta and Granularity" on page 92), we include important external concerns such as databases.

Laws of Software Architecture

While the scope of software architecture is almost impossibly broad, unifying elements do exist. The authors have first and foremost learned the *First Law of Software Architecture* by constantly stumbling across it:

> Everything in software architecture is a trade-off.
>
> —First Law of Software Architecture

Nothing exists on a nice, clean spectrum for software architects. Every decision must take into account many opposing factors.

> If an architect thinks they have discovered something that *isn't* a trade-off, more likely they just haven't *identified* the trade-off yet.
>
> —Corollary 1

We define software architecture in terms beyond structural scaffolding, incorporating principles, characteristics, and so on. Architecture is broader than just the combination of structural elements, reflected in our *Second Law of Software Architecture*:

> *Why* is more important than *how*.
>
> —Second Law of Software Architecture

The authors discovered the importance of this perspective when we tried keeping the results of exercises done by students during workshop as they crafted architecture solutions. Because the exercises were timed, the only artifacts we kept were the diagrams representing the topology. In other words, we captured *how* they solved the problem but not *why* the team made particular choices. An architect can look at an existing system they have no knowledge of and ascertain how the structure of the architecture works, but will struggle explaining why certain choices were made versus others.

Throughout the book, we highlight *why* architects make certain decisions along with trade-offs. We also highlight good techniques for capturing important decisions in "Architecture Decision Records" on page 285.

PART I

Foundations

To understand important trade-offs in architecture, developers must understand some basic concepts and terminology concerning components, modularity, coupling, and connascence.

CHAPTER 2

Architectural Thinking

An architect sees things differently from a developer's point of view, much in the same way a meteorologist might see clouds differently from an artist's point of view. This is called *architectural thinking*. Unfortunately, too many architects believe that architectural thinking is simply just "thinking about the architecture."

Architectural thinking is much more than that. It is seeing things with an architectural eye, or an architectural point of view. There are four main aspects of thinking like an architect. First, it's understanding the difference between architecture and design and knowing how to collaborate with development teams to make architecture work. Second, it's about having a wide breadth of technical knowledge while still maintaining a certain level of technical depth, allowing the architect to see solutions and possibilities that others do not see. Third, it's about understanding, analyzing, and reconciling trade-offs between various solutions and technologies. Finally, it's about understanding the importance of business drivers and how they translate to architectural concerns.

In this chapter we explore these four aspects of thinking like an architect and seeing things with an architectural eye.

Architecture Versus Design

The difference between architecture and design is often a confusing one. Where does architecture end and design begin? What responsibilities does an architect have versus those of a developer? Thinking like an architect is knowing the difference between architecture and design and seeing how the two integrate closely to form solutions to business and technical problems.

Consider Figure 2-1, which illustrates the traditional responsibilities an architect has, as compared to those of a developer. As shown in the diagram, an architect is responsible for things like analyzing business requirements to extract and define the architectural characteristics ("-ilities"), selecting which architecture patterns and styles would fit the problem domain, and creating components (the building blocks of the system). The artifacts created from these activities are then handed off to the development team, which is responsible for creating class diagrams for each component, creating user interface screens, and developing and testing source code.

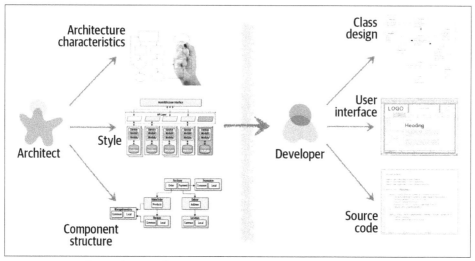

Figure 2-1. Traditional view of architecture versus design

There are several issues with the traditional responsibility model illustrated in Figure 2-1. As a matter of fact, this illustration shows exactly why architecture rarely works. Specifically, it is the unidirectional arrow passing though the virtual and physical barriers separating the architect from the developer that causes all of the problems associated with architecture. Decisions an architect makes sometimes never make it to the development teams, and decisions development teams make that change the architecture rarely get back to the architect. In this model the architect is disconnected from the development teams, and as such the architecture rarely provides what it was originally set out to do.

To make architecture work, both the physical and virtual barriers that exist between architects and developers must be broken down, thus forming a strong bidirectional relationship between architects and development teams. The architect and developer must be on the same virtual team to make this work, as depicted in Figure 2-2. Not only does this model facilitate strong bidirectional communication between architecture and development, but it also allows the architect to provide mentoring and coaching to developers on the team.

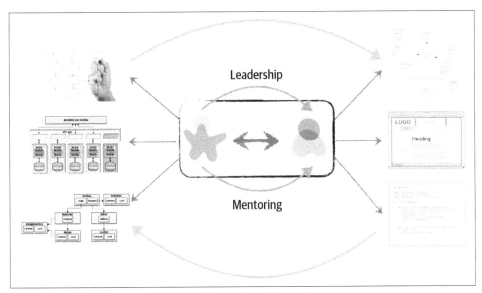

Figure 2-2. Making architecture work through collaboration

Unlike the old-school waterfall approaches to static and rigid software architecture, the architecture of today's systems changes and evolves every iteration or phase of a project. A tight collaboration between the architect and the development team is essential for the success of any software project. So where does architecture end and design begin? It doesn't. They are both part of the circle of life within a software project and must always be kept in synchronization with each other in order to succeed.

Technical Breadth

The scope of technological detail differs between developers and architects. Unlike a developer, who must have a significant amount of *technical depth* to perform their job, a software architect must have a significant amount of *technical breadth* to think like an architect and see things with an architecture point of view. This is illustrated by the knowledge pyramid shown in Figure 2-3, which encapsulates all the technical knowledge in the world. It turns out that the kind of information a technologist should value differs with career stages.

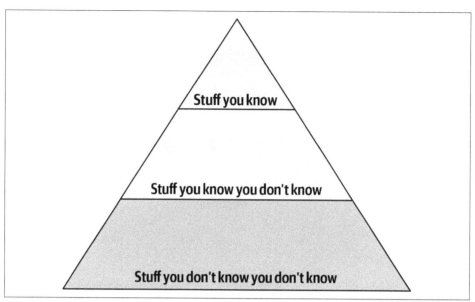

Figure 2-3. The pyramid representing all knowledge

As shown in Figure 2-3, any individual can partition all their knowledge into three sections: *stuff you know*, *stuff you know you don't know*, and *stuff you don't know you don't know*.

Stuff you know includes the technologies, frameworks, languages, and tools a technologist uses on a daily basis to perform their job, such as knowing Java as a Java programmer. *Stuff you know you don't know* includes those things a technologist knows a little about or has heard of but has little or no expertise in. A good example of this level of knowledge is the Clojure programming language. Most technologists have *heard* of Clojure and know it's a programming language based on Lisp, but they can't code in the language. *Stuff you don't know you don't know* is the largest part of the knowledge triangle and includes the entire host of technologies, tools, frameworks, and languages that would be the perfect solution to a problem a technologist is trying to solve, but the technologist doesn't even know those things exist.

A developer's early career focuses on expanding the top of the pyramid, to build experience and expertise. This is the ideal focus early on, because developers need more perspective, working knowledge, and hands-on experience. Expanding the top incidentally expands the middle section; as developers encounter more technologies and related artifacts, it adds to their stock of *stuff you know you don't know*.

In Figure 2-4, expanding the top of the pyramid is beneficial because expertise is valued. However, the *stuff you know* is also the *stuff you must maintain*—nothing is static in the software world. If a developer becomes an expert in Ruby on Rails, that expertise won't last if they ignore Ruby on Rails for a year or two. The things at the top of the pyramid require time investment to maintain expertise. Ultimately, the size of the top of an individual's pyramid is their *technical depth*.

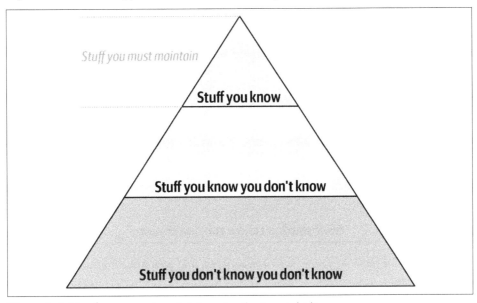

Figure 2-4. Developers must maintain expertise to retain it

However, the nature of knowledge changes as developers transition into the architect role. A large part of the value of an architect is a *broad* understanding of technology and how to use it to solve particular problems. For example, as an architect, it is more beneficial to know that five solutions exist for a particular problem than to have singular expertise in only one. The most important parts of the pyramid for architects are the top *and* middle sections; how far the middle section penetrates into the bottom section represents an architect's technical *breadth*, as shown in Figure 2-5.

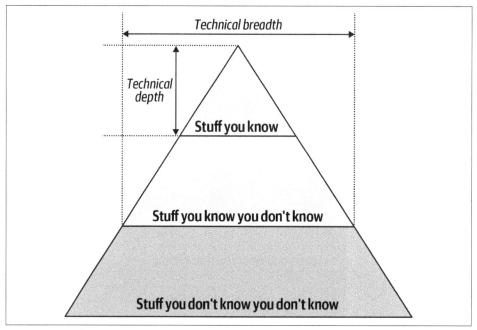

Figure 2-5. What someone knows is technical depth, and how much someone knows is technical breadth

As an architect, *breadth* is more important than *depth*. Because architects must make decisions that match capabilities to technical constraints, a broad understanding of a wide variety of solutions is valuable. Thus, for an architect, the wise course of action is to sacrifice some hard-won expertise and use that time to broaden their portfolio, as shown in Figure 2-6. As illustrated in the diagram, some areas of expertise will remain, probably in particularly enjoyable technology areas, while others usefully atrophy.

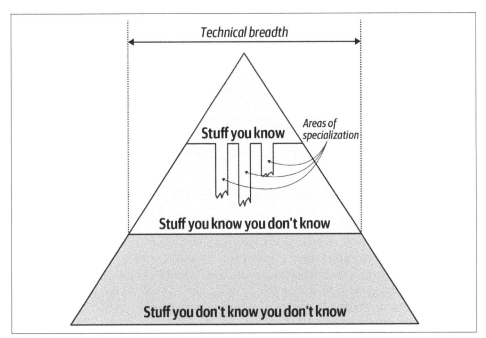

Figure 2-6. Enhanced breadth and shrinking depth for the architect role

Our knowledge pyramid illustrates how fundamentally different the role of *architect* compares to *developer*. Developers spend their whole careers honing expertise, and transitioning to the architect role means a shift in that perspective, which many individuals find difficult. This in turn leads to two common dysfunctions: first, an architect tries to maintain expertise in a wide variety of areas, succeeding in none of them and working themselves ragged in the process. Second, it manifests as *stale expertise* —the mistaken sensation that your outdated information is still cutting edge. We see this often in large companies where the developers who founded the company have moved into leadership roles yet still make technology decisions using ancient criteria (see "Frozen Caveman Anti-Pattern" on page 30).

Architects should focus on technical breadth so that they have a larger quiver from which to draw arrows. Developers transitioning to the architect role may have to change the way they view knowledge acquisition. Balancing their portfolio of knowledge regarding depth versus breadth is something every developer should consider throughout their career.

Frozen Caveman Anti-Pattern

A behavioral anti-pattern commonly observed in the wild, the *Frozen Caveman Anti-Pattern*, describes an architect who always reverts back to their pet irrational concern for every architecture. For example, one of Neal's colleagues worked on a system that featured a centralized architecture. Yet, each time they delivered the design to the client architects, the persistent question was "But what if we lose Italy?" Several years before, a freak communication problem had prevented headquarters from communicating with its stores in Italy, causing great inconvenience. While the chances of a reoccurrence were extremely small, the architects had become obsessed about this particular architectural characteristic.

Generally, this anti-pattern manifests in architects who have been burned in the past by a poor decision or unexpected occurrence, making them particularly cautious in the future. While risk assessment is important, it should be realistic as well. Understanding the difference between genuine versus perceived technical risk is part of the ongoing learning process for architects. Thinking like an architect requires overcoming these "frozen caveman" ideas and experiences, seeing other solutions, and asking more relevant questions.

Analyzing Trade-Offs

Thinking like an architect is all about seeing trade-offs in every solution, technical or otherwise, and analyzing those trade-offs to determine what is the best solution. To quote Mark (one of your authors):

> Architecture is the stuff you can't Google.

Everything in architecture is a trade-off, which is why the famous answer to every architecture question in the universe is "it depends." While many people get increasingly annoyed at this answer, it is unfortunately true. You cannot Google the answer to whether REST or messaging would be better, or whether microservices is the right architecture style, because it *does* depend. It depends on the deployment environment, business drivers, company culture, budgets, timeframes, developer skill set, and dozens of other factors. Everyone's environment, situation, and problem is different, hence why architecture is so hard. To quote Neal (another one of your authors):

> There are no right or wrong answers in architecture—only trade-offs.

For example, consider an item auction system, as illustrated in Figure 2-7, where someone places a bid for an item up for auction.

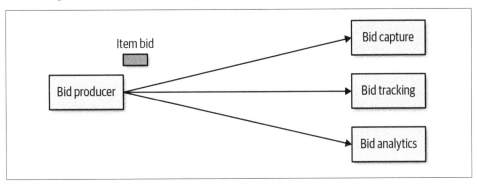

Figure 2-7. Auction system example of a trade-off—queues or topics?

The Bid Producer service generates a bid from the bidder and then sends that bid amount to the Bid Capture, Bid Tracking, and Bid Analytics services. This could be done by using queues in a point-to-point messaging fashion or by using a topic in a publish-and-subscribe messaging fashion. Which one should the architect use? You can't Google the answer. Architectural thinking requires the architect to analyze the trade-offs associated with each option and select the best one given the specific situation.

The two messaging options for the item auction system are shown in Figures 2-8 and 2-9, with Figure 2-8 illustrating the use of a topic in a publish-and-subscribe messaging model, and Figure 2-9 illustrating the use of queues in a point-to-point messaging model.

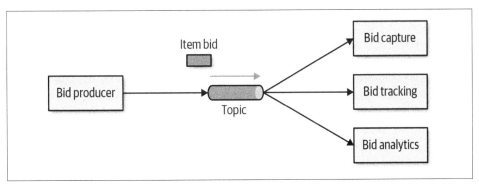

Figure 2-8. Use of a topic for communication between services

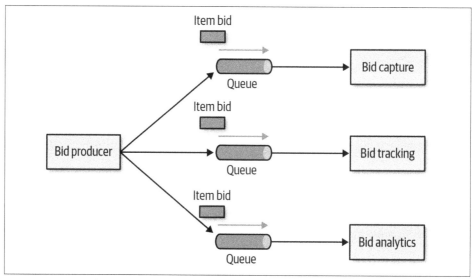

Figure 2-9. Use of queues for communication between services

The clear advantage (and seemingly obvious solution) to this problem in Figure 2-8 is that of *architectural extensibility*. The Bid Producer service only requires a single connection to a topic, unlike the queue solution in Figure 2-9 where the Bid Producer needs to connect to three different queues. If a new service called Bid History were to be added to this system due to the requirement to provide each bidder with a history of all the bids they made in each auction, no changes at all would be needed to the existing system. When the new Bid History service is created, it could simply subscribe to the topic already containing the bid information. In the queue option shown in Figure 2-9, however, a new queue would be required for the Bid History service, and the Bid Producer would need to be modified to add an additional connection to the new queue. The point here is that using queues requires significant change to the system when adding new bidding functionality, whereas with the topic approach no changes are needed at all in the existing infrastructure. Also, notice that the Bid Producer is more decoupled in the topic option—the Bid Producer doesn't know how the bidding information will be used or by which services. In the queue option the Bid Producer knows exactly how the bidding information is used (and by whom), and hence is more coupled to the system.

With this analysis it seems clear that the topic approach using the publish-and-subscribe messaging model is the obvious and best choice. However, to quote Rich Hickey, the creator of the Clojure programming language:

> Programmers know the benefits of everything and the trade-offs of nothing. Architects need to understand both.

Thinking architecturally is looking at the benefits of a given solution, but also analyzing the negatives, or trade-offs, associated with a solution. Continuing with the auction system example, a software architect would analyze the negatives of the topic solution. In analyzing the differences, notice first in Figure 2-8 that with a topic, *anyone* can access bidding data, which introduces a possible issue with data access and data security. In the queue model illustrated in Figure 2-9, the data sent to the queue can *only* be accessed by the specific consumer receiving that message. If a rogue service did listen in on a queue, those bids would not be received by the corresponding service, and a notification would immediately be sent about the loss of data (and hence a possible security breach). In other words, it is very easy to wiretap into a topic, but not a queue.

In addition to the security issue, the topic solution in Figure 2-8 only supports homogeneous contracts. All services receiving the bidding data must accept the same contract and set of bidding data. In the queue option in Figure 2-9, each consumer can have its own contract specific to the data it needs. For example, suppose the new Bid History service requires the current asking price along with the bid, but no other service needs that information. In this case, the contract would need to be modified, impacting all other services using that data. In the queue model, this would be a separate channel, hence a separate contract not impacting any other service.

Another disadvantage of the topic model illustrated in Figure 2-8 is that it does not support monitoring of the number of messages in the topic and hence auto-scaling capabilities. However, with the queue option in Figure 2-9, each queue can be monitored individually, and programmatic load balancing applied to each bidding consumer so that each can be automatically scaled independency from one another. Note that this trade-off is technology specific in that the Advanced Message Queuing Protocol (AMQP) (*https://www.amqp.org*) can support programmatic load balancing and monitoring because of the separation between an exchange (what the producer sends to) and a queue (what the consumer listens to).

Given this trade-off analysis, now which is the better option? And the answer? It depends! Table 2-1 summarizes these trade-offs.

Table 2-1. Trade-offs for topics

Topic advantages	Topic disadvantages
Architectural extensibility	Data access and data security concerns
Service decoupling	No heterogeneous contracts
	Monitoring and programmatic scalability

The point here is that *everything* in software architecture has a trade-off: an advantage and disadvantage. Thinking like an architect is analyzing these trade-offs, then asking "which is more important: extensibility or security?" The decision between different solutions will always depend on the business drivers, environment, and a host of other factors.

Understanding Business Drivers

Thinking like an architect is understanding the business drivers that are required for the success of the system and translating those requirements into architecture characteristics (such as scalability, performance, and availability). This is a challenging task that requires the architect to have some level of business domain knowledge and healthy, collaborative relationships with key business stakeholders. We've devoted several chapters in the book on this specific topic. In Chapter 4 we define various architecture characteristics. In Chapter 5 we describe ways to identify and qualify architecture characteristics. And in Chapter 6 we describe how to measure each of these characteristics to ensure the business needs of the system are met.

Balancing Architecture and Hands-On Coding

One of the difficult tasks an architect faces is how to balance hands-on coding with software architecture. We firmly believe that every architect should code and be able to maintain a certain level of technical depth (see "Technical Breadth" on page 25). While this may seem like an easy task, it is sometimes rather difficult to accomplish.

The first tip in striving for a balance between hands-on coding and being a software architect is avoiding the bottleneck trap. The bottleneck trap occurs when the architect has taken ownership of code within the critical path of a project (usually the underlying framework code) and becomes a bottleneck to the team. This happens because the architect is not a full-time developer and therefore must balance between playing the developer role (writing and testing source code) and the architect role (drawing diagrams, attending meetings, and well, attending more meetings).

One way to avoid the bottleneck trap as an effective software architect is to delegate the critical path and framework code to others on the development team and then focus on coding a piece of business functionality (a service or a screen) one to three iterations down the road. Three positive things happen by doing this. First, the architect is gaining hands-on experience writing production code while no longer becoming a bottleneck on the team. Second, the critical path and framework code is distributed to the development team (where it belongs), giving them ownership and a better understanding of the harder parts of the system. Third, and perhaps most important, the architect is writing the same business-related source code as the development team and is therefore better able to identify with the development team in terms of the pain they might be going through with processes, procedures, and the development environment.

Suppose, however, that the architect is not able to develop code with the development team. How can a software architect still remain hands-on and maintain some level of technical depth? There are four basic ways an architect can still remain hands-on at work without having to "practice coding from home" (although we recommend practicing coding at home as well).

The first way is to do frequent proof-of-concepts or POCs. This practice not only requires the architect to write source code, but it also helps validate an architecture decision by taking the implementation details into account. For example, if an architect is stuck trying to make a decision between two caching solutions, one effective way to help make this decision is to develop a working example in each caching product and compare the results. This allows the architect to see first-hand the implementation details and the amount of effort required to develop the full solution. It also allows the architect to better compare architectural characteristics such as scalability, performance, or overall fault tolerance of the different caching solutions.

Our advice when doing proof-of-concept work is that, whenever possible, the architect should write the best production-quality code they can. We recommend this practice for two reasons. First, quite often, throwaway proof-of-concept code goes into the source code repository and becomes the reference architecture or guiding example for others to follow. The last thing an architect would want is for their throwaway, sloppy code to be a representation of their typical work. The second reason is that by writing production-quality proof-of-concept code, the architect gets practice writing quality, well-structured code rather than continually developing bad coding practices.

Another way an architect can remain hands-on is to tackle some of the technical debt stories or architecture stories, freeing the development team up to work on the critical functional user stories. These stories are usually low priority, so if the architect does not have the chance to complete a technical debt or architecture story within a given iteration, it's not the end of the world and generally does not impact the success of the iteration.

Similarly, working on bug fixes within an iteration is another way of maintaining hands-on coding while helping the development team as well. While certainly not glamorous, this technique allows the architect to identify where issues and weakness may be within the code base and possibly the architecture.

Leveraging automation by creating simple command-line tools and analyzers to help the development team with their day-to-day tasks is another great way to maintain hands-on coding skills while making the development team more effective. Look for repetitive tasks the development team performs and automate the process. The development team will be grateful for the automation. Some examples are automated source validators to help check for specific coding standards not found in other lint tests, automated checklists, and repetitive manual code refactoring tasks.

Automation can also be in the form of architectural analysis and fitness functions to ensure the vitality and compliance of the architecture. For example, an architect can write Java code in ArchUnit (*https://www.archunit.org*) in the Java platform to automate architectural compliance, or write custom fitness functions (*https://evolutionaryarchitecture.com*) to ensure architectural compliance while gaining hands-on experience. We talk about these techniques in Chapter 6.

A final technique to remain hands-on as an architect is to do frequent code reviews. While the architect is not actually writing code, at least they are *involved* in the source code. Further, doing code reviews has the added benefits of being able to ensure compliance with the architecture and to seek out mentoring and coaching opportunities on the team.

CHAPTER 3

Modularity

First, we want to untangle some common terms used and overused in discussions about architecture surrounding modularity and provide definitions for use throughout the book.

> 95% of the words [about software architecture] are spent extolling the benefits of "modularity" and that little, if anything, is said about how to achieve it.
>
> —Glenford J. Myers (1978)

Different platforms offer different reuse mechanisms for code, but all support some way of grouping related code together into *modules*. While this concept is universal in software architecture, it has proven slippery to define. A casual internet search yields dozens of definitions, with no consistency (and some contradictions). As you can see from the quote from Myers, this isn't a new problem. However, because no recognized definition exists, we must jump into the fray and provide our own definitions for the sake of consistency throughout the book.

Understanding modularity and its many incarnations in the development platform of choice is critical for architects. Many of the tools we have to analyze architecture (such as metrics, fitness functions, and visualizations) rely on these modularity concepts. Modularity is an organizing principle. If an architect designs a system without paying attention to how the pieces wire together, they end up creating a system that presents myriad difficulties. To use a physics analogy, software systems model complex systems, which tend toward entropy (or disorder). Energy must be added to a physical system to preserve order. The same is true for software systems: architects must constantly expend energy to ensure good structural soundness, which won't happen by accident.

Preserving good modularity exemplifies our definition of an *implicit* architecture characteristic: virtually no project features a requirement that asks the architect to ensure good modular distinction and communication, yet sustainable code bases require order and consistency.

Definition

The dictionary defines *module* as "each of a set of standardized parts or independent units that can be used to construct a more complex structure." We use *modularity* to describe a logical grouping of related code, which could be a group of classes in an object-oriented language or functions in a structured or functional language. Most languages provide mechanisms for modularity (`package` in Java, `namespace` in .NET, and so on). Developers typically use modules as a way to group related code together. For example, the `com.mycompany.customer` package in Java should contain things related to customers.

Languages now feature a wide variety of packaging mechanisms, making a developer's chore of choosing between them difficult. For example, in many modern languages, developers can define behavior in functions/methods, classes, or packages/namespaces, each with different visibility and scoping rules. Other languages complicate this further by adding programming constructs such as the metaobject protocol (*https://oreil.ly/9Zw-J*) to provide developers even more extension mechanisms.

Architects must be aware of how developers package things because it has important implications in architecture. For example, if several packages are tightly coupled together, reusing one of them for related work becomes more difficult.

Modular Reuse Before Classes

Developers who predate object-oriented languages may puzzle over why so many different separation schemes commonly exist. Much of the reason has to do with backward compatibility, not of code but rather for how developers think about things. In March of 1968, Edsger Dijkstra published a letter in the *Communications of the ACM* entitled "Go To Statement Considered Harmful." He denigrated the common use of the `GOTO` statement common in programming languages at the time that allowed nonlinear leaping around within code, making reasoning and debugging difficult.

This paper helped usher in the era of *structured* programming languages, exemplified by Pascal and C, which encouraged deeper thinking about how things fit together. Developers quickly realized that most of the languages had no good way to group like things together logically. Thus, the short era of *modular* languages was born, such as Modula (Pascal creator Niklaus Wirth's next language) and Ada. These languages had the programming construct of a *module*, much as we think about packages or namespaces today (but without the classes).

The modular programming era was short-lived. Object-oriented languages became popular because they offered new ways to encapsulate and reuse code. Still, language designers realized the utility of modules, retaining them in the form of packages, namespaces, etc. Many odd compatibility features exist in languages to support these different paradigms. For example, Java supports modular (via packages and package-level initialization using static initializers), object-oriented, and functional paradigms, each programming style with its own scoping rules and quirks.

For discussions about architecture, we use modularity as a general term to denote a related grouping of code: classes, functions, or any other grouping. This doesn't imply a physical separation, merely a logical one; the difference is sometimes important. For example, lumping a large number of classes together in a monolithic application may make sense from a convenience standpoint. However, when it comes time to restructure the architecture, the coupling encouraged by loose partitioning becomes an impediment to breaking the monolith apart. Thus, it is useful to talk about modularity as a concept separate from the physical separation forced or implied by a particular platform.

It is worth noting the general concept of *namespace*, separate from the technical implementation in the .NET platform. Developers often need precise, fully qualified names for software assets to separate different software assets (components, classes, and so on) from each other. The most obvious example that people use every day is the internet: unique, global identifiers tied to IP addresses. Most languages have some modularity mechanism that doubles as a namespace to organize things: variables, functions, and/or methods. Sometimes the module structure is reflected physically. For example, Java requires that its package structure must reflect the directory structure of the physical class files.

A Language with No Name Conflicts: Java 1.0

The original designers of Java had extensive experience dealing with name conflicts and clashes in the various programming platforms at the time. The original design of Java used a clever hack to avoid the possibility of ambiguity between two classes that had the same name. For example, what if your problem domain included a catalog *order* and an installation *order*: both named *order* but with very different connotations (and classes). The solution in Java was to create the `package` namespace mechanism, along with the requirement that the physical directory structure just match the package name. Because filesystems won't allow the same named file to reside in the same directory, they leveraged the inherent features of the operating system to avoid the possibility of ambiguity. Thus, the original `classpath` in Java contained only directories, disallowing the possibility of name conflicts.

However, as the language designers discovered, forcing every project to have a fully formed directory structure was cumbersome, especially as projects became larger. Plus, building reusable assets was difficult: frameworks and libraries must be "exploded" into the directory structure. In the second major release of Java (1.2, called Java 2), designers added the `jar` mechanism, allowing an archive file to act as a directory structure on a classpath. For the next decade, Java developers struggled with getting the `classpath` exactly right, as a combination of directories and JAR files. And, of course, the original intent was broken: now two JAR files could create conflicting names on a classpath, leading to numerous war stories of debugging class loaders.

Measuring Modularity

Given the importance of modularity to architects, they need tools to understand it. Fortunately, researchers created a variety of language-agnostic metrics to help architects understand modularity. We focus on three key concepts: *cohesion*, *coupling*, and *connascence*.

Cohesion

Cohesion refers to what extent the parts of a module should be contained within the same module. In other words, it is a measure of how related the parts are to one another. Ideally, a cohesive module is one where all the parts should be packaged together, because breaking them into smaller pieces would require coupling the parts together via calls between modules to achieve useful results.

> Attempting to divide a cohesive module would only result in increased coupling and decreased readability.
>
> —Larry Constantine

Computer scientists have defined a range of cohesion measures, listed here from best to worst:

Functional cohesion
Every part of the module is related to the other, and the module contains everything essential to function.

Sequential cohesion
Two modules interact, where one outputs data that becomes the input for the other.

Communicational cohesion
Two modules form a communication chain, where each operates on information and/or contributes to some output. For example, add a record to the database and generate an email based on that information.

Procedural cohesion
> Two modules must execute code in a particular order.

Temporal cohesion
> Modules are related based on timing dependencies. For example, many systems have a list of seemingly unrelated things that must be initialized at system startup; these different tasks are temporally cohesive.

Logical cohesion
> The data within modules is related logically but not functionally. For example, consider a module that converts information from text, serialized objects, or streams. Operations are related, but the functions are quite different. A common example of this type of cohesion exists in virtually every Java project in the form of the `StringUtils` package: a group of static methods that operate on `String` but are otherwise unrelated.

Coincidental cohesion
> Elements in a module are not related other than being in the same source file; this represents the most negative form of cohesion.

Despite having seven variants listed, *cohesion* is a less precise metric than *coupling*. Often, the degree of cohesiveness of a particular module is at the discretion of a particular architect. For example, consider this module definition:

```
Customer Maintenance
```
- add customer
- update customer
- get customer
- notify customer
- get customer orders
- cancel customer orders

Should the last two entries reside in this module or should the developer create two separate modules, such as:

```
Customer Maintenance
```
- add customer
- update customer
- get customer
- notify customer

```
Order Maintenance
```
  • get customer orders
  • cancel customer orders

Which is the correct structure? As always, it depends:

  • Are those the only two operations for `Order Maintenance`? If so, it may make
    sense to collapse those operations back into `Customer Maintenance`.

  • Is `Customer Maintenance` expected to grow much larger, encouraging developers
    to look for opportunities to extract behavior?

  • Does `Order Maintenance` require so much knowledge of `Customer` information
    that separating the two modules would require a high degree of coupling to make
    it functional? This relates back to the Larry Constantine quote.

These questions represent the kind of trade-off analysis at the heart of the job of a
software architect.

Surprisingly, given the subjectiveness of cohesion, computer scientists have developed
a good structural metric to determine cohesion (or, more specifically, the lack of
cohesion). A well-known set of metrics named the Chidamber and Kemerer Object-
oriented metrics suite (*https://oreil.ly/-1lMh*) was developed by the eponymous
authors to measure particular aspects of object-oriented software systems. The suite
includes many common code metrics, such as cyclomatic complexity (see "Cyclomatic Complexity" on page 79) and several important coupling metrics discussed in
"Coupling" on page 44.

The Chidamber and Kemerer Lack of Cohesion in Methods (LCOM) metric measures the structural cohesion of a module, typically a component. The initial version
appears in Equation 3-1.

Equation 3-1. LCOM, version 1

$$LCOM = \begin{cases} |P| - |Q|, & \text{if } |P| > |Q| \\ 0, & \text{otherwise} \end{cases}$$

P increases by one for any method that doesn't access a particular shared field and *Q*
decreases by one for methods that do share a particular shared field. The authors
sympathize with those who don't understand this formulation. Worse, it has gradually
gotten more elaborate over time. The second variation introduced in 1996 (thus the
name *LCOM96B*) appears in Equation 3-2.

Equation 3-2. LCOM 96b

$$LCOM96b = \frac{1}{a} \sum_{j=1}^{a} \frac{m - \mu(Aj)}{m}$$

We wont bother untangling the variables and operators in Equation 3-2 because the following written explanation is clearer. Basically, the LCOM metric exposes incidental coupling within classes. Here's a better definition of LCOM:

LCOM
    The sum of sets of methods not shared via sharing fields

Consider a class with private fields a and b. Many of the methods only access a, and many other methods only access b. The *sum* of the sets of methods not shared via sharing fields (a and b) is high; therefore, this class reports a high LCOM score, indicating that it scores high in *lack of cohesion in methods*. Consider the three classes shown in Figure 3-1.

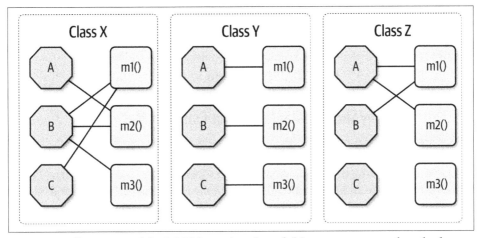

Figure 3-1. Illustration of the LCOM metric, where fields are octagons and methods are squares

In Figure 3-1, fields appear as single letters and methods appear as blocks. In Class X, the LCOM score is low, indicating good structural cohesion. Class Y, however, lacks cohesion; each of the field/method pairs in Class Y could appear in its own class without affecting behavior. Class Z shows mixed cohesion, where developers could refactor the last field/method combination into its own class.

The LCOM metric is useful to architects who are analyzing code bases in order to move from one architectural style to another. One of the common headaches when moving architectures are shared utility classes. Using the LCOM metric can help architects find classes that are incidentally coupled and should never have been a single class to begin with.

Many software metrics have serious deficiencies, and LCOM is not immune. All this metric can find is *structural* lack of cohesion; it has no way to determine logically if particular pieces fit together. This reflects back on our Second Law of Software Architecture: prefer *why* over *how*.

Coupling

Fortunately, we have better tools to analyze coupling in code bases, based in part on graph theory: because the method calls and returns form a call graph, analysis based on mathematics becomes possible. In 1979, Edward Yourdon and Larry Constantine published *Structured Design: Fundamentals of a Discipline of Computer Program and Systems Design* (Prentice-Hall), defining many core concepts, including the metrics *afferent* and *efferent* coupling. *Afferent* coupling measures the number of *incoming* connections to a code artifact (component, class, function, and so on). *Efferent* coupling measures the *outgoing* connections to other code artifacts. For virtually every platform tools exist that allow architects to analyze the coupling characteristics of code in order to assist in restructuring, migrating, or understanding a code base.

Why Such Similar Names for Coupling Metrics?

Why are two critical metrics in the architecture world that represent opposite concepts named virtually the same thing, differing in only the vowels that sound the most alike? These terms originate from Yourdon and Constantine's *Structured Design*. Borrowing concepts from mathematics, they coined the now-common afferent and efferent coupling terms, which should have been called incoming and outgoing coupling. However, because the original authors leaned toward mathematical symmetry rather than clarity, developers came up with several mnemonics to help out: *a* appears before *e* in the English alphabet, corresponding to *incoming* being before *outgoing*, or the observation that the letter *e* in efferent matches the initial letter in *exit*, corresponding to outgoing connections.

Abstractness, Instability, and Distance from the Main Sequence

While the raw value of component coupling has value to architects, several other derived metrics allow a deeper evaluation. These metrics were created by Robert Martin for a C++ book, but are widely applicable to other object-oriented languages.

Abstractness is the ratio of abstract artifacts (abstract classes, interfaces, and so on) to concrete artifacts (implementation). It represents a measure of abstractness versus implementation. For example, consider a code base with no abstractions, just a huge, single function of code (as in a single `main()` method). The flip side is a code base with too many abstractions, making it difficult for developers to understand how things wire together (for example, it takes developers a while to figure out what to do with an `AbstractSingletonProxyFactoryBean`).

The formula for abstractness appears in Equation 3-3.

Equation 3-3. Abstractness

$$A = \frac{\sum m^a}{\sum m^c}$$

In the equation, m^a represents *abstract* elements (interfaces or abstract classes) with the module, and m^c represents *concrete* elements (nonabstract classes). This metric looks for the same criteria. The easiest way to visualize this metric: consider an application with 5,000 lines of code, all in one `main()` method. The abstractness numerator is 1, while the denominator is 5,000, yielding an abstractness of almost 0. Thus, this metric measures the ratio of abstractions in your code.

Architects calculate *abstractness* by calculating the ratio of the sum of abstract artifacts to the sum of the concrete ones.

Another derived metric, *instability*, is defined as the ratio of efferent coupling to the sum of both efferent and afferent coupling, shown in Equation 3-4.

Equation 3-4. Instability

$$I = \frac{C^e}{C^e + C^a}$$

In the equation, c^e represents *efferent* (or outgoing) coupling, and c^a represents *afferent* (or incoming) coupling.

The *instability* metric determines the volatility of a code base. A code base that exhibits high degrees of instability breaks more easily when changed because of high coupling. For example, if a class calls to many other classes to delegate work, the calling class shows high susceptibility to breakage if one or more of the called methods change.

Distance from the Main Sequence

One of the few holistic metrics architects have for architectural structure is *distance from the main sequence*, a derived metric based on *instability* and *abstractness*, shown in Equation 3-5.

Equation 3-5. Distance from the main sequence

$$D = |A + I - 1|$$

In the equation, A = *abstractness* and I = *instability*.

Note that both *abstractness* and *instability* are fractions whose results will always fall between 0 and 1 (except in extreme cases of abstractness that wouldn't be practical). Thus, when graphing the relationship, we see the graph in Figure 3-2.

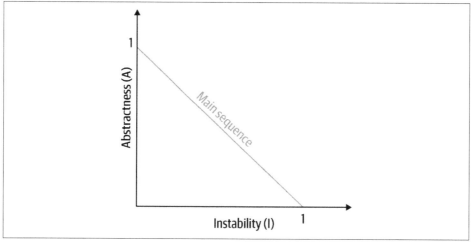

Figure 3-2. The main sequence defines the ideal relationship between abstractness and instability

The *distance* metric imagines an ideal relationship between abstractness and instability; classes that fall near this idealized line exhibit a healthy mixture of these two competing concerns. For example, graphing a particular class allows developers to calculate the *distance from the main sequence* metric, illustrated in Figure 3-3.

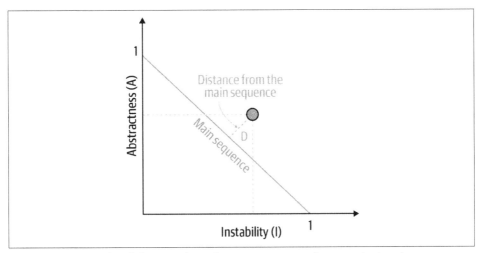

Figure 3-3. Normalized distance from the main sequence for a particular class

In Figure 3-3, developers graph the candidate class, then measure the distance from the idealized line. The closer to the line, the better balanced the class. Classes that fall too far into the upper-righthand corner enter into what architects call the *zone of uselessness*: code that is too abstract becomes difficult to use. Conversely, code that falls into the lower-lefthand corner enter the *zone of pain*: code with too much implementation and not enough abstraction becomes brittle and hard to maintain, illustrated in Figure 3-4.

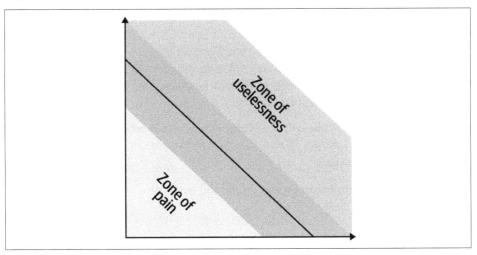

Figure 3-4. Zones of Uselessness and Pain

Tools exist in many platforms to provide these measures, which assist architects when analyzing code bases because of unfamiliarity, migration, or technical debt assessment.

Limitations of Metrics

While the industry has a few code-level metrics that provide valuable insight into code bases, our tools are extremely blunt compared to analysis tools from other engineering disciplines. Even metrics derived directly from the structure of code require interpretation. For example, cyclomatic complexity (see "Cyclomatic Complexity" on page 79) measures complexity in code bases but cannot distinguish from *essential* complexity (because the underlying problem is complex) or *accidental complexity* (the code is more complex than it should be). Virtually all code-level metrics require interpretation, but it is still useful to establish baselines for critical metrics such as cyclomatic complexity so that architects can assess which type they exhibit. We discuss setting up just such tests in "Governance and Fitness Functions" on page 82.

Notice that the previously mentioned book by Edward Yourdon and and Larry Constantine (*Structured Design: Fundamentals of a Discipline of Computer Program and Systems Design*) predates the popularity of object-oriented languages, focusing instead on structured programming constructs, such as functions (not methods). It also defined other types of coupling that we do not cover here because they have been supplanted by *connascence*.

Connascence

In 1996, Meilir Page-Jones published *What Every Programmer Should Know About Object-Oriented Design* (Dorset House), refining the afferent and efferent coupling metrics and recasting them to object-oriented languages with a concept he named *connascence*. Here's how he defined the term:

> Two components are connascent if a change in one would require the other to be modified in order to maintain the overall correctness of the system.
>
> —Meilir Page-Jones

He developed two types of connascence: *static* and *dynamic*.

Static connascence

Static connascence refers to source-code-level coupling (as opposed to execution-time coupling, covered in "Dynamic connascence" on page 50); it is a refinement of the afferent and efferent couplings defined by *Structured Design*. In other words, architects view the following types of static connascence as the *degree* to which something is coupled, either afferently or efferently:

Connascence of Name (CoN)

Multiple components must agree on the name of an entity.

Names of methods represents the most common way that code bases are coupled and the most desirable, especially in light of modern refactoring tools that make system-wide name changes trivial.

Connascence of Type (CoT)

Multiple components must agree on the type of an entity.

This type of connascence refers to the common facility in many statically typed languages to limit variables and parameters to specific types. However, this capability isn't purely a language feature—some dynamically typed languages offer selective typing, notably Clojure (*https://clojure.org*) and Clojure Spec (*https://clojure.org/about/spec*).

Connascence of Meaning (CoM) or Connascence of Convention (CoC)

Multiple components must agree on the meaning of particular values.

The most common obvious case for this type of connascence in code bases is hard-coded numbers rather than constants. For example, it is common in some languages to consider defining somewhere int TRUE = 1; int FALSE = 0. Imagine the problems if someone flips those values.

Connascence of Position (CoP)

Multiple components must agree on the order of values.

This is an issue with parameter values for method and function calls even in languages that feature static typing. For example, if a developer creates a method void updateSeat(String name, String seatLocation) and calls it with the values updateSeat("14D", "Ford, N"), the semantics aren't correct even if the types are.

Connascence of Algorithm (CoA)

Multiple components must agree on a particular algorithm.

A common case for this type of connascence occurs when a developer defines a security hashing algorithm that must run on both the server and client and produce identical results to authenticate the user. Obviously, this represents a high form of coupling—if either algorithm changes any details, the handshake will no longer work.

Dynamic connascence

The other type of connascence Page-Jones defined was *dynamic connascence*, which analyzes calls at runtime. The following is a description of the different types of dynamic connascence:

Connascence of Execution (CoE)
> The order of execution of multiple components is important.
>
> Consider this code:

```
email = new Email();
email.setRecipient("foo@example.com");
email.setSender("me@me.com");
email.send();
email.setSubject("whoops");
```

> It won't work correctly because certain properties must be set in order.

Connascence of Timing (CoT)
> The timing of the execution of multiple components is important.
>
> The common case for this type of connascence is a race condition caused by two threads executing at the same time, affecting the outcome of the joint operation.

Connascence of Values (CoV)
> Occurs when several values relate on one another and must change together.
>
> Consider the case where a developer has defined a rectangle as four points, representing the corners. To maintain the integrity of the data structure, the developer cannot randomly change one of points without considering the impact on the other points.
>
> The more common and problematic case involves transactions, especially in distributed systems. When an architect designs a system with separate databases, yet needs to update a single value across all of the databases, all the values must change together or not at all.

Connascence of Identity (CoI)
> Occurs when multiple components must reference the same entity.

The common example of this type of connascence involves two independent components that must share and update a common data structure, such as a distributed queue.

Architects have a harder time determining dynamic connascence because we lack tools to analyze runtime calls as effectively as we can analyze the call graph.

Connascence properties

Connascence is an analysis tool for architect and developers, and some properties of connascence help developers use it wisely. The following is a description of each of these connascence properties:

Strength

Architects determine the *strength* of connascence by the ease with which a developer can refactor that type of coupling; different types of connascence are demonstrably more desirable, as shown in Figure 3-5. Architects and developers can improve the coupling characteristics of their code base by refactoring toward better types of connascence.

Architects should prefer static connascence to dynamic because developers can determine it by simple source code analysis, and modern tools make it trivial to improve static connascence. For example, consider the case of *connascence of meaning*, which developers can improve by refactoring to *connascence of name* by creating a named constant rather than a magic value.

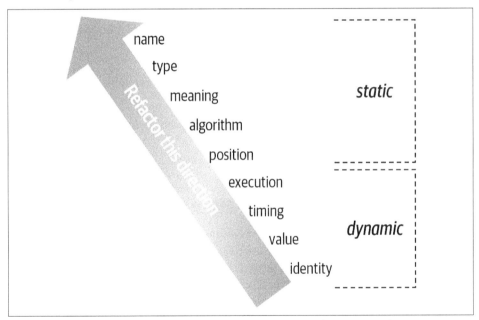

Figure 3-5. The strength on connascence provides a good refactoring guide

Locality

The *locality* of connascence measures how proximal the modules are to each other in the code base. Proximal code (in the same module) typically has more and higher forms of connascence than more separated code (in separate modules or code bases). In other words, forms of connascence that indicate poor coupling when far apart are fine when closer together. For example, if two classes in the same component have connascence of meaning, it is less damaging to the code base than if two components have the same form of connascence.

Developers must consider strength and locality together. Stronger forms of connascence found within the same module represent less code smell than the same connascence spread apart.

Degree

The *degree* of connascence relates to the size of its impact—does it impact a few classes or many? Lesser degrees of connascence damage code bases less. In other words, having high dynamic connascence isn't terrible if you only have a few modules. However, code bases tend to grow, making a small problem correspondingly bigger.

Page-Jones offers three guidelines for using connascence to improve systems modularity:

1. Minimize overall connascence by breaking the system into encapsulated elements

2. Minimize any remaining connascence that crosses encapsulation boundaries

3. Maximize the connascence within encapsulation boundaries

The legendary software architecture innovator Jim Weirich repopularized the concept of connascence and offers two great pieces of advice:

Rule of Degree: convert strong forms of connascence into weaker forms of connascence

Rule of Locality: as the distance between software elements increases, use weaker forms of connascence

Unifying Coupling and Connascence Metrics

So far, we've discussed both coupling and connascence, measures from different eras and with different targets. However, from an architect's point of view, these two views overlap. What Page-Jones identifies as static connascence represents degrees of either incoming or outgoing coupling. Structured programming only cares about in or out, whereas connascence cares about how things are coupled together.

To help visualize the overlap in concepts, consider Figure 3-6. The structured programming coupling concepts appear on the left, while the connascence characteristics appear on the right. What structured programming called *data coupling* (method calls), connascence provides advice for how that coupling should manifest. Structured programming didn't really address the areas covered by dynamic connascence; we encapsulate that concept shortly in "Architectural Quanta and Granularity" on page 92.

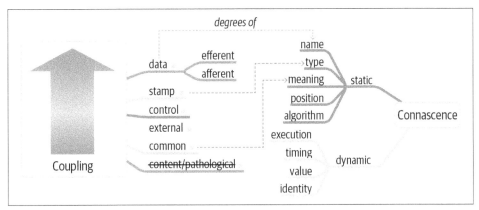

Figure 3-6. Unifying coupling and connascence

The problems with 1990s connascence

Several problems exist for architects when applying these useful metrics for analyzing and designing systems. First, these measures look at details at a low level of code, focusing on code quality and hygiene than necessarily architectural structure. Architects tend to care more about *how* modules are coupled rather than the *degree* of coupling. For example, an architect cares about synchronous versus asynchronous communication, and doesn't care so much about how that's implemented.

The second problem with connascence lies with the fact that it doesn't really address a fundamental decision that many modern architects must make—synchronous or asynchronous communication in distributed architectures like microservices? Referring back to the First Law of Software Architecture, everything is a trade-off. After we discuss the scope of architecture characteristics in Chapter 7, we'll introduce new ways to think about modern connascence.

From Modules to Components

We use the term *module* throughout as a generic name for a bundling of related code. However, most platforms support some form of *component*, one of the key building blocks for software architects. The concept and corresponding analysis of the logical or physical separation has existed since the earliest days of computer science. Yet, with all the writing and thinking about components and separation, developers and architects still struggle with achieving good outcomes.

We'll discuss deriving components from problem domains in Chapter 8, but we must first discuss another fundamental aspect of software architecture: architecture characteristics and their scope.

CHAPTER 4

Architecture Characteristics Defined

A company decides to solve a particular problem using software, so it gathers a list of requirements for that system. A wide variety of techniques exist for the exercise of requirements gathering, generally defined by the software development process used by the team. But the architect must consider many other factors in designing a software solution, as illustrated in Figure 4-1.

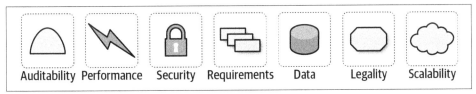

Figure 4-1. A software solution consists of both domain requirements and architectural characteristics

Architects may collaborate on defining the domain or business requirements, but one key responsibility entails defining, discovering, and otherwise analyzing all the things the software must do that isn't directly related to the domain functionality: *architectural characteristics*.

What distinguishes software architecture from coding and design? Many things, including the role that architects have in defining architectural characteristics, the important aspects of the system independent of the problem domain. Many organizations describe these features of software with a variety of terms, including *nonfunctional requirements*, but we dislike that term because it is self-denigrating. Architects created that term to distinguish architecture characteristics from *functional requirements*, but naming something *nonfunctional* has a negative impact from a language standpoint: how can teams be convinced to pay enough attention to something "nonfunctional"? Another popular term is *quality attributes*, which we dislike because it implies after-the-fact quality assessment rather than design. We prefer *architecture characteristics* because it describes concerns critical to the success of the architecture, and therefore the system as a whole, without discounting its importance.

An architecture characteristic meets three criteria:

- Specifies a nondomain design consideration
- Influences some structural aspect of the design
- Is critical or important to application success

These interlocking parts of our definition are illustrated in Figure 4-2.

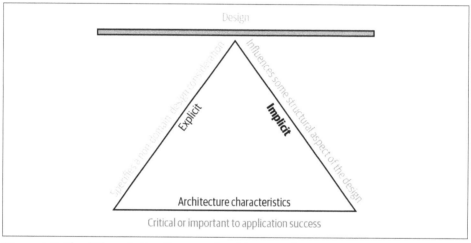

Figure 4-2. The differentiating features of architecture characteristics

The definition illustrated in Figure 4-2 consists of the three components listed, in addition to a few modifiers:

Specifies a nondomain design consideration

When designing an application, the requirements specify what the application should do; architecture characteristics specify operational and design criteria for success, concerning how to implement the requirements and why certain choices were made. For example, a common important architecture characteristic specifies a certain level of performance for the application, which often doesn't appear in a requirements document. Even more pertinent: no requirements document states "prevent technical debt," but it is a common design consideration for architects and developers. We cover this distinction between explicit and implicit characteristics in depth in "Extracting Architecture Characteristics from Domain Concerns" on page 65.

Influences some structural aspect of the design

The primary reason architects try to describe architecture characteristics on projects concerns design considerations: does this architecture characteristic require special structural consideration to succeed? For example, *security* is a concern in virtually every project, and all systems must take a baseline of precautions during design and coding. However, it rises to the level of architecture characteristic when the architect needs to design something special. Consider two cases surrounding payment in a example system:

Third-party payment processor

If an integration point handles payment details, then the architecture shouldn't require special structural considerations. The design should incorporate standard security hygiene, such as encryption and hashing, but doesn't require special structure.

In-application payment processing

If the application under design must handle payment processing, the architect may design a specific module, component, or service for that purpose to isolate the critical security concerns structurally. Now, the architecture characteristic has an impact on both architecture and design.

Of course, even these two criteria aren't sufficient in many cases to make this determination: past security incidents, the nature of the integration with the third party, and a host of other criteria may be present during this decision. Still, it shows some of the considerations architects must make when determining how to design for certain capabilities.

Critical or important to application success

Applications *could* support a huge number of architecture characteristics…but shouldn't. Support for each architecture characteristic adds complexity to the design. Thus, a critical job for architects lies in choosing the fewest architecture characteristics rather than the most possible.

We further subdivide architecture characteristics into implicit versus explicit architecture characteristics. Implicit ones rarely appear in requirements, yet they're necessary for project success. For example, availability, reliability, and security underpin virtually all applications, yet they're rarely specified in design documents. Architects must use their knowledge of the problem domain to uncover these architecture characteristics during the analysis phase. For example, a high-frequency trading firm may not have to specify low latency in every system, yet the architects in that problem domain know how critical it is. Explicit architecture characteristics appear in requirements documents or other specific instructions.

In Figure 4-2, the choice of a triangle is intentional: each of the definition elements supports the others, which in turn support the overall design of the system. The fulcrum created by the triangle illustrates the fact that these architecture characteristics often interact with one another, leading to the pervasive use among architects of the term *trade-off*.

Architectural Characteristics (Partially) Listed

Architecture characteristics exist along a broad spectrum of the software system, ranging from low-level code characteristics, such as modularity, to sophisticated operational concerns, such as scalability and elasticity. No true universal standard exists despite attempts to codify ones in the past. Instead, each organization creates its own interpretation of these terms. Additionally, because the software ecosystem changes so fast, new concepts, terms, measures, and verifications constantly appear, providing new opportunities for architecture characteristics definitions.

Despite the volume and scale, architects commonly separate architecture characteristics into broad categories. The following sections describe a few, along with some examples.

Operational Architecture Characteristics

Operational architecture characteristics cover capabilities such as performance, scalability, elasticity, availability, and reliability. Table 4-1 lists some operational architecture characteristics.

Table 4-1. Common operational architecture characteristics

Term	Definition
Availability	How long the system will need to be available (if 24/7, steps need to be in place to allow the system to be up and running quickly in case of any failure).
Continuity	Disaster recovery capability.
Performance	Includes stress testing, peak analysis, analysis of the frequency of functions used, capacity required, and response times. Performance acceptance sometimes requires an exercise of its own, taking months to complete.
Recoverability	Business continuity requirements (e.g., in case of a disaster, how quickly is the system required to be online again?). This will affect the backup strategy and requirements for duplicated hardware.
Reliability/ safety	Assess if the system needs to be fail-safe, or if it is mission critical in a way that affects lives. If it fails, will it cost the company large sums of money?
Robustness	Ability to handle error and boundary conditions while running if the internet connection goes down or if there's a power outage or hardware failure.
Scalability	Ability for the system to perform and operate as the number of users or requests increases.

Operational architecture characteristics heavily overlap with operations and DevOps concerns, forming the intersection of those concerns in many software projects.

Structural Architecture Characteristics

Architects must concern themselves with code structure. In many cases, the architect has sole or shared responsibility for code quality concerns, such as good modularity, controlled coupling between components, readable code, and a host of other internal quality assessments. Table 4-2 lists a few structural architecture characteristics.

Table 4-2. Structural architecture characteristics

Term	Definition
Configurability	Ability for the end users to easily change aspects of the software's configuration (through usable interfaces).
Extensibility	How important it is to plug new pieces of functionality in.
Installability	Ease of system installation on all necessary platforms.
Leverageability/ reuse	Ability to leverage common components across multiple products.
Localization	Support for multiple languages on entry/query screens in data fields; on reports, multibyte character requirements and units of measure or currencies.
Maintainability	How easy it is to apply changes and enhance the system?
Portability	Does the system need to run on more than one platform? (For example, does the frontend need to run against Oracle as well as SAP DB?)
Supportability	What level of technical support is needed by the application? What level of logging and other facilities are required to debug errors in the system?
Upgradeability	Ability to easily/quickly upgrade from a previous version of this application/solution to a newer version on servers and clients.

Cross-Cutting Architecture Characteristics

While many architecture characteristics fall into easily recognizable categories, many fall outside or defy categorization yet form important design constraints and considerations. Table 4-3 describes a few of these.

Table 4-3. Cross-cutting architecture characteristics

Term	Definition
Accessibility	Access to all your users, including those with disabilities like colorblindness or hearing loss.
Archivability	Will the data need to be archived or deleted after a period of time? (For example, customer accounts are to be deleted after three months or marked as obsolete and archived to a secondary database for future access.)
Authentication	Security requirements to ensure users are who they say they are.
Authorization	Security requirements to ensure users can access only certain functions within the application (by use case, subsystem, webpage, business rule, field level, etc.).
Legal	What legislative constraints is the system operating in (data protection, Sarbanes Oxley, GDPR, etc.)? What reservation rights does the company require? Any regulations regarding the way the application is to be built or deployed?

Term	Definition
Privacy	Ability to hide transactions from internal company employees (encrypted transactions so even DBAs and network architects cannot see them).
Security	Does the data need to be encrypted in the database? Encrypted for network communication between internal systems? What type of authentication needs to be in place for remote user access?
Supportability	What level of technical support is needed by the application? What level of logging and other facilities are required to debug errors in the system?
Usability/ achievability	Level of training required for users to achieve their goals with the application/solution. Usability requirements need to be treated as seriously as any other architectural issue.

Any list of architecture characteristics will necessarily be an incomplete list; any software may invent important architectural characteristics based on unique factors (see "Italy-ility" on page 60 for an example).

Italy-ility

One of Neal's colleagues recounts a story about the unique nature of architectural characteristics. She worked for a client whose mandate required a centralized architecture. Yet, for each proposed design, the first question from the client was "But what happens if we lose Italy?" Years ago, because of a freak communication outage, the head office had lost communication with the Italian branches, and it was organizationally traumatic. Thus, a firm requirement of all future architectures insisted upon what the team eventually called *Italy-ility*, which they all knew meant a unique combination of availability, recoverability, and resilience.

Additionally, many of the preceding terms are imprecise and ambiguous, sometimes because of subtle nuance or the lack of objective definitions. For example, *interoperability* and *compatibility* may appear equivalent, which will be true for some systems. However, they differ because *interoperability* implies ease of integration with other systems, which in turn implies published, documented APIs. *Compatibility*, on the other hand, is more concerned with industry and domain standards. Another example is *learnability*. One definition is how easy it is for users to learn to use the software, and another definition is the level at which the system can automatically learn about its environment in order to become self-configuring or self-optimizing using machine learning algorithms.

Many of the definitions overlap. For example, consider availability and reliability, which seem to overlap in almost all cases. Yet consider the internet protocol UDP, which underlies TCP. UDP is available over IP but not reliable: the packets may arrive out of order, and the receiver may have to ask for missing packets again.

No complete list of standards exists. The International Organization for Standards (ISO) publishes a list organized by capabilities (*https://oreil.ly/SKc_Y*), overlapping many of the ones we've listed, but mainly establishing an incomplete category list. The following are some of the ISO definitions:

Performance efficiency
Measure of the performance relative to the amount of resources used under known conditions. This includes *time behavior* (measure of response, processing times, and/or throughput rates), *resource utilization* (amounts and types of resources used), and *capacity* (degree to which the maximum established limits are exceeded).

Compatibility
Degree to which a product, system, or component can exchange information with other products, systems, or components and/or perform its required functions while sharing the same hardware or software environment. It includes *coexistence* (can perform its required functions efficiently while sharing a common environment and resources with other products) and *interoperability* (degree to which two or more systems can exchange and utilize information).

Usability
Users can use the system effectively, efficiently, and satisfactorily for its intended purpose. It includes *appropriateness recognizability* (users can recognize whether the software is appropriate for their needs), *learnability* (how easy users can learn how to use the software), *user error protection* (protection against users making errors), and *accessibility* (make the software available to people with the widest range of characteristics and capabilities).

Reliability
Degree to which a system functions under specified conditions for a specified period of time. This characteristic includes subcategories such as *maturity* (does the software meet the reliability needs under normal operation), *availability* (software is operational and accessible), *fault tolerance* (does the software operate as intended despite hardware or software faults), and *recoverability* (can the software recover from failure by recovering any affected data and reestablish the desired state of the system.

Security
Degree the software protects information and data so that people or other products or systems have the degree of data access appropriate to their types and levels of authorization. This family of characteristics includes *confidentiality* (data is accessible only to those authorized to have access), *integrity* (the software prevents unauthorized access to or modification of software or data), *nonrepudiation*, (can actions or events be proven to have taken place), *accountability* (can user actions of a user be traced), and *authenticity* (proving the identity of a user).

Maintainability

> Represents the degree of effectiveness and efficiency to which developers can modify the software to improve it, correct it, or adapt it to changes in environment and/or requirements. This characteristic includes *modularity* (degree to which the software is composed of discrete components), *reusability* (degree to which developers can use an asset in more than one system or in building other assets), *analyzability* (how easily developers can gather concrete metrics about the software), *modifiability* (degree to which developers can modify the software without introducing defects or degrading existing product quality), and *testability* (how easily developers and others can test the software).

Portability

> Degree to which developers can transfer a system, product, or component from one hardware, software, or other operational or usage environment to another. This characteristic includes the subcharacteristics of *adaptability* (can developers effectively and efficiently adapt the software for different or evolving hardware, software, or other operational or usage environments), *installability* (can the software be installed and/or uninstalled in a specified environment), and *replaceability* (how easily developers can replace the functionality with other software).

The last item in the ISO list addresses the functional aspects of software, which we do not believe belongs in this list:

Functional suitability

> This characteristic represents the degree to which a product or system provides functions that meet stated and implied needs when used under specified conditions. This characteristic is composed of the following subcharacteristics:

Functional completeness

> Degree to which the set of functions covers all the specified tasks and user objectives.

Functional correctness

> Degree to which a product or system provides the correct results with the needed degree of precision.

Functional appropriateness

> Degree to which the functions facilitate the accomplishment of specified tasks and objectives. These are not architecture characteristics but rather the motivational requirements to build the software. This illustrates how thinking about the relationship between architecture characteristics and the problem domain has evolved. We cover this evolution in Chapter 7.

Trade-Offs and Least Worst Architecture

Applications can only support a few of the architecture characteristics we've listed for a variety of reasons. First, each of the supported characteristics requires design effort and perhaps structural support. Second, the bigger problem lies with the fact that each architecture characteristic often has an impact on others. For example, if an architect wants to improve *security*, it will almost certainly negatively impact *performance*: the application must do more on-the-fly encryption, indirection for secrets hiding, and other activities that potentially degrade performance.

A metaphor will help illustrate this interconnectivity. Apparently, pilots often struggle learning to fly helicopters because it requires a control for each hand and each foot, and changing one impacts the others. Thus, flying a helicopter is a balancing exercise, which nicely describes the trade-off process when choosing architecture characteristics. Each architecture characteristic that an architect designs support for potentially complicates the overall design.

Thus, architects rarely encounter the situation where they are able to design a system and maximize every single architecture characteristic. More often, the decisions come down to trade-offs between several competing concerns.

 Never shoot for the *best* architecture, but rather the *least worst* architecture.

Too many architecture characteristics leads to generic solutions that are trying to solve every business problem, and those architectures rarely work because the design becomes unwieldy.

This suggests that architects should strive to design architecture to be as iterative as possible. If you can make changes to the architecture more easily, you can stress less about discovering the exact correct thing in the first attempt. One of the most important lessons of Agile software development is the value of iteration; this holds true at all levels of software development, including architecture.

CHAPTER 5

Identifying Architectural Characteristics

Identifying the driving architectural characteristics is one of the first steps in creating an architecture or determining the validity of an existing architecture. Identifying the correct architectural characteristics ("-ilities") for a given problem or application requires an architect to not only understand the domain problem, but also collaborate with the problem domain stakeholders to determine what is truly important from a domain perspective.

An architect uncovers architecture characteristics in at least three ways by extracting from domain concerns, requirements, and implicit domain knowledge. We previously discussed implicit characteristics and we cover the other two here.

Extracting Architecture Characteristics from Domain Concerns

An architect must be able to translate domain concerns to identify the right architectural characteristics. For example, is scalability the most important concern, or is it fault tolerance, security, or performance? Perhaps the system requires all four characteristics combined. Understanding the key domain goals and domain situation allows an architect to translate those domain concerns to "-ilities," which then forms the basis for correct and justifiable architecture decisions.

One tip when collaborating with domain stakeholders to define the driving architecture characteristics is to work hard to keep the final list as short as possible. A common anti-pattern in architecture entails trying to design a *generic architecture*, one that supports *all* the architecture characteristics. Each architecture characteristic the architecture supports complicates the overall system design; supporting too many architecture characteristics leads to greater and greater complexity before the architect and developers have even started addressing the problem domain, the original motivation for writing the software. Don't obsess over the number of charateristics, but rather the motivation to keep design simple.

Case Study: The Vasa

The original story of over-specifying architecture characteristics and ultimately killing a project must be the Vasa. It was a Swedish warship built between 1626 and 1628 by a king who wanted the most magnificent ship ever created. Up until that time, ships were either troop transports or gunships—the Vasa would be both! Most ships had one deck—the Vasa had two! All the cannons were twice the size of those on similar ships. Despite some trepidation by the expert ship builders (who ultimately couldn't say no to King Adolphus), the shipbuilders finished the construction. In celebration, the ship sailed out into the harbor and shot a cannon salute off one side. Unfortunately, because the ship was top-heavy, it capsized and sank to the bottom of the bay in Sweden. In the early 20th century, salvagers rescued the ship, which now resides in a museum in Stockholm.

Many architects and domain stakeholders want to prioritize the final list of architecture characteristics that the application or system must support. While this is certainly desirable, in most cases it is a fool's errand and will not only waste time, but also produce a lot of unnecessary frustration and disagreement with the key stakeholders. Rarely will all stakeholders agree on the priority of each and every characteristic. A better approach is to have the domain stakeholders select the top three most important characteristics from the final list (in any order). Not only is this much easier to gain consensus on, but it also fosters discussions about what is most important and helps the architect analyze trade-offs when making vital architecture decisions.

Most architecture characteristics come from listening to key domain stakeholders and collaborating with them to determine what is important from a domain perspective. While this may seem like a straightforward activity, the problem is that architects and domain stakeholders speak different languages. Architects talk about scalability, interoperability, fault tolerance, learnability, and availability. Domain stakeholders talk about mergers and acquisitions, user satisfaction, time to market, and competitive advantage. What happens is a "lost in translation" problem where the architect and domain stakeholder don't understand each other. Architects have no idea how to create an architecture to support user satisfaction, and domain stakeholders don't understand why there is so much focus and talk about availability, interoperability, learnability, and fault tolerance in the application. Fortunately, there is usually a translation from domain concerns to architecture characteristics. Table 5-1 shows some of the more common domain concerns and the corresponding "-ilities" that support them.

Table 5-1. Translation of domain concerns to architecture characteristics

Domain concern	Architecture characteristics
Mergers and acquisitions	Interoperability, scalability, adaptability, extensibility
Time to market	Agility, testability, deployability
User satisfaction	Performance, availability, fault tolerance, testability, deployability, agility, security
Competitive advantage	Agility, testability, deployability, scalability, availability, fault tolerance
Time and budget	Simplicity, feasibility

One important thing to note is that agility does not equal time to market. Rather, it is agility + testability + deployability. This is a trap many architects fall into when translating domain concerns. Focusing on only one of the ingredients is like forgetting to put the flour in the cake batter. For example, a domain stakeholder might say something like "Due to regulatory requirements, it is absolutely imperative that we complete end-of-day fund pricing on time." An ineffective architect might just focus on performance because that seems to be the primary focus of that domain concern. However, that architect will fail for many reasons. First, it doesn't matter how fast the system is if it isn't available when needed. Second, as the domain grows and more funds are created, the system must be able to also scale to finish end-of-day processing in time. Third, the system must not only be available, but must also be reliable so that it doesn't crash as end-of-day fund prices are being calculated. Forth, what happens if the end-of-day fund pricing is about 85% complete and the system crashes? It must be able to recover and restart where the pricing left off. Finally, the system may be fast, but are the fund prices being calculated correctly? So, in addition to performance, the architect must also equally place a focus on availability, scalability, reliability, recoverability, and auditability.

Extracting Architecture Characteristics from Requirements

Some architecture characteristics come from explicit statements in requirements documents. For example, explicit expected numbers of users and scale commonly appear in domain or domain concerns. Others come from inherent domain knowledge by architects, one of the many reasons that domain knowledge is always beneficial for architects. For example, suppose an architect designs an application that handles class registration for university students. To make the math easy, assume that the school has 1,000 students and 10 hours for registration. Should an architect design a system assuming consistent scale, making the implicit assumption that the students during the registration process will distribute themselves evenly over time? Or, based on knowledge of university students habits and proclivities, should the architect design a system that can handle all 1,000 students attempting to register in the last 10 minutes? Anyone who understands how much students stereotypically procrastinate knows the answer to this question! Rarely will details like this appear in requirements documents, yet they do inform the design decisions.

The Origin of Architecture Katas

A few years ago, Ted Neward, a well-known architect, devised architecture katas, a clever method to allow nascent architects a way to practice deriving architecture characteristics from domain-targeted descriptions. From Japan and martial arts, a *kata* is an individual training exercise, where the emphasis lies on proper form and technique.

> How do we get great designers? Great designers design, of course.
>
> —Fred Brooks

So how are we supposed to get great architects if they only get the chance to architect fewer than a half dozen times in their career?

To provide a curriculum for aspiring architects, Ted created the first architecture katas site, which your authors Neal and Mark adapted and updated. The basic premise of the kata exercise provides architects with a problem stated in domain terms and additional context (things that might not appear in requirements yet impact design). Small teams work for 45 minutes on a design, then show results to the other groups, who vote on who came up with the best architecture. True to its original purpose, architecture katas provide a useful laboratory for aspiring architects.

Each kata has predefined sections:

Description
: The overall domain problem the system is trying to solve

Users
: The expected number and/or types of users of the system

Requirements
: Domain/domain-level requirements, as an architect might expect from domain users/domain experts

Neal updated the format a few years later on his blog (*http://nealford.com/katas*) to add the *additional context* section to each kata with important additional considerations, making the exercises more realistic.

Additional context
: Many of the considerations an architect must make aren't explicitly expressed in requirements but rather by implicit knowledge of the problem domain

We encourage burgeoning architects to use the site to do their own kata exercise. Anyone can host a brown-bag lunch where a team of aspiring architects can solve a problem and get an experienced architect to evaluate the design and trade-off

---

analysis, either on the spot or from a short analysis after the fact. The design won't be elaborate because the exercise is timeboxed. Team members ideally get feedback from the experienced architecture about missed trade-offs and alternative designs.

Case Study: Silicon Sandwiches

To illustrate several concepts, we use an *architecture kata* (see "The Origin of Architecture Katas" on page 68 for the origin of the concept). To show how architects derive architecture characteristics from requirements, we introduce the Silicon Sandwiches kata.

Description
> A national sandwich shop wants to enable online ordering (in addition to its current call-in service).

Users
> Thousands, perhaps one day millions

Requirements
- Users will place their order, then be given a time to pick up their sandwich and directions to the shop (which must integrate with several external mapping services that include traffic information)
- If the shop offers a delivery service, dispatch the driver with the sandwich to the user
- Mobile-device accessibility
- Offer national daily promotions/specials
- Offer local daily promotions/specials
- Accept payment online, in person, or upon delivery

Additional context
- Sandwich shops are franchised, each with a different owner
- Parent company has near-future plans to expand overseas
- Corporate goal is to hire inexpensive labor to maximize profit

Given this scenario, how would an architect derive architecture characteristics? Each part of the requirement might contribute to one or more aspects of architecture (and many will not). The architect doesn't design the entire system here—considerable effort must still go into crafting code to solve the domain statement. Instead, the architect looks for things that influence or impact the design, particularly structural.

First, separate the candidate architecture characteristics into explicit and implicit characteristics.

Explicit Characteristics

Explicit architecture characteristics appear in a requirements specification as part of the necessary design. For example, a shopping website may aspire to support a particular number of concurrent users, which domain analysts specify in the requirements. An architect should consider each part of the requirements to see if it contributes to an architecture characteristic. But first, an architect should consider domain-level predictions about expected metrics, as represented in the Users section of the kata.

One of the first details that should catch an architect's eye is the number of users: currently thousands, perhaps one day millions (this is a very ambitious sandwich shop!). Thus, *scalability*—the ability to handle a large number of concurrent users without serious performance degradation—is one of the top architecture characteristics. Notice that the problem statement didn't explicitly ask for scalability, but rather expressed that requirement as an expected number of users. Architects must often decode domain language into engineering equivalents.

However, we also probably need *elasticity*—the ability to handle bursts of requests. These two characteristics often appear lumped together, but they have different constraints. Scalability looks like the graph shown in Figure 5-1.

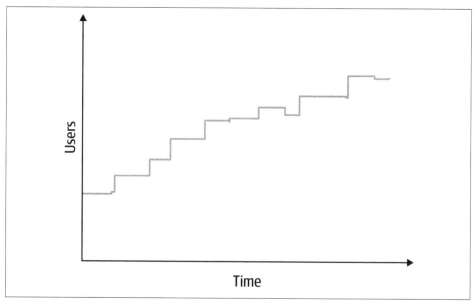

Figure 5-1. Scalability measures the performance of concurrent users

Elasticity, on the other hand, measures bursts of traffic, as shown in Figure 5-2.

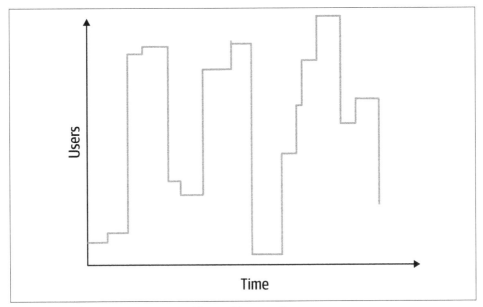

Figure 5-2. Elastic systems must withstand bursts of users

Some systems are scalable but not elastic. For example, consider a hotel reservation system. Absent special sales or events, the number of users is probably consistent. In contrast, consider a concert ticket booking system. As new tickets go on sale, fervent fans will flood the site, requiring high degrees of elasticity. Often, elastic systems also need scalability: the ability to handle bursts and high numbers of concurrent users.

The requirement for elasticity did not appear in the Silicon Sandwiches requirements, yet the architect should identify this as an important consideration. Requirements sometimes state architecture characteristics outright, but some lurk inside the problem domain. Consider a sandwich shop. Is its traffic consistent throughout the day? Or does it endure bursts of traffic around mealtimes? Almost certainly the latter. Thus, a good architect should identify this potential architecture characteristic.

An architect should consider each of these business requirements in turn to see if architecture characteristics exist:

1. Users will place their order, then be given a time to pick up their sandwich and directions to the shop (which must provide the option to integrate with external mapping services that include traffic information).

   External mapping services imply integration points, which may impact aspects such as reliability. For example, if a developer builds a system that relies on a third-party system, yet calling it fails, it impacts the reliability of the calling system. However, architects must also be wary of over-specifying architecture characteristics. What if the external traffic service is down? Should the Silicon

Sandwiches site fail, or should it just offer slightly less efficiency without traffic information? Architects should always guard against building unnecessary brittleness or fragility into designs.

2. If the shop offers a delivery service, dispatch the driver with the sandwich to the user.

   No special architecture characteristics seem necessary to support this requirement.

3. Mobile-device accessibility.

   This requirement will primarily affect the *design* of the application, pointing toward building either a portable web application or several native web applications. Given the budget constraints and simplicity of the application, an architect would likely deem it overkill to build multiple applications, so the design points toward a mobile-optimized web application. Thus, the architect may want to define some specific performance architecture characteristics for page load time and other mobile-sensitive characteristics. Notice that the architect shouldn't act alone in situations like this, but should instead collaborate with user experience designers, domain stakeholders, and other interested parties to vet decisions like this.

4. Offer national daily promotions/specials.

5. Offer local daily promotions/specials.

   Both of these requirements specify customizability across both promotions and specials. Notice that requirement 1 also implies customized traffic information based on address. Based on all three of these requirements, the architect may consider customizability as an architecture characteristic. For example, an architecture style such as microkernel architecture supports customized behavior extremely well by defining a plug-in architecture. In this case, the default behavior appears in the core, and developers write the optional customized parts, based on location, via plug-ins. However, a traditional design can also accommodate this requirement via design patterns (such as Template Method). This conundrum is common in architecture and requires architects to constantly weight trade-offs between competing options. We discuss particular trade-off in more detail in "Design Versus Architecture and Trade-Offs" on page 74.

6. Accept payment online, in person, or upon delivery.

   Online payments imply security, but nothing in this requirement suggests a particularly heightened level of security beyond what's implicit.

7. Sandwich shops are franchised, each with a different owner.

   This requirement may impose cost restrictions on the architecture—the architect should check the feasibility (applying constraints like cost, time, and staff skill set) to see if a simple or sacrificial architecture is warranted.

8. Parent company has near-future plans to expand overseas.

   This requirement implies *internationalization*, or *i18n*. Many design techniques exist to handle this requirement, which shouldn't require special structure to accommodate. This will, however, certainly drive design decisions.

9. Corporate goal is to hire inexpensive labor to maximize profit.

   This requirement suggests that usability will be important, but again is more concerned with design than architecture characteristics.

The third architecture characteristic we derive from the preceding requirements is *performance*: no one wants to buy from a sandwich shop that has poor performance, especially at peak times. However, *performance* is a nuanced concept—what *kind* of performance should the architect design for? We cover the various nuances of performance in Chapter 6.

We also want to define performance numbers in conjunction with scalability numbers. In other words, we must establish a baseline of performance without particular scale, as well as determine what an acceptable level of performance is given a certain number of users. Quite often, architecture characteristics interact with one another, forcing architects to define them in relation to one another.

Implicit Characteristics

Many architecture characteristics aren't specified in requirements documents, yet they make up an important aspect of the design. One implicit architecture characteristic the system might want to support is *availability*: making sure users can access the sandwich site. Closely related to availability is *reliability*: making sure the site stays up during interactions—no one wants to purchase from a site that continues dropping connections, forcing them to log in again.

Security appears as an implicit characteristic in every system: no one wants to create insecure software. However, it may be prioritized depending on criticality, which illustrates the interlocking nature of our definition. An architect considers security an architecture characteristic if it influences some structural aspect of the design and is critical or important to the application.

For Silicon Sandwiches, an architect might assume that payments should be handled by a third party. Thus, as long as developers follow general security hygiene (not passing credit card numbers as plain text, not storing too much information, and so on), the architect shouldn't need any special structural design to accommodate security; good design in the application will suffice. Each architecture characteristic interacts with the others, leading to the common pitfall of architects of over-specifying architecture characteristics, which is just as damaging as under-specifying them because it overcomplicates the system design.

The last major architecture characteristic that Silicon Sandwiches needs to support encompasses several details from the requirements: *customizability*. Notice that several parts of the problem domain offer custom behavior: recipes, local sales, and directions that may be locally overridden. Thus, the architecture should support the ability to facilitate custom behavior. Normally, this would fall into the design of the application. However, as our definition specifies, a part of the problem domain that relies on custom structure to support it moves into the realm of an architecture characteristic. This design element isn't critical to the success of the application though. It is important to note that there are no correct answers in choosing architecture characteristics, only incorrect ones (or, as Mark notes in one of his well-known quotes):

> There are no wrong answers in architecture, only expensive ones.

Design Versus Architecture and Trade-Offs

In the Silicon Sandwiches kata, an architect would likely identify customizability as a part of the system, but the question then becomes: architecture or design? The architecture implies some structural component, whereas design resides within the architecture. In the customizability case of Silicon Sandwiches, the architect could choose an architecture style like microkernel and build structural support for customization. However, if the architect chose another style because of competing concerns, developers could implement the customization using the Template Method design pattern, which allows parent classes to define workflow that can be overridden in child classes. Which design is better?

Like in all architecture, it depends on a number of factors. First, are there good reasons, such as performance and coupling, not to implement a microkernel architecture? Second, are other desirable architecture characteristics more difficult in one design versus the other? Third, how much would it cost to support all the architecture characteristics in each design versus pattern? This type of architectural trade-off analysis makes up an important part of an architect's role.

Above all, it is critical for the architect to collaborate with the developers, project manager, operations team, and other co-constructors of the software system. No architecture decision should be made isolated from the implementation team (which leads to the dreaded *Ivory Tower Architect* anti-pattern). In the case of Silicon Sandwiches, the architect, tech lead, developers, and domain analysts should collaborate to decide how best to implement customizability.

An architect could design an architecture that doesn't accommodate customizability structurally, requiring the design of the application itself to support that behavior (see "Design Versus Architecture and Trade-Offs" on page 74). Architects shouldn't stress too much about discovering the exactly correct set of architecture characteristics—developers can implement functionality in a variety of ways. However, correctly identifying important structural elements may facilitate a simpler or more elegant design. Architects must remember: there is no best design in architecture, only a least worst collection of trade-offs.

Architects must also prioritize these architecture characteristics toward trying to find the simplest required sets. A useful exercise once the team has made a first pass at identifying the architecture characteristics is to try to determine the least important one—if you must eliminate one, which would it be? Generally, architects are more likely to cull the explicit architecture characteristics, as many of the implicit ones support general success. The way we define what's critical or important to success assists architects in determining if the application truly requires each architecture characteristic. By attempting to determine the least applicable one, architects can help determine critical necessity. In the case of Silicon Sandwiches, which architecture characteristic that we have identified is least important? Again, no absolute correct answer exists. However, in this case, the solution could lose either customizability or performance. We could eliminate customizability as an architecture characteristic and plan to implement that behavior as part of application design. Of the operational architecture characteristics, performance is likely the least critical for success. Of course, the developers don't mean to build an application that has terrible performance, but rather one that doesn't prioritize performance over other characteristics, such as scalability or availability.

CHAPTER 6

Measuring and Governing Architecture Characteristics

Architects must deal with the extraordinarily wide variety of architecture characteristics across all different aspects of software projects. Operational aspects like performance, elasticity, and scalability comingle with structural concerns such as modularity and deployability. This chapter focuses on concretely defining some of the more common architecture characteristics and building governance mechanisms for them.

Measuring Architecture Characteristics

Several common problems exist around the definition of architecture characteristics in organizations:

They aren't physics
> Many architecture characteristics in common usage have vague meanings. For example, how does an architect design for *agility* or *deployability*? The industry has wildly differing perspectives on common terms, sometimes driven by legitimate differing contexts, and sometimes accidental.

Wildly varying definitions
> Even within the same organization, different departments may disagree on the definition of critical features such as *performance*. Until developers, architecture, and operations can unify on a common definition, a proper conversation is difficult.

Too composite

> Many desirable architecture characteristics comprise many others at a smaller scale. For example, developers can decompose agility into characteristics such as modularity, deployability, and testability.

Objective definitions for architecture characteristics solve all three problems: by agreeing organization-wide on concrete definitions for architecture characteristics, teams create a ubiquitous language around architecture. Also, by encouraging objective definitions, teams can unpack composite characteristics to uncover measurable features they can objectively define.

Operational Measures

Many architecture characteristics have obvious direct measurements, such as performance or scalability. However, even these offer many nuanced interpretations, depending on the team's goals. For example, perhaps a team measures the average response time for certain requests, a good example of an operational architecture characteristics measure. But if teams only measure the average, what happens if some boundary condition causes 1% of requests to take 10 times longer than others? If the site has enough traffic, the outliers may not even show up. Therefore, a team may also want to measure the maximum response times to catch outliers.

The Many Flavors of Performance

Many of the architecture characteristics we describe have multiple, nuanced definitions. Performance is a great example. Many projects look at general performance: for example, how long request and response cycles take for a web application. However, architects and DevOps engineers have performed a tremendous amount of work on establishing performance budgets: specific budgets for specific parts of the application. For example, many organizations have researched user behavior and determined that the optimum time for first-page render (the first visible sign of progress for a webpage, in a browser or mobile device) is 500 ms—half a second; Most applications fall in the double-digit range for this metric. But, for modern sites that attempt to capture as many users as possible, this is an important metric to track, and the organizations behind them have built extremely nuanced measures.

Some of these metrics have additional implications for the design of applications. Many forward-thinking organizations place *K-weight budgets* for page downloads: a maximum number of bytes' worth of libraries and frameworks allowed on a particular page. Their rationale behind this structure derives from physics constraints: only so many bytes can travel over a network at a time, especially for mobile devices in high-latency areas.

High-level teams don't just establish hard performance numbers; they base their definitions on statistical analysis. For example, say a video streaming service wants to monitor scalability. Rather than set an arbitrary number as the goal, engineers measure the scale over time and build statistical models, then raise alarms if the real-time metrics fall outside the prediction models. A failure can mean two things: the model is incorrect (which teams like to know) or something is amiss (which teams also like to know).

The kinds of characteristics that teams can now measure are evolving rapidly, in conjunction with tools and nuanced understanding. For example, many teams recently focused on performance budgets for metrics such as *first contentful paint* and *first CPU idle*, both of which speak volumes about performance issues for users of webpages on mobile devices. As devices, targets, capabilities, and myriad other things change, teams will find new things and ways to measure.

Structural Measures

Some objective measures are not so obvious as performance. What about internal structural characteristics, such as well-defined modularity? Unfortunately, comprehensive metrics for internal code quality don't yet exist. However, some metrics and common tools do allow architects to address some critical aspects of code structure, albeit along narrow dimensions.

An obvious measurable aspect of code is complexity, defined by the *cyclomatic complexity* metric.

Cyclomatic Complexity

Cyclomatic Complexity (CC) (*https://oreil.ly/mAHFZ*) is a code-level metric designed to provide an object measure for the complexity of code, at the function/method, class, or application level, developed by Thomas McCabe, Sr., in 1976.

It is computed by applying graph theory to code, specifically decision points, which cause different execution paths. For example, if a function has no decision statements (such as `if` statements), then `CC = 1`. If the function had a single conditional, then `CC = 2` because two possible execution paths exist.

The formula for calculating the CC for a single function or method is $CC = E - N + 2$, where N represents *nodes* (lines of code), and E represents *edges* (possible decisions). Consider the C-like code shown in Example 6-1.

Example 6-1. Sample code for cyclomatic complexity evaluation

```
public void decision(int c1, int c2) {
    if (c1 < 100)
        return 0;
    else if (c1 + C2 > 500)
        return 1;
    else
      return -1;
}
```

The cyclomatic complexity for Example 6-1 is 3 (=3 − 2 + 2); the graph appears in Figure 6-1.

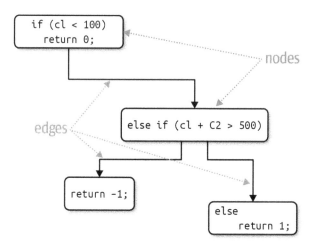

Figure 6-1. Cyclomatic Complexity for the decision function

The number 2 appearing in the cyclomatic complexity formula represents a simplification for a single function/method. For fan-out calls to other methods (known as *connected components* in graph theory), the more general formula is $CC = E − N + 2P$, where P represents the number of connected components.

Architects and developers universally agree that overly complex code represents a code smell; it harms virtually every one of the desirable characteristics of code bases: modularity, testability, deployability, and so on. Yet if teams don't keep an eye on gradually growing complexity, that complexity will dominate the code base.

What's a Good Value for Cyclomatic Complexity?

A common question the authors receive when talking about this subject is: what's a good threshold value for CC? Of course, like all answers in software architecture: it depends! It depends on the complexity of the problem domain. For example, if you have an algorithmically complex problem, the solution will yield complex functions. Some of the key aspects of CC for architects to monitor: are functions complex because of the problem domain or because of poor coding? Alternatively, is the code partitioned poorly? In other words, could a large method be broken down into smaller, logical chunks, distributing the work (and complexity) into more well-factored methods?

In general, the industry thresholds for CC suggest that a value under 10 is acceptable, barring other considerations such as complex domains. We consider that threshold very high and would prefer code to fall under five, indicating cohesive, well-factored code. A metrics tool in the Java world, Crap4J (*http://www.crap4j.org*), attempts to determine how poor (crappy) your code is by evaluating a combination of CC and code coverage; if CC grows to over 50, no amount of code coverage rescues that code from crappiness. The most terrifying professional artifact Neal ever encountered was a single C function that served as the heart of a commercial software package whose CC was over 800! It was a single function with over 4,000 lines of code, including the liberal use of GOTO statements (to escape impossibly deeply nested loops).

Engineering practices like test-driven development have the accidental (but positive) side effect of generating smaller, less complex methods on average for a given problem domain. When practicing TDD, developers try to write a simple test, then write the smallest amount of code to pass the test. This focus on discrete behavior and good test boundaries encourages well-factored, highly cohesive methods that exhibit low CC.

Process Measures

Some architecture characteristics intersect with software development processes. For example, agility often appears as a desirable feature. However, it is a composite architecture characteristic that architects may decompose into features such as testability, and deployability.

Testability is measurable through code coverage tools for virtually all platforms that assess the completeness of testing. Like all software checks, it cannot replace thinking and intent. For example, a code base can have 100% code coverage yet poor assertions that don't actually provide confidence in code correctness. However, testability is clearly an objectively measurable characteristic. Similarly, teams can measure deployability via a variety of metrics: percentage of successful to failed deployments, how long deployments take, issues/bugs raised by deployments, and a host of others. Each team bears the responsibility to arrive at a good set of measurements that capture useful data for their organization, both in quality and quantity. Many of these measures come down to team priorities and goals.

Agility and its related parts clearly relate to the software development process. However, that process may impact the structure of the architecture. For example, if ease of deployment and testability are high priorities, then an architect would place more emphasis on good modularity and isolation at the architecture level, an example of an architecture characteristic driving a structural decision. Virtually anything within the scope of a software project may rise to the level of an architecture characteristic if it manages to meet our three criteria, forcing an architect to make design decisions to account for it.

Governance and Fitness Functions

Once architects have established architecture characteristics and prioritized them, how can they make sure that developers will respect those priorities? Modularity is a great example of an aspect of architecture that is important but not urgent; on many software projects, urgency dominates, yet architects still need a mechanism for governance.

Governing Architecture Characteristics

Governance, derived from the Greek word *kubernan* (to steer) is an important responsibility of the architect role. As the name implies, the scope of architecture governance covers any aspect of the software development process that architects (including roles like enterprise architects) want to exert an influence upon. For example, ensuring software quality within an organization falls under the heading of architectural governance because it falls within the scope of architecture, and negligence can lead to disastrous quality problems.

Fortunately, increasingly sophisticated solutions exist to relieve this problem from architects, a good example of the incremental growth in capabilities within the software development ecosystem. The drive toward automation on software projects spawned by Extreme Programming (*http://www.extremeprogramming.org*) created continuous integration, which led to further automation into operations, which we now call DevOps, continuing through to architectural governance. The book *Building Evolutionary Architectures* (O'Reilly) describes a family of techniques, called fitness functions, used to automate many aspects of architecture governance.

Fitness Functions

The word "evolutionary" in *Building Evolutionary Architectures* comes more from evolutionary computing than biology. One of the authors, Dr. Rebecca Parsons, spent some time in the evolutionary computing space, including tools like genetic algorithms. A genetic algorithm executes and produces an answer and then undergoes mutation by well-known techniques defined within the evolutionary computing world. If a developer tries to design a genetic algorithm to produce some beneficial outcome, they often want to guide the algorithm, providing an objective measure indicating the quality of the outcome. That guidance mechanism is called a *fitness function*: an object function used to assess how close the output comes to achieving the aim. For example, suppose a developer needed to solve the traveling salesperson problem (*https://oreil.ly/GApjt*), a famous problem used as a basis for machine learning. Given a salesperson and a list of cities they must visit, with distances between them, what is the optimum route? If a developer designs a genetic algorithm to solve this problem, one fitness function might evaluate the length of the route, as the shortest possible one represents highest success. Another fitness function might be to evaluate the overall cost associated with the route and attempt to keep cost at a minimum. Yet another might be to evaluate the time the traveling salesperson is away and optimize to shorten the total travel time.

Practices in evolutionary architecture borrow this concept to create an *architecture fitness function*:

Architecture fitness function
> Any mechanism that provides an objective integrity assessment of some architecture characteristic or combination of architecture characteristics

Fitness functions are not some new framework for architects to download, but rather a new perspective on many existing tools. Notice in the definition the phrase *any mechanism*—the verification techniques for architecture characteristics are as varied as the characteristics are. Fitness functions overlap many existing verification mechanisms, depending on the way they are used: as metrics, monitors, unit testing libraries, chaos engineering, and so on, illustrated in Figure 6-2.

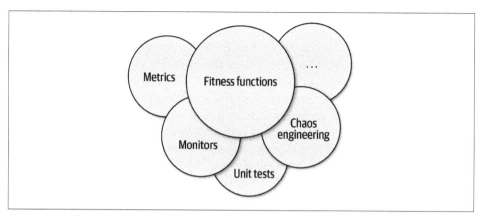

Figure 6-2. The mechanisms of fitness functions

Many different tools may be used to implement fitness functions, depending on the architecture characteristics. For example, in "Coupling" on page 44 we introduced metrics to allow architects to assess modularity. Here are a couple of examples of fitness functions that test various aspects of modularity.

Cyclic dependencies

Modularity is an implicit architecture characteristic that most architects care about, because poorly maintained modularity harms the structure of a code base; thus, architects should place a high priority on maintaining good modularity. However, forces work against the architect's good intentions on many platforms. For example, when coding in any popular Java or .NET development environment, as soon as a developer references a class not already imported, the IDE helpfully presents a dialog asking the developers if they would like to auto-import the reference. This occurs so often that most programmers develop the habit of swatting the auto-import dialog away like a reflex action. However, arbitrarily importing classes or components between one another spells disaster for modularity. For example, Figure 6-3 illustrates a particularly damaging anti-pattern that architects aspire to avoid.

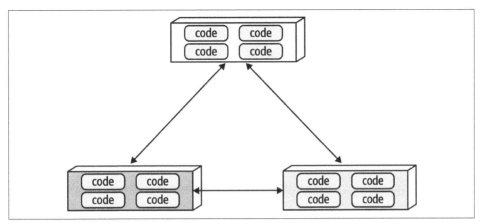

Figure 6-3. Cyclic dependencies between components

In Figure 6-3, each component references something in the others. Having a network of components such as this damages modularity because a developer cannot reuse a single component without also bringing the others along. And, of course, if the other components are coupled to other components, the architecture tends more and more toward the Big Ball of Mud (*https://oreil.ly/usx7p*) anti-pattern. How can architects govern this behavior without constantly looking over the shoulders of trigger-happy developers? Code reviews help but happen too late in the development cycle to be effective. If an architect allows a development team to rampantly import across the code base for a week until the code review, serious damage has already occurred in the code base.

The solution to this problem is to write a fitness function to look after cycles, as shown in Example 6-2.

Example 6-2. Fitness function to detect component cycles

```
public class CycleTest {
    private JDepend jdepend;

    @BeforeEach
    void init() {
        jdepend = new JDepend();
        jdepend.addDirectory("/path/to/project/persistence/classes");
        jdepend.addDirectory("/path/to/project/web/classes");
        jdepend.addDirectory("/path/to/project/thirdpartyjars");
    }

    @Test
    void testAllPackages() {
        Collection packages = jdepend.analyze();
        assertEquals("Cycles exist", false, jdepend.containsCycles());
```

```
    }
}
```

In the code, an architect uses the metrics tool JDepend (*https://oreil.ly/ozzzk*) to check the dependencies between packages. The tool understands the structure of Java packages and fails the test if any cycles exist. An architect can wire this test into the continuous build on a project and stop worrying about the accidental introduction of cycles by trigger-happy developers. This is a great example of a fitness function guarding the important rather than urgent practices of software development: it's an important concern for architects yet has little impact on day-to-day coding.

Distance from the main sequence fitness function

In "Coupling" on page 44, we introduced the more esoteric metric of distance from the main sequence, which architects can also verify using fitness functions, as shown in Example 6-3.

Example 6-3. Distance from the main sequence fitness function

```
@Test
void AllPackages() {
    double ideal = 0.0;
    double tolerance = 0.5; // project-dependent
    Collection packages = jdepend.analyze();
    Iterator iter = packages.iterator();
    while (iter.hasNext()) {
      JavaPackage p = (JavaPackage)iter.next();
      assertEquals("Distance exceeded: " + p.getName(),
            ideal, p.distance(), tolerance);
    }
}
```

In the code, the architect uses JDepend to establish a threshold for acceptable values, failing the test if a class falls outside the range.

This is both an example of an objective measure for an architecture characteristic and the importance of collaboration between developers and architects when designing and implementing fitness functions. The intent is not for a group of architects to ascend to an ivory tower and develop esoteric fitness functions that developers cannot understand.

 Architects must ensure that developers understand the purpose of the fitness function before imposing it on them.

The sophistication of fitness function tools has increased over the last few years, including some special purpose tools. One such tool is ArchUnit (*https://www.archu nit.org*), a Java testing framework inspired by and using several parts of the JUnit (*https://junit.org*) ecosystem. ArchUnit provides a variety of predefined governance rules codified as unit tests and allows architects to write specific tests that address modularity. Consider the layered architecture illustrated in Figure 6-4.

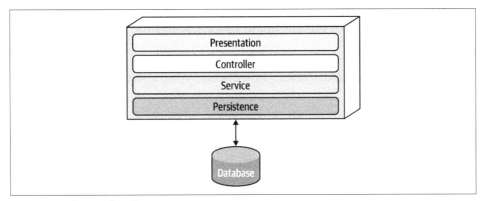

Figure 6-4. Layered architecture

When designing a layered monolith such as the one in Figure 6-4, the architect defines the layers for good reason (motivations, trade-offs, and other aspects of the layered architecture are described in Chapter 10). However, how can the architect ensure that developers will respect those layers? Some developers may not understand the importance of the patterns, while others may adopt a "better to ask forgiveness than permission" attitude because of some overriding local concern such as performance. But allowing implementers to erode the reasons for the architecture hurts the long-term health of the architecture.

ArchUnit allows architects to address this problem via a fitness function, shown in Example 6-4.

Example 6-4. ArchUnit fitness function to govern layers

```
layeredArchitecture()
    .layer("Controller").definedBy("..controller..")
    .layer("Service").definedBy("..service..")
    .layer("Persistence").definedBy("..persistence..")

    .whereLayer("Controller").mayNotBeAccessedByAnyLayer()
    .whereLayer("Service").mayOnlyBeAccessedByLayers("Controller")
    .whereLayer("Persistence").mayOnlyBeAccessedByLayers("Service")
```

In Example 6-4, the architect defines the desirable relationship between layers and writes a verification fitness function to govern it.

A similar tool in the .NET space, NetArchTest (*https://oreil.ly/EMXpv*), allows similar tests for that platform; a layer verification in C# appears in Example 6-5.

Example 6-5. NetArchTest for layer dependencies

```
// Classes in the presentation should not directly reference repositories
var result = Types.InCurrentDomain()
    .That()
    .ResideInNamespace("NetArchTest.SampleLibrary.Presentation")
    .ShouldNot()
    .HaveDependencyOn("NetArchTest.SampleLibrary.Data")
    .GetResult()
    .IsSuccessful;
```

Another example of fitness functions is Netflix's Chaos Monkey and the attendant Simian Army (*https://oreil.ly/GipHq*). In particular, the *Conformity*, *Security*, and *Janitor* Monkeys exemplify this approach. The Conformity Monkey allows Netflix architects to define governance rules enforced by the monkey in production. For example, if the architects decided that each service should respond usefully to all RESTful verbs, they build that check into the Conformity Monkey. Similarly, the Security Monkey checks each service for well-known security defects, like ports that shouldn't be active and configuration errors. Finally, the Janitor Monkey looks for instances that no other services route to anymore. Netflix has an evolutionary architecture, so developers routinely migrate to newer services, leaving old services running with no collaborators. Because services running on the cloud consume money, the Janitor Monkey looks for orphan services and disintegrates them out of production.

The Origin of the Simian Army

When Netflix decided to move its operations to Amazon's cloud, the architects worried over the fact that they no longer had control over operations—what happens if a defect appears operationally? To solve this problem, they spawned the discipline of Chaos Engineering with the original Chaos Monkey, and eventually the Simian Army. The Chaos Monkey simulated general chaos within the production environment to see how well their system would endure it. Latency was a problem with some AWS instances, thus the Chaos Monkey would simulate high latency (which was such a problem, they eventually created a specialized monkey for it, the Latency Monkey). Tools such as the Chaos Kong, which simulates an entire Amazon data center failure, helped Netflix avoid such outages when they occured for real.

Chaos engineering offers an interesting new perspective on architecture: it's not a question of if something will eventually break, but when. Anticipating those breakages and tests to prevent them makes systems much more robust.

A few years ago, the influential book *The Checklist Manifesto* (*https://oreil.ly/XNcV9*) by Atul Gawande (Picador) described how professions such as airline pilots and surgeons use checklists (sometimes legally mandated). It's not because those professionals don't know their jobs or are forgetful. Rather, when professionals do a highly detailed job over and over, it becomes easy for details to slip by; a succinct checklist forms an effective reminder. This is the correct perspective on fitness functions— rather than a heavyweight governance mechanism, fitness functions provide a mechanism for architects to express important architectural principles and automatically verify them. Developers know that they shouldn't release insecure code, but that priority competes with dozens or hundreds of other priorities for busy developers. Tools like the Security Monkey specifically, and fitness functions generally, allow architects to codify important governance checks into the substrate of the architecture.

CHAPTER 7

Scope of Architecture Characteristics

A prevailing axiomatic assumption in the software architecture world had traditionally placed the scope of architecture characteristics at the system level. For example, when architects talk about scalability, they generally couch that discussion around the scalability of the entire system. That was a safe assumption a decade ago, when virtually all systems were monolithic. With the advent of modern engineering techniques and the architecture styles they enabled, such as microservices, the scope of architecture characteristics has narrowed considerably. This is a prime example of an axiom slowly becoming outdated as the software development ecosystem continues its relentless evolution.

During the writing of the *Building Evolutionary Architectures* (*http://evolutionaryarchitecture.com*) book, the authors needed a technique to measure the structural evolvability of particular architecture styles. None of the existing measures offered the correct level of detail. In "Structural Measures" on page 79, we discuss a variety of code-level metrics that allow architects to analyze structural aspects of an architecture. However, all these metrics only reveal low-level details about the code, and cannot evaluate dependent components (such as databases) outside the code base that still impact many architecture characteristics, especially operational ones. For example, no matter how much an architect puts effort into designing a performant or elastic code base, if the system uses a database that doesn't match those characteristics, the application won't be successful.

When evaluating many operational architecture characteristics, an architect must consider dependent components outside the code base that will impact those characteristics. Thus, architects need another method to measure these kinds of dependencies. That lead the *Building Evolutionary Architectures* authors to define the term *architecture quantum*. To understand the architecture quantum definition, we must preview one key metric here, connascence.

Coupling and Connascence

Many of the code-level coupling metrics, such as *afferent* and *efferent* coupling (described in "Structural Measures" on page 79), reveal details at a too fine-grained level for architectural analysis. In 1996, Meilir Page-Jones published a book titled *What Every Programmer Should Know About Object Oriented Design* (Dorset House) that included several new measures of coupling he named *connascence*, which is defined as follows:

Connascence
> Two components are connascent if a change in one would require the other to be modified in order to maintain the overall correctness of the system

He defined two types of connascence: *static*, discoverable via static code analysis, and *dynamic*, concerning runtime behavior. To define the architecture quantum, we needed a measure of how components are "wired" together, which corresponds to the connascence concept. For example, if two services in a microservices architecture share the same class definition of some class, like *address*, we say they are *statically* connascent with each other—changing the shared class requires changes to both services.

For dynamic connascence, we define two types: *synchronous* and *asynchronous*. Synchronous calls between two distributed services have the caller wait for the response from the callee. On the other hand, *asynchronous* calls allow fire-and-forget semantics in event-driven architectures, allowing two different services to differ in operational architecture

Architectural Quanta and Granularity

Component-level coupling isn't the only thing that binds software together. Many business concepts semantically bind parts of the system together, creating *functional cohesion*. To successfully design, analyze, and evolve software, developers must consider all the coupling points that could break.

Many science-literate developers know of the concept of quantum from physics, the minimum amount of any physical entity involved in an interaction. The word quantum derives from Latin, meaning "how great" or "how much." We have adopted this notion to define an *architecture quantum*:

Architecture quantum
> An independently deployable artifact with high functional cohesion and synchronous connascence

This definition contains several parts, dissected here:

Independently deployable

An architecture quantum includes all the necessary components to function independently from other parts of the architecture. For example, if an application uses a database, it is part of the quantum because the system won't function without it. This requirement means that virtually all legacy systems deployed using a single database by definition form a quantum of one. However, in the microservices architecture style, each service includes its own database (part of the *bounded context* driving philosophy in microservices, described in detail in Chapter 17), creating multiple quanta within that architecture.

High functional cohesion

Cohesion in component design refers to how well the contained code is unified in purpose. For example, a `Customer` component with properties and methods all pertaining to a *Customer* entity exhibits high cohesion; whereas a `Utility` component with a random collection of miscellaneous methods would not.

High functional cohesion implies that an architecture quantum does something purposeful. This distinction matters little in traditional monolithic applications with a single database. However, in microservices architectures, developers typically design each service to match a single workflow (a *bounded context*, as described in "Domain-Driven Design's Bounded Context" on page 94), thus exhibiting high functional cohesion.

Synchronous connascence

Synchronous connascence implies synchronous calls within an application context or between distributed services that form this architecture quantum. For example, if one service in a microservices architecture calls another one synchronously, each service cannot exhibit extreme differences in operational architecture characteristics. If the caller is much more scalable than the callee, timeouts and other reliability concerns will occur. Thus, synchronous calls create dynamic connascence for the length of the call—if one is waiting for the other, their operational architecture characteristics must be the same for the duration of the call.

Back in Chapter 6, we defined the relationship between traditional coupling metrics and connascence, which didn't include our new *communication connascence* measure. We update this diagram in Figure 7-1.

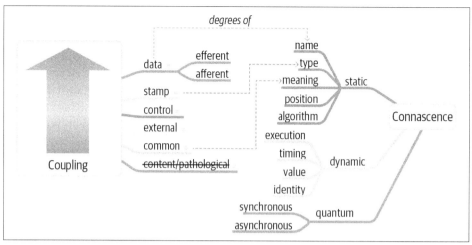

Figure 7-1. Adding quantum connascence to the unified diagram

For another example, consider a microservices architecture with a `Payment` service and an `Auction` service. When an auction ends, the `Auction` service sends payment information to the `Payment` service. However, let's say that the payment service can only handle a payment every 500 ms—what happens when a large number of auctions end at once? A poorly designed architecture would allow the first call to go through and allow the others to time out. Alternatively, an architect might design an asynchronous communication link between `Payment` and `Auction`, allowing the message queue to temporarily buffer differences. In this case, asynchronous connascence creates a more flexible architecture. We cover this subject in great detail in Chapter 14.

Domain-Driven Design's Bounded Context

Eric Evans' book *Domain-Driven Design* (Addison-Wesley Professional) has deeply influenced modern architectural thinking. *Domain-driven design* (DDD) (*https://dddcommunity.org*) is a modeling technique that allows for organized decomposition of complex problem domains. DDD defines the *bounded context*, where everything related to the domain is visible internally but opaque to other bounded contexts. Before DDD, developers sought holistic reuse across common entities within the organization. Yet creating common shared artifacts causes a host of problems, such as coupling, more difficult coordination, and increased complexity. The *bounded context* concept recognizes that each entity works best within a localized context. Thus, instead of creating a unified `Customer` class across the entire organization, each problem domain can create its own and reconcile differences at integration points.

The architecture quantum concept provides the new scope for architecture characteristics. In modern systems, architects define architecture characteristics at the quantum level rather than system level. By looking at a narrower scope for important operational concerns, architects may identify architectural challenges early, leading to hybrid architectures. To illustrate scoping provided by the architecture quantum measure, consider another architecture kata, *Going, Going, Gone*.

Case Study: Going, Going, Gone

In Chapter 5, we introduced the concept of an architecture kata. Consider this one, concerning an online auction company. Here is the description of the architecture kata:

Description
> An auction company wants to take its auctions online to a nationwide scale. Customers choose the auction to participate in, wait until the auction begins, then bid as if they are there in the room with the auctioneer.

Users
> Scale up to hundreds of participants per auction, potentially up to thousands of participants, and as many simultaneous auctions as possible.

Requirements
- Auctions must be as real-time as possible.
- Bidders register with a credit card; the system automatically charges the card if the bidder wins.
- Participants must be tracked via a reputation index.
- Bidders can see a live video stream of the auction and all bids as they occur.
- Both online and live bids must be received in the order in which they are placed.

Additional context
- Auction company is expanding aggressively by merging with smaller competitors.
- Budget is not constrained. This is a strategic direction.
- Company just exited a lawsuit where it settled a suit alleging fraud.

Just as in "Case Study: Silicon Sandwiches" on page 69, an architect must consider each of these requirements to ascertain architecture characteristics:

1. "Nationwide scale," "scale up to hundreds of participants per auction, potentially up to thousands of participants, and as many simultaneous auctions as possible," "auctions must be as real-time as possible."

Each of these requirements implies both scalability to support the sheer number of users and elasticity to support the bursty nature of auctions. While the requirements explicitly call out scalability, elasticity represents an implicit characteristics based on the problem domain. When considering auctions, do users all politely spread themselves out during the course of bidding, or do they become more frantic near the end? Domain knowledge is crucial for architects to pick up implicit architecture characteristics. Given the real-time nature of auctions, an architect will certainly consider performance a key architecture characteristic.

2. "Bidders register with a credit card; the system automatically charges the card if the bidder wins," "company just exited a lawsuit where it settled a suit alleging fraud."

   Both these requirements clearly point to security as an architecture characteristic. As covered in Chapter 5, security is an implicit architecture characteristic in virtually every application. Thus, architects rely on the second part of the definition of architecture characteristics, that they influence some structural aspect of the design. Should an architect design something special to accommodate security, or will general design and coding hygiene suffice? Architects have developed techniques for handling credit cards safely via design without necessarily building special structure. For example, as long as developers make sure not to store credit card numbers in plain text, to encrypt while in transit, and so on, then the architect shouldn't have to build special considerations for security.

   However, the second phrase should make an architect pause and ask for further clarification. Clearly, some aspect of security (fraud) was a problem in the past, thus the architect should ask for further input no matter what level of security they design.

3. "Participants must be tracked via a reputation index."

   This requirement suggests some fanciful names such as "anti-trollability," but the *track* part of the requirement might suggest some architecture characteristics such as auditability and loggability. The deciding factor again goes back to the defining characteristic—is this outside the scope of the problem domain? Architects must remember that the analysis to yield architecture characteristics represents only a small part of the overall effort to design and implement an application—a lot of design work happens past this phase! During this part of architecture definition, architects look for requirements with structural impact not already covered by the domain.

   Here's a useful litmus test architects use to make the determination between domain versus architecture characteristics is: does it require domain knowledge to implement, or is it an abstract architecture characteristic? In the Going, Going, Gone kata, an architect upon encountering the phrase "reputation index" would seek out a business analyst or other subject matter expert to explain what they had in mind. In other words, the phrase "reputation index" isn't a standard definition like more common architecture characteristics. As a counter example, when architects discuss *elasticity*, the ability to handle bursts of users, they can talk about the architecture characteristic purely in the abstract—it doesn't matter what kind of application they consider: banking, catalog site, streaming video, and so on. Architects must determine whether a requirement isn't already encompassed by the domain *and* requires particular structure, which elevates a consideration to architecture characteristic.

4. "Auction company is expanding aggressively by merging with smaller competitors."

   While this requirement may not have an immediate impact on application design, it might become the determining factor in a trade-off between several options. For example, architects must often choose details such as communication protocols for integration architecture: if integration with newly merged companies isn't a concern, it frees the architect to choose something highly specific to the problem. On the other hand, an architect may choose something that's less than perfect to accommodate some additional trade-off, such as interoperability. Subtle implicit architecture characteristics such as this pervade architecture, illustrating why doing the job well presents challenges.

5. "Budget is not constrained. This is a strategic direction."

   Some architecture katas impose budget restrictions on the solution to represent a common real-world trade-off. However, in the Going, Going, Gone kata, it does not. This allows the architect to choose more elaborate and/or special-purpose architectures, which will be beneficial given the next requirements.

6. "Bidders can see a live video stream of the auction and all bids as they occur," "both online and live bids must be received in the order in which they are placed."

   This requirement presents an interesting architectural challenge, definitely impacting the structure of the application and exposing the futility of treating architecture characteristics as a system-wide evaluation. Consider availability—is that need uniform throughout the architecture? In other words, is the availability of the one bidder more important than availability for one of the hundreds of bidders? Obviously, the architect desires good measures for both, but one is clearly more critical: if the auctioneer cannot access the site, online bids cannot occur for anyone. Reliability commonly appears with availability; it addresses operational aspects such as uptime, as well as data integrity and other measures of how reliable an application is. For example, in an auction site, the architect must ensure that the message ordering is reliably correct, eliminating race conditions and other problems.

This last requirement in the Going, Going, Gone kata highlights the need for a more granular scope in architecture than the system level. Using the architecture quantum measure, architects scope architecture characteristics at the quantum level. For example, in Going, Going, Gone, an architect would notice that different parts of this architecture need different characteristics: streaming bids, online bidders, and the auctioneer are three obvious choices. Architects use the architecture quantum measure as a way to think about deployment, coupling, where data should reside, and communication styles within architectures. In this kata, an architect can analyze the differing architecture characteristics per architecture quantum, leading to hybrid architecture design earlier in the process.

Thus, for Going, Going, Gone, we identified the following quanta and corresponding architecture characteristics:

Bidder feedback
Encompasses the bid stream and video stream of bids

- Availability
- Scalability
- Performance

Auctioneer
The live auctioneer

- Availability
- Reliability
- Scalability
- Elasticity
- Performance
- Security

Bidder
Online bidders and bidding

- Reliability
- Availability
- Scalability
- Elasticity

CHAPTER 8

Component-Based Thinking

In Chapter 3, we discussed *modules* as a collection of related code. However, architects typically think in terms of *components*, the physical manifestation of a module.

Developers physically package modules in different ways, sometimes depending on their development platform. We call physical packaging of modules *components*. Most languages support physical packaging as well: `jar` files in Java, `dll` in .NET, `gem` in Ruby, and so on. In this chapter, we discuss architectural considerations around components, ranging from scope to discovery.

Component Scope

Developers find it useful to subdivide the concept of *component* based on a wide host of factors, a few of which appear in Figure 8-1.

Components offer a language-specific mechanism to group artifacts together, often nesting them to create stratification. As shown in Figure 8-1, the simplest component wraps code at a higher level of modularity than classes (or functions, in nonobject-oriented languages). This simple wrapper is often called a *library*, which tends to run in the same memory address as the calling code and communicate via language function call mechanisms. Libraries are usually compile-time dependencies (with notable exceptions like dynamic link libraries [DLLs] that were the bane of Windows users for many years).

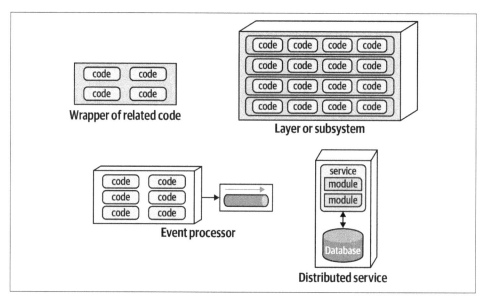

Figure 8-1. Different varieties of components

Components also appear as subsystems or layers in architecture, as the deployable unit of work for many event processors. Another type of component, a *service*, tends to run in its own address space and communicates via low-level networking protocols like TCP/IP or higher-level formats like REST or message queues, forming stand-alone, deployable units in architectures like microservices.

Nothing requires an architect to use components—it just so happens that it's often useful to have a higher level of modularity than the lowest level offered by the language. For example, in microservices architectures, simplicity is one of the architectural principles. Thus, a service may consist of enough code to warrant components or may be simple enough to just contain a small bit of code, as illustrated in Figure 8-2.

Components form the fundamental modular building block in architecture, making them a critical consideration for architects. In fact, one of the primary decisions an architect must make concerns the top-level partitioning of components in the architecture.

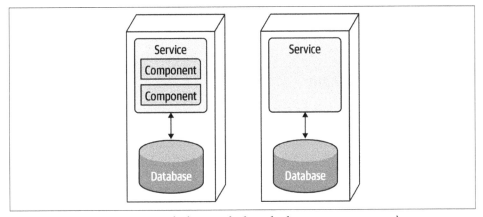

Figure 8-2. A microservice might have so little code that components aren't necessary

Architect Role

Typically, the architect defines, refines, manages, and governs components within an architecture. Software architects, in collaboration with business analysts, subject matter experts, developers, QA engineers, operations, and enterprise architects, create the initial design for software, incorporating the architecture characteristics discussed in Chapter 4 and the requirements for the software system.

Virtually all the details we cover in this book exist independently from whatever software development process teams use: architecture is independent from the development process. The primary exception to this rule entails the engineering practices pioneered in the various flavors of Agile software development, particularly in the areas of deployment and automating governance. However, in general, software architecture exists separate from the process. Thus, architects ultimately don't care where requirements originate: a formal Joint Application Design (JAD) process, lengthy waterfall-style analysis and design, Agile story cards…or any hybrid variation of those.

Generally the component is the lowest level of the software system an architect interacts directly with, with the exception of many of the code quality metrics discussed in Chapter 6 that affect code bases holistically. Components consist of classes or functions (depending on the implementation platform), whose design falls under the responsibility of tech leads or developers. It's not that architects shouldn't involve themselves in class design (particularly when discovering or applying design patterns), but they should avoid micromanaging each decision from top to bottom in the system. If architects never allow other roles to make decisions of consequence, the organization will struggle with empowering the next generation of architects.

An architect must identify components as one of the first tasks on a new project. But before an architect can identify components, they must know how to partition the architecture.

Architecture Partitioning

The First Law of Software Architecture states that everything in software is a trade-off, including how architects create components in an architecture. Because components represent a general containership mechanism, an architect can build any type of partitioning they want. Several common styles exist, with different sets of trade-offs. We discuss architecture styles in depth in Part II. Here we discuss an important aspect of styles, the *top-level partitioning* in an architecture.

Consider the two types of architecture styles shown in Figure 8-3.

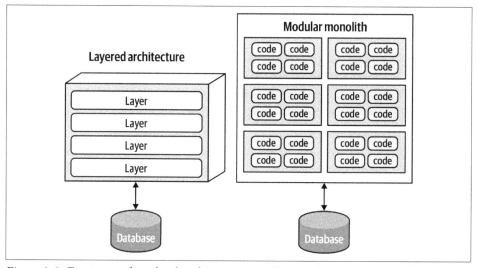

Figure 8-3. Two types of top-level architecture partitioning: layered and modular

In Figure 8-3, one type of architecture familiar to many is the *layered monolith* (discussed in detail in Chapter 10). The other is an architecture style popularized by Simon Brown (*https://www.codingthearchitecture.com*) called a *modular monolith*, a single deployment unit associated with a database and partitioned around domains rather than technical capabilities. These two styles represent different ways to *top-level partition* the architecture. Note that in each variation, each of the top-level components (layers or components) likely has other components embedded within. The top-level partitioning is of particular interest to architects because it defines the fundamental architecture style and way of partitioning code.

Organizing architecture based on technical capabilities like the layered monolith represents *technical top-level partitioning*. A common version of this appears in Figure 8-4.

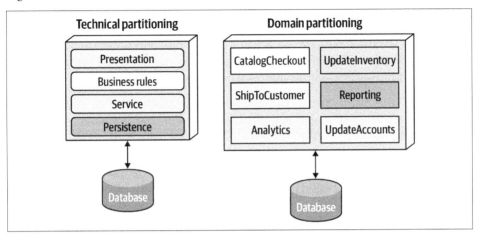

Figure 8-4. Two types of top-level partitioning in architecture

In Figure 8-4, the architect has partitioned the functionality of the system into *technical* capabilities: presentation, business rules, services, persistence, and so on. This way of organizing a code base certainly makes sense. All the persistence code resides in one layer in the architecture, making it easy for developers to find persistence-related code. Even though the basic concept of layered architecture predates it by decades, the Model-View-Controller design pattern matches with this architectural pattern, making it easy for developers to understand. Thus, it is often the default architecture in many organizations.

An interesting side effect of the predominance of the layered architecture relates to how companies seat different project roles. When using a layered architecture, it makes some sense to have all the backend developers sit together in one department, the DBAs in another, the presentation team in another, and so on. Because of *Conway's law*, this makes some sense in those organizations.

Conway's Law

Back in the late 1960s, Melvin Conway (*https://oreil.ly/z2Swa*) made an observation that has become known as *Conway's law*:

> Organizations which design systems … are constrained to produce designs which are copies of the communication structures of these organizations.

Paraphrased, this law suggests that when a group of people designs some technical artifact, the communication structures between the people end up replicated in the

---

design. People at all levels of organizations see this law in action, and they sometimes make decisions based on it. For example, it is common for organizations to partition workers based on technical capabilities, which makes sense from a pure organizational sense but hampers collaboration because of artificial separation of common concerns.

A related observation coined by Jonny Leroy of ThoughtWorks is the Inverse Conway Maneuver (*https://oreil.ly/9EYd6*), which suggests evolving team and organizational structure together to promote the desired architecture.

The other architectural variation in Figure 8-4 represents *domain partitioning*, inspired by the Eric Evan book *Domain-Driven Design*, which is a modeling technique for decomposing complex software systems. In DDD, the architect identifies domains or workflows independent and decoupled from each other. The microservices architecture style (discussed in Chapter 17) is based on this philosophy. In a modular monolith, the architect partitions the architecture around domains or workflows rather than technical capabilities. As components often nest within one another, each of the components in Figure 8-4 in the domain partitioning (for example, *Catalog-Checkout*) may use a persistence library and have a separate layer for business rules, but the top-level partitioning revolves around domains.

One of the fundamental distinctions between different architecture patterns is what type of top-level partitioning each supports, which we cover for each individual pattern. It also has a huge impact on how an architect decides how to initially identify components—does the architect want to partition things technically or by domain?

Architects using technical partitioning organize the components of the system by technical capabilities: presentation, business rules, persistence, and so on. Thus, one of the organizing principles of this architecture is *separation of technical concerns.* This in turn creates useful levels of decoupling: if the service layer is only connected to the persistence layer below and business rules layer above, then changes in persistence will only potentially affect those layers. This style of partitioning provides a decoupling technique, reducing rippling side effects on dependent components. We cover more details of this architecture style in the layered architecture pattern in Chapter 10. It is certainly logical to organize systems using technical partitioning, but, like all things in software architecture, this offers some trade-offs.

The separation enforced by technical partitioning enables developers to find certain categories of the code base quickly, as it is organized by capabilities. However, most realistic software systems require workflows that cut across technical capabilities. Consider the common business workflow of *CatalogCheckout*. The code to handle *CatalogCheckout* in the technically layered architecture appears in all the layers, as shown in Figure 8-5.

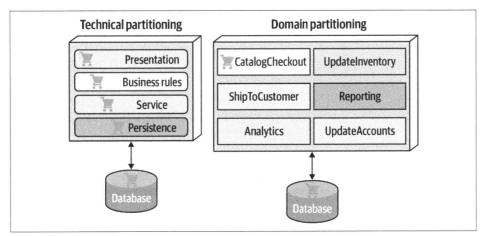

Figure 8-5. Where domains/workflows appear in technical- and domain-partitioned architectures

In Figure 8-5, in the technically partitioned architecture, *CatalogCheckout* appears in all the layers; the domain is smeared across the technical layers. Contrast this with domain partitioning, which uses a top-level partitioning that organizes components by domain rather than technical capabilities. In Figure 8-5, architects designing the domain-partitioned architecture build top-level components around workflows and/or domains. Each component in the domain partitioning may have subcomponents, including layers, but the top-level partitioning focuses on domains, which better reflects the kinds of changes that most often occur on projects.

Neither of these styles is more correct than the other—refer to the First Law of Software Architecture. That said, we have observed a decided industry trend over the last few years toward domain partitioning for the monolithic and distributed (for example, microservices) architectures. However, it is one of the first decisions an architect must make.

Case Study: Silicon Sandwiches: Partitioning

Consider the case of one of our example katas, "Case Study: Silicon Sandwiches" on page 69. When deriving components, one of the fundamental decisions facing an architect is the top-level partitioning. Consider the first of two different possibilities for Silicon Sandwiches, a domain partitioning, illustrated in Figure 8-6.

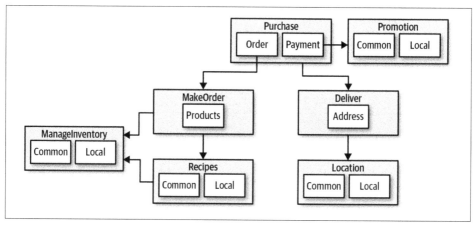

Figure 8-6. A domain-partitioned design for Silicon Sandwiches

In Figure 8-6, the architect has designed around domains (workflows), creating discrete components for Purchase, Promotion, MakeOrder, ManageInventory, Recipes, Delivery, and Location. Within many of these components resides a subcomponent to handle the various types of customization required, covering both common and local variations.

An alternative design isolates the common and local parts into their own partition, illustrated in Figure 8-7. Common and Local represent top-level components, with Pur chase and Delivery remaining to handle the workflow.

Which is better? It depends! Each partitioning offers different advantages and drawbacks.

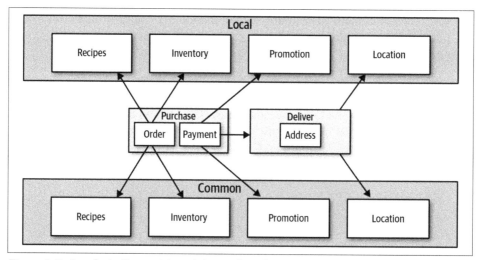

Figure 8-7. A technically partitioned design for Silicon Sandwiches

Domain partitioning

Domain-partitioned architectures separate top-level components by workflows and/or domains.

Advantages
- Modeled more closely toward how the business functions rather than an implementation detail
- Easier to utilize the Inverse Conway Maneuver to build cross-functional teams around domains
- Aligns more closely to the modular monolith and microservices architecture styles
- Message flow matches the problem domain
- Easy to migrate data and components to distributed architecture

Disadvantage
- Customization code appears in multiple places

Technical partitioning

Technically partitioned architectures separate top-level components based on technical capabilities rather than discrete workflows. This may manifest as layers inspired by Model-View-Controller separation or some other ad hoc technical partitioning. Figure 8-7 separates components based on customization.

Advantages
- Clearly separates customization code.
- Aligns more closely to the layered architecture pattern.

Disadvantages
- Higher degree of global coupling. Changes to either the Common or Local component will likely affect all the other components.
- Developers may have to duplicate domain concepts in both common and local layers.
- Typically higher coupling at the data level. In a system like this, the application and data architects would likely collaborate to create a single database, including customization and domains. That in turn creates difficulties in untangling the data relationships if the architects later want to migrate this architecture to a distributed system.

Many other factors contribute to an architect's decision on what architecture style to base their design upon, covered in Part II.

Developer Role

Developers typically take components, jointly designed with the architect role, and further subdivide them into classes, functions, or subcomponents. In general, class and function design is the shared responsibility of architects, tech leads, and developers, with the lion's share going to developer roles.

Developers should never take components designed by architects as the last word; all software design benefits from iteration. Rather, that initial design should be viewed as a first draft, where implementation will reveal more details and refinements.

Component Identification Flow

Component identification works best as an iterative process, producing candidates and refinements through feedback, illustrated in Figure 8-8.

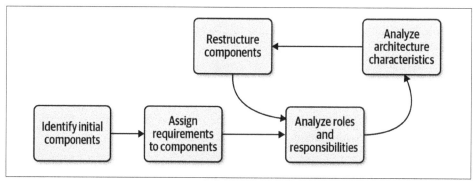

Figure 8-8. Component identification cycle

This cycle describes a generic architecture exposition cycle. Certain specialized domains may insert other steps in this process or change it altogether. For example, in some domains, some code must undergo security or auditing steps in this process. Descriptions of each step in Figure 8-8 appear in the following sections.

Identifying Initial Components

Before any code exists for a software project, the architect must somehow determine what top-level components to begin with, based on what type of top-level partitioning they choose. Outside that, an architect has the freedom to make up whatever components they want, then map domain functionality to them to see where behavior should reside. While this may sound arbitrary, it's hard to start with anything more concrete if an architect designs a system from scratch. The likelihood of achieving a good design from this initial set of components is disparagingly small, which is why architects must iterate on component design to improve it.

Assign Requirements to Components

Once an architect has identified initial components, the next step aligns requirements (or user stories) to those components to see how well they fit. This may entail creating new components, consolidating existing ones, or breaking components apart because they have too much responsibility. This mapping doesn't have to be exact—the architect is attempting to find a good coarse-grained substrate to allow further design and refinement by architects, tech leads, and/or developers.

Analyze Roles and Responsibilities

When assigning stories to components, the architect also looks at the roles and responsibilities elucidated during the requirements to make sure that the granularity matches. Thinking about both the roles and behaviors the application must support allows the architect to align the component and domain granularity. One of the greatest challenges for architects entails discovering the correct granularity for components, which encourages the iterative approach described here.

Analyze Architecture Characteristics

When assigning requirements to components, the architect should also look at the architecture characteristics discovered earlier in order to think about how they might impact component division and granularity. For example, while two parts of a system might deal with user input, the part that deals with hundreds of concurrent users will need different architecture characteristics than another part that needs to support only a few. Thus, while a purely functional view of component design might yield a single component to handle user interaction, analyzing the architecture characteristics will lead to a subdivision.

Restructure Components

Feedback is critical in software design. Thus, architects must continually iterate on their component design with developers. Designing software provides all kinds of unexpected difficulties—no one can anticipate all the unknown issues that usually occur during software projects. Thus, an iterative approach to component design is key. First, it's virtually impossible to account for all the different discoveries and edge cases that will arise that encourage redesign. Secondly, as the architecture and developers delve more deeply into building the application, they gain a more nuanced understanding of where behavior and roles should lie.

Component Granularity

Finding the proper granularity for components is one of an architect's most difficult tasks. Too fine-grained a component design leads to too much communication between components to achieve results. Too coarse-grained components encourage high internal coupling, which leads to difficulties in deployability and testability, as well as modularity-related negative side effects.

Component Design

No accepted "correct" way exists to design components. Rather, a wide variety of techniques exist, all with various trade-offs. In all processes, an architect takes requirements and tries to determine what coarse-grained building blocks will make up the application. Lots of different techniques exist, all with varying trade-offs and coupled to the software development process used by the team and organization. Here, we talk about a few general ways to discover components and traps to avoid.

Discovering Components

Architects, often in collaboration with other roles such as developers, business analysts, and subject matter experts, create an initial component design based on general knowledge of the system and how they choose to decompose it, based on technical or domain partitioning. The team goal is an initial design that partitions the problem space into coarse chunks that take into account differing architecture characteristics.

Entity trap

While there is no one true way to ascertain components, a common anti-pattern lurks: the *entity trap*. Say that an architect is working on designing components for our kata Going, Going, Gone and ends up with a design resembling Figure 8-9.

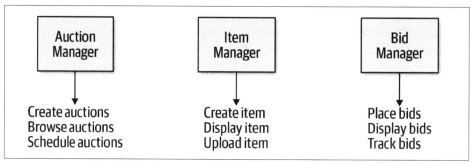

Figure 8-9. Building an architecture as an object-relational mapping

In Figure 8-9, the architect has basically taken each entity identified in the requirements and made a `Manager` component based on that entity. This isn't an architecture; it's an object-relational mapping (ORM) of a framework to a database. In other words, if a system only needs simple database CRUD operations (create, read, update, delete), then the architect can download a framework to create user interfaces directly from the database. Many popular ORM frameworks exist to solve this common CRUD behavior.

Naked Objects and Similar Frameworks

More than a decade ago, a family of frameworks appeared that makes building simple CRUD applications trivial, exemplified by Naked Objects (which has since split into two projects, a .NET version still called NakedObjects (*https://oreil.ly/RQ8XQ*), and a Java version that moved to the Apache open source foundation under the name Isis (*http://isis.apache.org*)). The premise behind these frameworks offers to build a user interface frontend on database entities. For example, in Naked Objects, the developer points the framework to database tables, and the framework builds a user interface based on the tables and their defined relationships.

Several other popular frameworks exist that basically provide a default user interface based on database table structure: the scaffolding feature of the Ruby on Rails (*https://rubyonrails.org*) framework provides the same kind of default mappings from website to database (with many options to extend and add sophistication to the resulting application).

If an architect's needs require merely a simple mapping from a database to a user interface, full-blown architecture isn't necessary; one of these frameworks will suffice.

The entity trap anti-pattern arises when an architect incorrectly identifies the database relationships as workflows in the application, a correspondence that rarely manifests in the real world. Rather, this anti-pattern generally indicates lack of thought about the actual workflows of the application. Components created with the entity trap also tend to be too coarse-grained, offering no guidance whatsoever to the development team in terms of the packaging and overall structuring of the source code.

Actor/Actions approach

The *actor/actions* approach is a popular way that architects use to map requirements to components. In this approach, originally defined by the Rational Unified Process, architects identify actors who perform activities with the application and the actions those actors may perform. It provides a technique for discovering the typical users of the system and what kinds of things they might do with the system.

The actor/actions approach became popular in conjunction with particular software development processes, especially more formal processes that favor a significant portion of upfront design. It is still popular and works well when the requirements feature distinct roles and the kinds of actions they can perform. This style of component decomposition works well for all types of systems, monolithic or distributed.

Event storming

Event storming as a component discovery technique comes from domain-driven design (DDD) and shares popularity with microservices, also heavily influenced by DDD. In event storming, the architect assumes the project will use messages and/or events to communicate between the various components. To that end, the team tries to determine which events occur in the system based on requirements and identified roles, and build components around those event and message handlers. This works well in distributed architectures like microservices that use events and messages, because it helps architects define the messages used in the eventual system.

Workflow approach

An alternative to event storming offers a more generic approach for architects not using DDD or messaging. The *workflow approach* models the components around workflows, much like event storming, but without the explicit constraints of building a message-based system. A workflow approach identifies the key roles, determines the kinds of workflows these roles engage in, and builds components around the identified activities.

None of these techniques is superior to the others; all offer a different set of trade-offs. If a team uses a waterfall approach or other older software development processes, they might prefer the Actor/Actions approach because it is general. When using DDD and corresponding architectures like microservices, *event storming* matches the software development process exactly.

Case Study: Going, Going, Gone: Discovering Components

If a team has no special constraints and is looking for a good general-purpose component decomposition, the Actor/Actions approach works well as a generic solution. It's the one we use in our case study for Going, Going, Gone.

In Chapter 7, we introduced the architecture kata for Going, Going, Gone (GGG) and discovered architecture characteristics for this system. This system has three obvious roles: the *bidder*, the *auctioneer*, and a frequent participant in this modeling technique, the *system*, for internal actions. The roles interact with the application, represented here by the system, which identifies when the application initiates an event rather than one of the roles. For example, in GGG, once the auction is complete, the system triggers the payment system to process payments.

We can also identify a starting set of actions for each of these roles:

Bidder

View live video stream, view live bid stream, place a bid

Auctioneer

Enter live bids into system, receive online bids, mark item as sold

System

Start auction, make payment, track bidder activity

Given these actions, we can iteratively build a set of starter components for GGG; one such solution appears in Figure 8-10.

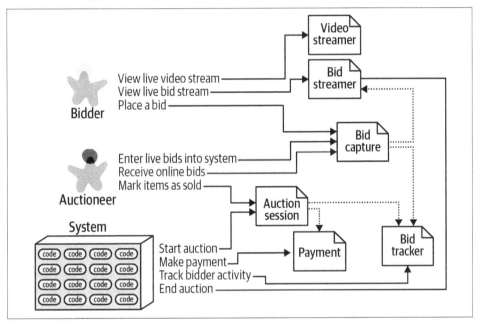

Figure 8-10. Initial set of components for Going, Going, Gone

In Figure 8-10, each of the roles and actions maps to a component, which in turn may need to collaborate on information. These are the components we identified for this solution:

VideoStreamer

Streams a live auction to users.

BidStreamer

Streams bids as they occur to the users. Both VideoStreamer and BidStreamer offer read-only views of the auction to the bidder.

BidCapture

   This component captures bids from both the auctioneer and bidders.

BidTracker

   Tracks bids and acts as the system of record.

AuctionSession

   Starts and stops an auction. When the bidder ends the auction, performs the payment and resolution steps, including notifying bidders of ending.

Payment

   Third-party payment processor for credit card payments.

Referring to the component identification flow diagram in Figure 8-8, after the initial identification of components, the architect next analyzes architecture characteristics to determine if that will change the design. For this system, the architect can definitely identify different sets of architecture characteristics. For example, the current design features a BidCapture component to capture bids from both bidders and the auctioneer, which makes sense functionally: capturing bids from anyone can be handled the same. However, what about architecture characteristics around bid capture? The auctioneer doesn't need the same level of scalability or elasticity as potentially thousands of bidders. By the same token, an architect must ensure that architecture characteristics like reliability (connections don't drop) and availability (the system is up) for the auctioneer could be higher than other parts of the system. For example, while it's bad for business if a bidder can't log in to the site or if they suffer from a dropped connection, it's disastrous to the auction if either of those things happen to the auctioneer.

Because they have differing levels of architecture characteristics, the architect decides to split the Bid Capture component into Bid Capture and Auctioneer Capture so that each of the two components can support differing architecture characteristics. The updated design appears in Figure 8-11.

The architect creates a new component for Auctioneer Capture and updates information links to both Bid Streamer (so that online bidders see the live bids) and Bid Tracker, which is managing the bid streams. Note that Bid Tracker is now the component that will unify the two very different information streams: the single stream of information from the auctioneer and the multiple streams from bidders.

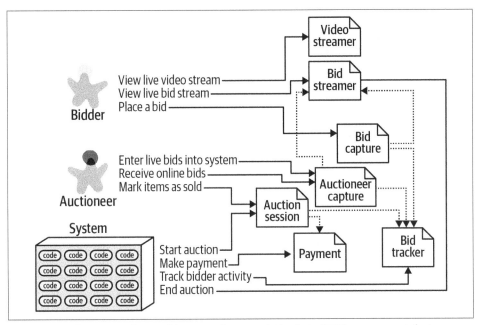

Figure 8-11. Incorporating architecture characteristics into GGG component design

The design shown in Figure 8-11 isn't likely the final design. More requirements must be uncovered (how do people register, administration functions around payment, and so on). However, this example provides a good starting point to start iterating further on the design.

This is one possible set of components to solve the GGG problem—but it's not necessarily correct, nor is it the only one. Few software systems have only one way that developers can implement them; every design has different sets of trade-offs. As an architect, don't obsess over finding the one true design, because many will suffice (and less likely overengineered). Rather, try to objectively assess the trade-offs between different design decisions, and choose the one that has the least worst set of trade-offs.

Architecture Quantum Redux: Choosing Between Monolithic Versus Distributed Architectures

Recalling the discussion defining architecture quantum in "Architectural Quanta and Granularity" on page 92, the architecture quantum defines the scope of architecture characteristics. That in turn leads an architect toward an important decision as they finish their initial component design: should the architecture be monolithic or distributed?

A *monolithic* architecture typically features a single deployable unit, including all functionality of the system that runs in the process, typically connected to a single database. Types of monolithic architectures include the layered and modular monolith, discussed fully in Chapter 10. A *distributed* architecture is the opposite—the application consists of multiple services running in their own ecosystem, communicating via networking protocols. Distributed architectures may feature finer-grained deployment models, where each service may have its own release cadence and engineering practices, based on the development team and their priorities.

Each architecture style offers a variety of trade-offs, covered in Part II. However, the fundamental decision rests on how many quanta the architecture discovers during the design process. If the system can manage with a single quantum (in other words, one set of architecture characteristics), then a monolith architecture offers many advantages. On the other hand, differing architecture characteristics for components, as illustrated in the GGG component analysis, requires a distributed architecture to accommodate differing architecture characteristics. For example, the `VideoStreamer` and `BidStreamer` both offer read-only views of the auction to bidders. From a design standpoint, an architect would rather not deal with read-only streaming mixed with high-scale updates. Along with the aforementioned differences between bidder and auctioneer, these differing characteristics lead an architect to choose a distributed architecture.

The ability to determine a fundamental design characteristic of architecture (monolith versus distributed) early in the design process highlights one of the advantages of using the architecture quantum as a way of analyzing architecture characteristics scope and coupling.

PART II

Architecture Styles

The difference between an architecture style and an architecture pattern can be confusing. We define an *architecture style* as the overarching structure of how the user interface and backend source code are organized (such as within layers of a monolithic deployment or separately deployed services) and how that source code interacts with a datastore. *Architecture patterns*, on the other hand, are lower-level design structures that help form specific solutions within an architecture style (such as how to achieve high scalability or high performance within a set of operations or between sets of services).

Understanding architecture styles occupies much of the time and effort for new architects because they share importance and abundance. Architects must understand the various styles and the trade-offs encapsulated within each to make effective decisions; each architecture style embodies a well-known set of trade-offs that help an architect make the right choice for a particular business problem.

CHAPTER 9

Foundations

Architecture styles, sometimes called architecture patterns, describe a named relationship of components covering a variety of architecture characteristics. An architecture style name, similar to design patterns, creates a single name that acts as shorthand between experienced architects. For example, when an architect talks about a layered monolith, their target in the conversation understands aspects of structure, which kinds of architecture characteristics work well (and which ones can cause problems), typical deployment models, data strategies, and a host of other information. Thus, architects should be familiar with the basic names of fundamental generic architecture styles.

Each name captures a wealth of understood detail, one of the purposes of design patterns. An architecture style describes the topology, assumed and default architecture characteristics, both beneficial and detrimental. We cover many common modern architecture patterns in the remainder of this section of the book (Part II). However, architects should be familiar with several fundamental patterns that appear embedded within the larger patterns.

Fundamental Patterns

Several fundamental patterns appear again and again throughout the history of software architecture because they provide a useful perspective on organizing code, deployments, or other aspects of architecture. For example, the concept of layers in architecture, separating different concerns based on functionality, is as old as software itself. Yet, the layered pattern continues to manifest in different guises, including modern variants discussed in Chapter 10.

Big Ball of Mud

Architects refer to the absence of any discernible architecture structure as a *Big Ball of Mud*, named after the eponymous anti-pattern defined in a paper released in 1997 by Brian Foote and Joseph Yoder:

> A *Big Ball of Mud* is a haphazardly structured, sprawling, sloppy, duct-tape-and-baling-wire, spaghetti-code jungle. These systems show unmistakable signs of unregulated growth, and repeated, expedient repair. Information is shared promiscuously among distant elements of the system, often to the point where nearly all the important information becomes global or duplicated.
>
> The overall structure of the system may never have been well defined.
>
> If it was, it may have eroded beyond recognition. Programmers with a shred of architectural sensibility shun these quagmires. Only those who are unconcerned about architecture, and, perhaps, are comfortable with the inertia of the day-to-day chore of patching the holes in these failing dikes, are content to work on such systems.
>
> —Brian Foote and Joseph Yoder

In modern terms, a *big ball of mud* might describe a simple scripting application with event handlers wired directly to database calls, with no real internal structure. Many trivial applications start like this then become unwieldy as they continue to grow.

In general, architects want to avoid this type of architecture at all costs. The lack of structure makes change increasingly difficult. This type of architecture also suffers from problems in deployment, testability, scalability, and performance.

Unfortunately, this architecture anti-pattern occurs quite commonly in the real world. Few architects intend to create one, but many projects inadvertently manage to create a mess because of lack of governance around code quality and structure. For example, Neal worked with a client project whose structure appears in Figure 9-1.

The client (whose name is withheld for obvious reasons) created a Java-based web application as quickly as possible over several years. The technical visualization[1] shows their architectural coupling: each dot on the perimeter of the circle represents a class, and each line represents connections between the classes, where bolder lines indicate stronger connections. In this code base, any change to a class makes it difficult to predict rippling side effects to other classes, making change a terrifying affair.

---

1 Made with a now-retired tool called XRay, an Eclipse plug-in.

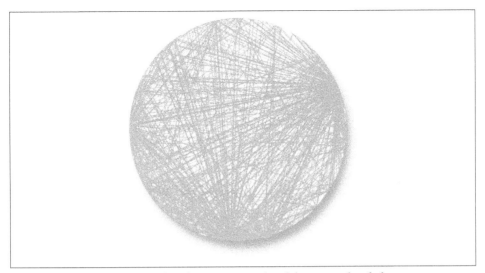

Figure 9-1. A Big Ball of Mud architecture visualized from a real code base

Unitary Architecture

When software originated, there was only the computer, and software ran on it. Through the various eras of hardware and software evolution, the two started as a single entity, then split as the need for more sophisticated capabilities grew. For example, mainframe computers started as singular systems, then gradually separated data into its own kind of system. Similarly, when personal computers first appeared, much of the commercial development focused on single machines. As networking PCs became common, distributed systems (such as client/server) appeared.

Few unitary architectures exist outside embedded systems and other highly constrained environments. Generally, software systems tend to grow in functionality over time, requiring separation of concerns to maintain operational architecture characteristics, such as performance and scale.

Client/Server

Over time, various forces required partitioning away from a single system; how to do that forms the basis for many of these styles. Many architecture styles deal with how to efficiently separate parts of the system.

A fundamental style in architecture separates technical functionality between frontend and backend, called a *two-tier*, or *client/server*, architecture. Many different flavors of this architecture exist, depending on the era and computing capabilities.

Desktop + database server

An early personal computer architecture encouraged developers to write rich desktop applications in user interfaces like Windows, separating the data into a separate database server. This architecture coincided with the appearance of standalone database servers that could connect via standard network protocols. It allowed presentation logic to reside on the desktop, while the more computationally intense action (both in volume and complexity) occurred on more robust database servers.

Browser + web server

Once modern web development arrived, the common split became web browser connected to web server (which in turn was connected to a database server). The separation of responsibilities was similar to the desktop variant but with even thinner clients as browsers, allowing a wider distribution both inside and outside firewalls. Even though the database is separate from the web server, architects often still consider this a two-tier architecture because the web and database servers run on one class of machine within the operations center and the user interface runs on the user's browser.

Three-tier

An architecture that became quite popular during the late 1990s was a *three-tier architecture*, which provided even more layers of separation. As tools like application servers became popular in Java and .NET, companies started building even more layers in their topology: a database tier using an industrial-strength database server, an application tier managed by an application server, frontend coded in generated HTML, and increasingly, JavaScript, as its capabilities expanded.

The three-tier architecture corresponded with network-level protocols such as Common Object Request Broker Architecture (CORBA) (*https://www.corba.org*) and Distributed Component Object Model (DCOM) (*https://oreil.ly/1TEqv*) that facilitated building distributed architectures.

Just as developers today don't worry about how network protocols like TCP/IP work (they just work), most architects don't have to worry about this level of plumbing in distributed architectures. The capabilities offered by such tools in that era exist today as either tools (like message queues) or architecture patterns (such as event-driven architecture, covered in Chapter 14).

Monolithic Versus Distributed Architectures

Architecture styles can be classified into two main types: *monolithic* (single deployment unit of all code) and *distributed* (multiple deployment units connected through remote access protocols). While no classification scheme is perfect, distributed architectures all share a common set of challenges and issues not found in the monolithic architecture styles, making this classification scheme a good separation between the various architecture styles. In this book we will describe in detail the following architecture styles:

Monolithic
- Layered architecture (Chapter 10)
- Pipeline architecture (Chapter 11)
- Microkernel architecture (Chapter 12)

Distributed
- Service-based architecture (Chapter 13)
- Event-driven architecture (Chapter 14)
- Space-based architecture (Chapter 15)
- Service-oriented architecture (Chapter 16)
- Microservices architecture (Chapter 17)

Distributed architecture styles, while being much more powerful in terms of performance, scalability, and availability than monolithic architecture styles, have significant trade-offs for this power. The first group of issues facing all distributed architectures are described in *the fallacies of distributed computing (https://oreil.ly/fVAEY)*, first coined by L. Peter Deutsch and other colleagues from Sun Microsystems in 1994. A *fallacy* is something that is believed or assumed to be true but is not. All eight of the fallacies of distributed computing apply to distributed architectures today. The following sections describe each fallacy.

Fallacy #1: The Network Is Reliable

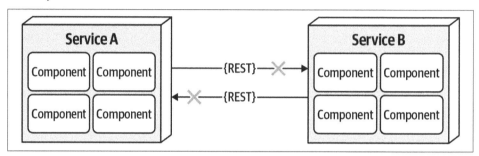

Figure 9-2. The network is not reliable

Developers and architects alike assume that the network is reliable, but it is not. While networks have become more reliable over time, the fact of the matter is that networks still remain generally unreliable. This is significant for all distributed architectures because all distributed architecture styles rely on the network for communication to and from services, as well as between services. As illustrated in Figure 9-2, `Service B` may be totally healthy, but `Service A` cannot reach it due to a network problem; or even worse, `Service A` made a request to `Service B` to process some data and does not receive a response because of a network issue. This is why things like timeouts and circuit breakers exist between services. The more a system relies on the network (such as microservices architecture), the potentially less reliable it becomes.

Fallacy #2: Latency Is Zero

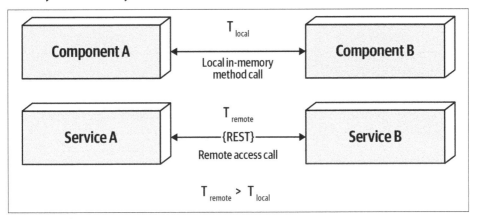

Figure 9-3. Latency is not zero

As Figure 9-3 shows, when a local call is made to another component via a method or function call, that time (t_local) is measured in nanoseconds or microseconds. However, when that same call is made through a remote access protocol (such as REST, messaging, or RPC), the time measured to access that service (t_remote) is measured in milliseconds. Therefore, t_remote will always be greater that t_local. Latency in any distributed architecture is not zero, yet most architects ignore this fallacy, insisting that they have fast networks. Ask yourself this question: do you know what the average round-trip latency is for a RESTful call in your production environment? Is it 60 milliseconds? Is it 500 milliseconds?

When using any distributed architecture, architects must know this latency average. It is the only way of determining whether a distributed architecture is feasible, particularly when considering microservices (see Chapter 17) due to the fine-grained nature of the services and the amount of communication between those services. Assuming an average of 100 milliseconds of latency per request, chaining together 10 service calls to perform a particular business function adds 1,000 milliseconds to the request! Knowing the average latency is important, but even more important is also knowing the 95th to 99th percentile. While an average latency might yield only 60 milliseconds (which is good), the 95th percentile might be 400 milliseconds! It's usually this "long tail" latency that will kill performance in a distributed architecture. In most cases, architects can get latency values from a network administrator (see "Fallacy #6: There Is Only One Administrator" on page 129).

Fallacy #3: Bandwidth Is Infinite

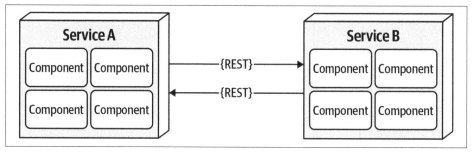

Figure 9-4. Bandwidth is not infinite

Bandwidth is usually not a concern in monolithic architectures, because once processing goes into a monolith, little or no bandwidth is required to process that business request. However, as shown in Figure 9-4, once systems are broken apart into smaller deployment units (services) in a distributed architecture such as microservices, communication to and between these services significantly utilizes bandwidth, causing networks to slow down, thus impacting latency (fallacy #2) and reliability (fallacy #1).

To illustrate the importance of this fallacy, consider the two services shown in Figure 9-4. Let's say the lefthand service manages the wish list items for the website, and the righthand service manages the customer profile. Whenever a request for a wish list comes into the lefthand service, it must make an interservice call to the righthand customer profile service to get the customer name because that data is needed in the response contract for the wish list, but the wish list service on the lefthand side doesn't have the name. The customer profile service returns 45 attributes totaling 500 kb to the wish list service, which only needs the name (200 bytes). This is a form of coupling referred to as *stamp coupling*. This may not sound significant, but requests for the wish list items happen about 2,000 times a second. This means that this interservice call from the wish list service to the customer profile service happens 2,000 times a second. At 500 kb for each request, the amount of bandwidth used for that *one* interservice call (out of hundreds being made that second) is 1 Gb!

Stamp coupling in distributed architectures consumes significant amounts of bandwidth. If the customer profile service were to only pass back the data needed by the wish list service (in this case 200 bytes), the total bandwidth used to transmit the data is only 400 kb. Stamp coupling can be resolved in the following ways:

- Create private RESTful API endpoints
- Use field selectors in the contract
- Use GraphQL (*https://graphql.org*) to decouple contracts
- Use value-driven contracts with consumer-driven contracts (CDCs)
- Use internal messaging endpoints

Regardless of the technique used, ensuring that the minimal amount of data is passed between services or systems in a distributed architecture is the best way to address this fallacy.

Fallacy #4: The Network Is Secure

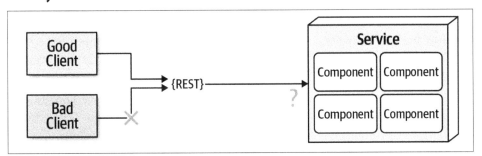

Figure 9-5. The network is not secure

Most architects and developers get so comfortable using virtual private networks (VPNs), trusted networks, and firewalls that they tend to forget about this fallacy of distributed computing: *the network is not secure*. Security becomes much more challenging in a distributed architecture. As shown in Figure 9-5, each and every endpoint to each distributed deployment unit must be secured so that unknown or bad requests do not make it to that service. The surface area for threats and attacks increases by magnitudes when moving from a monolithic to a distributed architecture. Having to secure every endpoint, even when doing interservice communication, is another reason performance tends to be slower in synchronous, highly-distributed architectures such as microservices or service-based architecture.

Fallacy #5: The Topology Never Changes

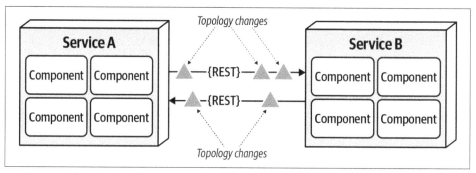

Figure 9-6. The network topology always changes

This fallacy refers to the overall network topology, including all of the routers, hubs, switches, firewalls, networks, and appliances used within the overall network. Architects assume that the topology is fixed and never changes. *Of course it changes.* It changes all the time. What is the significance of this fallacy?

Suppose an architect comes into work on a Monday morning, and everyone is running around like crazy because services keep timing out in production. The architect works with the teams, frantically trying to figure out why this is happening. No new services were deployed over the weekend. What could it be? After several hours the architect discovers that a minor network upgrade happened at 2 a.m. that morning. This supposedly "minor" network upgrade invalidated all of the latency assumptions, triggering timeouts and circuit breakers.

Architects must be in constant communication with operations and network administrators to know what is changing and when so that they can make adjustments accordingly to reduce the type of surprise previously described. This may seem obvious and easy, but it is not. As a matter of fact, this fallacy leads directly to the next fallacy.

Fallacy #6: There Is Only One Administrator

Figure 9-7. There are many network administrators, not just one

Architects all the time fall into this fallacy, assuming they only need to collaborate and communicate with one administrator. As shown in Figure 9-7, there are dozens of network administrators in a typical large company. Who should the architect talk to with regard to latency ("Fallacy #2: Latency Is Zero" on page 125) or topology changes ("Fallacy #5: The Topology Never Changes" on page 128)? This fallacy points to the complexity of distributed architecture and the amount of coordination that must happen to get everything working correctly. Monolithic applications do not require this level of communication and collaboration due to the single deployment unit characteristics of those architecture styles.

Fallacy #7: Transport Cost Is Zero

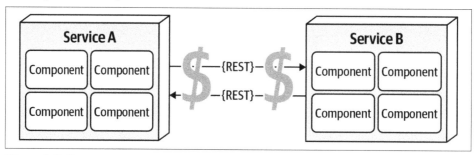

Figure 9-8. Remote access costs money

Many software architects confuse this fallacy for latency ("Fallacy #2: Latency Is Zero" on page 125). Transport cost here does not refer to latency, but rather to actual *cost* in terms of money associated with making a "simple RESTful call." Architects assume (incorrectly) that the necessary infrastructure is in place and sufficient for making a simple RESTful call or breaking apart a monolithic application. *It is usually not.* Distributed architectures cost significantly more than monolithic architectures, primarily due to increased needs for additional hardware, servers, gateways, firewalls, new subnets, proxies, and so on.

Whenever embarking on a distributed architecture, we encourage architects to analyze the current server and network topology with regard to capacity, bandwidth, latency, and security zones to not get caught up in the trap of surprise with this fallacy.

Fallacy #8: The Network Is Homogeneous

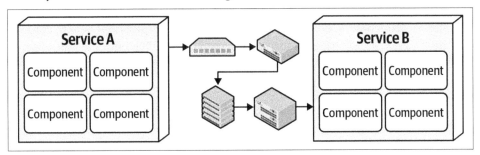

Figure 9-9. The network is not homogeneous

Most architects and developers assume a network is homogeneous—made up by only one network hardware vendor. Nothing could be farther from the truth. Most companies have multiple network hardware vendors in their infrastructure, if not more.

So what? The significance of this fallacy is that not all of those heterogeneous hardware vendors play together well. Most of it works, but does Juniper hardware seamlessly integrate with Cisco hardware? Networking standards have evolved over the years, making this less of an issue, but the fact remains that not all situations, load, and circumstances have been fully tested, and as such, network packets occasionally get lost. This in turn impacts network reliability ("Fallacy #1: The Network Is Reliable" on page 124), latency assumptions and assertions ("Fallacy #2: Latency Is Zero" on page 125), and assumptions made about the bandwidth ("Fallacy #3: Bandwidth Is Infinite" on page 126). In other words, this fallacy ties back into all of the other fallacies, forming an endless loop of confusion and frustration when dealing with networks (which is necessary when using distributed architectures).

Other Distributed Considerations

In addition to the eight fallacies of distributed computing previously described, there are other issues and challenges facing distributed architecture that aren't present in monolithic architectures. Although the details of these other issues are out of scope for this book, we list and summarize them in the following sections.

Distributed logging

Performing root-cause analysis to determine why a particular order was dropped is very difficult and time-consuming in a distributed architecture due to the distribution of application and system logs. In a monolithic application there is typically only one log, making it easier to trace a request and determine the issue. However, distributed architectures contain dozens to hundreds of different logs, all located in a different place and all with a different format, making it difficult to track down a problem.

Logging consolidation tools such as Splunk (*https://www.splunk.com*) help to consolidate information from various sources and systems together into one consolidated log and console, but these tools only scratch the surface of the complexities involved with distributed logging. Detailed solutions and patterns for distributed logging are outside the scope of this book.

Distributed transactions

Architects and developers take transactions for granted in a monolithic architecture world because they are so straightforward and easy to manage. Standard `commits` and `rollbacks` executed from persistence frameworks leverage ACID (atomicity, consistency, isolation, durability) transactions to guarantee that the data is updated in a correct way to ensure high data consistency and integrity. Such is not the case with distributed architectures.

Distributed architectures rely on what is called *eventual consistency* to ensure the data processed by separate deployment units is at some unspecified point in time all synchronized into a consistent state. This is one of the trade-offs of distributed architecture: high scalability, performance, and availability at the sacrifice of data consistency and data integrity.

Transactional sagas (*https://oreil.ly/1lLmj*) are one way to manage distributed transactions. Sagas utilize either event sourcing for compensation or finite state machines to manage the state of transaction. In addition to sagas, *BASE* transactions are used. BASE stands for (B)asic availability, (S)oft state, and (E)ventual consistency. BASE transactions are not a piece of software, but rather a technique. *Soft state* in BASE refers to the transit of data from a source to a target, as well as the inconsistency between data sources. Based on the *basic availability* of the systems or services involved, the systems will *eventually* become consistent through the use of architecture patterns and messaging.

Contract maintenance and versioning

Another particularly difficult challenge within distributed architecture is contract creation, maintenance, and versioning. A contract is behavior and data that is agreed upon by both the client and the service. Contract maintenance is particularly difficult in distributed architectures, primarily due to decoupled services and systems owned by different teams and departments. Even more complex are the communication models needed for version deprecation.

CHAPTER 10

Layered Architecture Style

The *layered* architecture, also known as the *n-tiered* architecture style, is one of the most common architecture styles. This style of architecture is the de facto standard for most applications, primarily because of its simplicity, familiarity, and low cost. It is also a very natural way to develop applications due to Conway's law (*https://oreil.ly/Rb4uN*), which states that organizations that design systems are constrained to produce designs which are copies of the communication structures of these organizations. In most organizations there are user interface (UI) developers, backend developers, rules developers, and database experts (DBAs). These organizational layers fit nicely into the tiers of a traditional layered architecture, making it a natural choice for many business applications. The layered architecture style also falls into several architectural anti-patterns, including the *architecture by implication* anti-pattern and the *accidental architecture* anti-pattern. If a developer or architect is unsure which architecture style they are using, or if an Agile development team "just starts coding," chances are good that it is the layered architecture style they are implementing.

Topology

Components within the layered architecture style are organized into logical horizontal layers, with each layer performing a specific role within the application (such as presentation logic or business logic). Although there are no specific restrictions in terms of the number and types of layers that must exist, most layered architectures consist of four standard layers: presentation, business, persistence, and database, as illustrated in Figure 10-1. In some cases, the business layer and persistence layer are combined into a single business layer, particularly when the persistence logic (such as SQL or HSQL) is embedded within the business layer components. Thus, smaller applications may have only three layers, whereas larger and more complex business applications may contain five or more layers.

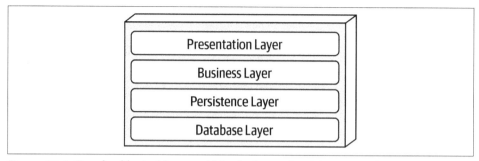

Figure 10-1. Standard logical layers within the layered architecture style

Figure 10-2 illustrates the various topology variants from a physical layering (deployment) perspective. The first variant combines the presentation, business, and persistence layers into a single deployment unit, with the database layer typically represented as a separate external physical database (or filesystem). The second variant physically separates the presentation layer into its own deployment unit, with the business and persistence layers combined into a second deployment unit. Again, with this variant, the database layer is usually physically separated through an external database or filesystem. A third variant combines all four standard layers into a single deployment, including the database layer. This variant might be useful for smaller applications with either an internally embedded database or an in-memory database. Many on-premises ("on-prem") products are built and delivered to customers using this third variant.

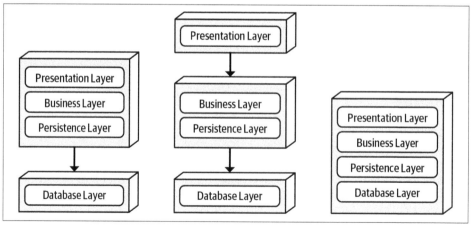

Figure 10-2. Physical topology (deployment) variants

Each layer of the layered architecture style has a specific role and responsibility within the architecture. For example, the presentation layer would be responsible for handling all user interface and browser communication logic, whereas the business layer would be responsible for executing specific business rules associated with the request. Each layer in the architecture forms an abstraction around the work that needs to be done to satisfy a particular business request. For example, the presentation layer doesn't need to know or worry about how to get customer data; it only needs to display that information on a screen in a particular format. Similarly, the business layer doesn't need to be concerned about how to format customer data for display on a screen or even where the customer data is coming from; it only needs to get the data from the persistence layer, perform business logic against the data (such as calculating values or aggregating data), and pass that information up to the presentation layer.

This *separation of concerns* concept within the layered architecture style makes it easy to build effective roles and responsibility models within the architecture. Components within a specific layer are limited in scope, dealing only with the logic that pertains to that layer. For example, components in the presentation layer only handle presentation logic, whereas components residing in the business layer only handle business logic. This allows developers to leverage their particular technical expertise to focus on the technical aspects of the domain (such as presentation logic or persistence logic). The trade-off of this benefit, however, is a lack of overall agility (the ability to respond quickly to change).

The layered architecture is a *technically partitioned* architecture (as opposed to a *domain-partitioned* architecture). Groups of components, rather than being grouped by domain (such as customer), are grouped by their technical role in the architecture (such as presentation or business). As a result, any particular business domain is spread throughout all of the layers of the architecture. For example, the domain of "customer" is contained in the presentation layer, business layer, rules layer, services layer, and database layer, making it difficult to apply changes to that domain. As a result, a domain-driven design approach does not work as well with the layered architecture style.

Layers of Isolation

Each layer in the layered architecture style can be either *closed* or *open*. A closed layer means that as a request moves top-down from layer to layer, the request cannot skip any layers, but rather must go through the layer immediately below it to get to the next layer (see Figure 10-3). For example, in a closed-layered architecture, a request originating from the presentation layer must first go through the business layer and then to the persistence layer before finally making it to the database layer.

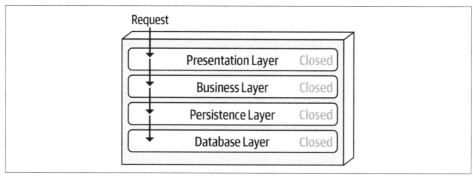

Figure 10-3. Closed layers within the layered architecture

Notice that in Figure 10-3 it would be much faster and easier for the presentation layer to access the database directly for simple retrieval requests, bypassing any unnecessary layers (what used to be known in the early 2000s as the *fast-lane reader pattern*). For this to happen, the business and persistence layers would have to be *open*, allowing requests to bypass other layers. Which is better—open layers or closed layers? The answer to this question lies in a key concept known as *layers of isolation*.

The *layers of isolation* concept means that changes made in one layer of the architecture generally don't impact or affect components in other layers, providing the contracts between those layers remain unchanged. Each layer is independent of the other layers, thereby having little or no knowledge of the inner workings of other layers in the architecture. However, to support layers of isolation, layers involved with the major flow of the request necessarily have to be closed. If the presentation layer can directly access the persistence layer, then changes made to the persistence layer would impact both the business layer *and* the presentation layer, producing a very tightly coupled application with layer interdependencies between components. This type of architecture then becomes very brittle, as well as difficult and expensive to change.

The layers of isolation concept also allows any layer in the architecture to be replaced without impacting any other layer (again, assuming well-defined contracts and the use of the business delegate pattern (*https://oreil.ly/WeKWs*)). For example, you can leverage the layers of isolation concept within the layered architecture style to replace your older JavaServer Faces (JSF) presentation layer with React.js without impacting any other layer in the application.

Adding Layers

While closed layers facilitate layers of isolation and therefore help isolate change within the architecture, there are times when it makes sense for certain layers to be open. For example, suppose there are shared objects within the business layer that contain common functionality for business components (such as date and string util-

ity classes, auditing classes, logging classes, and so on). Suppose there is an architecture decision stating that the presentation layer is restricted from using these shared business objects. This constraint is illustrated in Figure 10-4, with the dotted line going from a presentation component to a shared business object in the business layer. This scenario is difficult to govern and control because *architecturally* the presentation layer has access to the business layer, and hence has access to the shared objects within that layer.

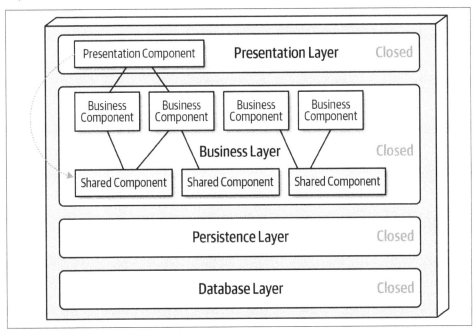

Figure 10-4. Shared objects within the business layer

One way to architecturally mandate this restriction is to add to the architecture a new services layer containing all of the shared business objects. Adding this new layer now architecturally restricts the presentation layer from accessing the shared business objects because the business layer is closed (see Figure 10-5). However, the new services layer must be marked as *open*; otherwise the business layer would be forced to go through the services layer to access the persistence layer. Marking the services layer as open allows the business layer to either access that layer (as indicated by the solid arrow), or bypass the layer and go to the next one down (as indicated by the dotted arrow in Figure 10-5).

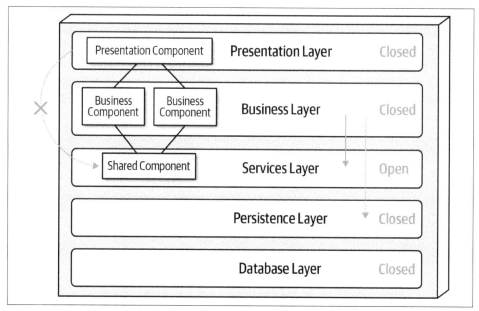

Figure 10-5. Adding a new services layer to the architecture

Leveraging the concept of open and closed layers helps define the relationship between architecture layers and request flows. It also provides developers with the necessary information and guidance to understand various layer access restrictions within the architecture. Failure to document or properly communicate which layers in the architecture are open and closed (and why) usually results in tightly coupled and brittle architectures that are very difficult to test, maintain, and deploy.

Other Considerations

The layered architecture makes for a good starting point for most applications when it is not known yet exactly which architecture style will ultimately be used. This is a common practice for many microservices efforts when architects are still determining whether microservices is the right architecture choice, but development must begin. However, when using this technique, be sure to keep reuse at a minimum and keep object hierarchies (depth of inheritance tree) fairly shallow so as to maintain a good level of modularity. This will help facilitate the move to another architecture style later on.

One thing to watch out for with the layered architecture is the *architecture sinkhole* anti-pattern. This anti-pattern occurs when requests move from layer to layer as simple pass-through processing with no business logic performed within each layer. For example, suppose the presentation layer responds to a simple request from the user to retrieve basic customer data (such as name and address). The presentation layer passes the request to the business layer, which does nothing but pass the request on to the rules layer, which in turn does nothing but pass the request on to the persistence layer, which then makes a simple SQL call to the database layer to retrieve the customer data. The data is then passed all the way back up the stack with no additional processing or logic to aggregate, calculate, apply rules, or transform the data. This results in unnecessary object instantiation and processing, impacting both memory consumption and performance.

Every layered architecture will have at least some scenarios that fall into the architecture sinkhole anti-pattern. The key to determining whether the architecture sinkhole anti-pattern is at play is to analyze the percentage of requests that fall into this category. The 80-20 rule is usually a good practice to follow. For example, it is acceptable if only 20 percent of the requests are sinkholes. However, if 80 percent of the requests are sinkholes, it a good indicator that the layered architecture is not the correct architecture style for the problem domain. Another approach to solving the architecture sinkhole anti-pattern is to make all the layers in the architecture open, realizing, of course, that the trade-off is increased difficulty in managing change within the architecture.

Why Use This Architecture Style

The layered architecture style is a good choice for small, simple applications or websites. It is also a good architecture choice, particularly as a starting point, for situations with very tight budget and time constraints. Because of the simplicity and familiarity among developers and architects, the layered architecture is perhaps one of the lowest-cost architecture styles, promoting ease of development for smaller applications. The layered architecture style is also a good choice when an architect is still analyzing business needs and requirements and is unsure which architecture style would be best.

As applications using the layered architecture style grow, characteristics like maintainability, agility, testability, and deployability are adversely affected. For this reason, large applications and systems using the layered architecture might be better suited for other, more modular architecture styles.

Architecture Characteristics Ratings

A one-star rating in the characteristics ratings table (shown in Figure 10-6) means the specific architecture characteristic isn't well supported in the architecture, whereas a five-star rating means the architecture characteristic is one of the strongest features in the architecture style. The definition for each characteristic identified in the scorecard can be found in Chapter 4.

Architecture characteristic	Star rating
Partitioning type	Technical
Number of quanta	1
Deployability	☆
Elasticity	☆
Evolutionary	☆
Fault tolerance	☆
Modularity	☆
Overall cost	☆☆☆☆☆
Performance	☆☆
Reliability	☆☆☆
Scalability	☆
Simplicity	☆☆☆☆☆
Testability	☆☆

Figure 10-6. Layered architecture characteristics ratings

Overall cost and simplicity are the primary strengths of the layered architecture style. Being monolithic in nature, layered architectures don't have the complexities associated with distributed architecture styles, are simple and easy to understand, and are relatively low cost to build and maintain. However, as a cautionary note, these ratings start to quickly diminish as monolithic layered architectures get bigger and consequently more complex.

Both deployability and testability rate very low for this architecture style. Deployability rates low due to the ceremony of deployment (effort to deploy), high risk, and lack of frequent deployments. A simple three-line change to a class file in the layered architecture style requires the entire deployment unit to be redeployed, taking in potential database changes, configuration changes, or other coding changes sneaking in alongside the original change. Furthermore, this simple three-line change is usually bundled with dozens of other changes, thereby increasing deployment risk even further (as well as increasing the frequency of deployment). The low testability rating also reflects this scenario; with a simple three-line change, most developers are not going to spend hours executing the entire regression test suite (even if such a thing were to exist in the first place), particularly along with dozens of other changes being made to the monolithic application at the same time. We gave testability a two-star rating (rather than one star) due to the ability to mock or stub components (or even an entire layer), which eases the overall testing effort.

Overall reliability rates medium (three stars) in this architecture style, mostly due to the lack of network traffic, bandwidth, and latency found in most distributed architectures. We only gave the layered architecture three stars for reliability because of the nature of the monolithic deployment, combined with the low ratings for testability (completeness of testing) and deployment risk.

Elasticity and scalability rate very low (one star) for the layered architecture, primarily due to monolithic deployments and the lack of architectural modularity. Although it is possible to make certain functions within a monolith scale more than others, this effort usually requires very complex design techniques such as multithreading, internal messaging, and other parallel processing practices, techniques this architecture isn't well suited for. However, because the layered architecture is always a single system quantum due to the monolithic user interface, backend processing, and monolithic database, applications can only scale to a certain point based on the single quantum.

Performance is always an interesting characteristic to rate for the layered architecture. We gave it only two stars because the architecture style simply does not lend itself to high-performance systems due to the lack of parallel processing, closed layering, and the sinkhole architecture anti-pattern. Like scalability, performance can be addressed through caching, multithreading, and the like, but it is not a natural characteristic of this architecture style; architects and developers have to work hard to make all this happen.

Layered architectures don't support fault tolerance due to monolithic deployments and the lack of architectural modularity. If one small part of a layered architecture causes an out-of-memory condition to occur, the entire application unit is impacted and crashes. Furthermore, overall availability is impacted due to the high mean-time-to-recovery (MTTR) usually experienced by most monolithic applications, with startup times ranging anywhere from 2 minutes for smaller applications, up to 15 minutes or more for most large applications.

CHAPTER 11

Pipeline Architecture Style

One of the fundamental styles in software architecture that appears again and again is the *pipeline* architecture (also known as the *pipes and filters* architecture). As soon as developers and architects decided to split functionality into discrete parts, this pattern followed. Most developers know this architecture as this underlying principle behind Unix terminal shell languages, such as Bash (*https://oreil.ly/uP2Bo*) and Zsh (*https://oreil.ly/40UyF*).

Developers in many functional programming languages will see parallels between language constructs and elements of this architecture. In fact, many tools that utilize the MapReduce (*https://oreil.ly/veX6W*) programming model follow this basic topology. While these examples show a low-level implementation of the pipeline architecture style, it can also be used for higher-level business applications.

Topology

The topology of the pipeline architecture consists of pipes and filters, illustrated in Figure 11-1.

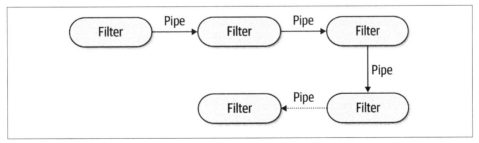

Figure 11-1. Basic topology for pipeline architecture

The pipes and filters coordinate in a specific fashion, with pipes forming one-way communication between filters, usually in a point-to-point fashion.

Pipes

Pipes in this architecture form the communication channel between filters. Each pipe is typically unidirectional and point-to-point (rather than broadcast) for performance reasons, accepting input from one source and always directing output to another. The payload carried on the pipes may be any data format, but architects favor smaller amounts of data to enable high performance.

Filters

Filters are self-contained, independent from other filters, and generally stateless. Filters should perform one task only. Composite tasks should be handled by a sequence of filters rather than a single one.

Four types of filters exist within this architecture style:

Producer
> The starting point of a process, outbound only, sometimes called the *source*.

Transformer
> Accepts input, optionally performs a transformation on some or all of the data, then forwards it to the outbound pipe. Functional advocates will recognize this feature as *map*.

Tester
> Accepts input, tests one or more criteria, then optionally produces output, based on the test. Functional programmers will recognize this as similar to *reduce*.

Consumer
> The termination point for the pipeline flow. Consumers sometimes persist the final result of the pipeline process to a database, or they may display the final results on a user interface screen.

The unidirectional nature and simplicity of each of the pipes and filters encourages compositional reuse. Many developers have discovered this ability using shells. A famous story from the blog "More Shell, Less Egg" (*https://oreil.ly/ljeb5*) illustrates just how powerful these abstractions are. Donald Knuth was asked to write a program to solve this text handling problem: read a file of text, determine the *n* most frequently used words, and print out a sorted list of those words along with their frequencies. He wrote a program consisting of more than 10 pages of Pascal, designing (and documenting) a new algorithm along the way. Then, Doug McIlroy demonstrated a shell script that would easily fit within a Twitter post that solved the problem more simply, elegantly, and understandably (if you understand shell commands):

```
tr -cs A-Za-z '\n' |
tr A-Z a-z |
sort |
uniq -c |
sort -rn |
sed ${1}q
```

Even the designers of Unix shells are often surprised at the inventive uses developers have wrought with their simple but powerfully composite abstractions.

Example

The pipeline architecture pattern appears in a variety of applications, especially tasks that facilitate simple, one-way processing. For example, many Electronic Data Interchange (EDI) tools use this pattern, building transformations from one document type to another using pipes and filters. ETL tools (extract, transform, and load) leverage the pipeline architecture as well for the flow and modification of data from one database or data source to another. Orchestrators and mediators such as Apache Camel (*https://camel.apache.org*) utilize the pipeline architecture to pass information from one step in a business process to another.

To illustrate how the pipeline architecture can be used, consider the following example, as illustrated in Figure 11-2, where various service telemetry information is sent from services via streaming to Apache Kafka (*https://kafka.apache.org*).

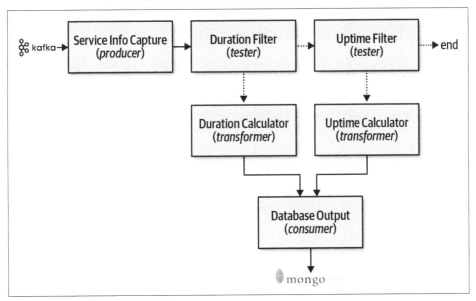

Figure 11-2. Pipeline architecture example

Example | 145

Notice in Figure 11-2 the use of the pipeline architecture style to process the different kinds of data streamed to Kafka. The Service Info Capture filter (producer filter) subscribes to the Kafka topic and receives service information. It then sends this captured data to a tester filter called Duration Filter to determine whether the data captured from Kafka is related to the duration (in milliseconds) of the service request. Notice the separation of concerns between the filters; the Service Metrics Capture filter is only concerned about how to connect to a Kafka topic and receive streaming data, whereas the Duration Filter is only concerned about qualifying the data and optionally routing it to the next pipe. If the data is related to the duration (in milliseconds) of the service request, then the Duration Filter passes the data on to the Duration Calculator transformer filter. Otherwise, it passes it on to the Uptime Filter tester filter to check if the data is related to uptime metrics. If it is not, then the pipeline ends—the data is of no interest to this particular processing flow. Otherwise, if it is uptime metrics, it then passes the data along to the Uptime Calculator to calculate the uptime metrics for the service. These transformers then pass the modified data to the Database Output consumer, which then persists the data in a MongoDB (*https://www.mongodb.com*) database.

This example shows the extensibility properties of the pipeline architecture. For example, in Figure 11-2, a new tester filter could easily be added after the Uptime Filter to pass the data on to another newly gathered metric, such as the database connection wait time.

Architecture Characteristics Ratings

A one-star rating in the characteristics ratings table Figure 11-3 means the specific architecture characteristic isn't well supported in the architecture, whereas a five-star rating means the architecture characteristic is one of the strongest features in the architecture style. The definition for each characteristic identified in the scorecard can be found in Chapter 4.

The pipeline architecture style is a technically partitioned architecture due to the partitioning of application logic into filter types (producer, tester, transformer, and consumer). Also, because the pipeline architecture is usually implemented as a monolithic deployment, the architectural quantum is always one.

Architecture characteristic	Star rating
Partitioning type	Technical
Number of quanta	1
Deployability	☆☆
Elasticity	☆
Evolutionary	☆☆☆
Fault tolerance	☆
Modularity	☆☆☆
Overall cost	☆☆☆☆☆
Performance	☆☆
Reliability	☆☆☆
Scalability	☆
Simplicity	☆☆☆☆☆
Testability	☆☆☆

Figure 11-3. Pipeline architecture characteristics ratings

Overall cost and simplicity combined with modularity are the primary strengths of the pipeline architecture style. Being monolithic in nature, pipeline architectures don't have the complexities associated with distributed architecture styles, are simple and easy to understand, and are relatively low cost to build and maintain. Architectural modularity is achieved through the separation of concerns between the various filter types and transformers. Any of these filters can be modified or replaced without impacting the other filters. For instance, in the Kafka example illustrated in Figure 11-2, the Duration Calculator can be modified to change the duration calculation without impacting any other filter.

Deployability and testability, while only around average, rate slightly higher than the layered architecture due to the level of modularity achieved through filters. That said, this architecture style is still a monolith, and as such, ceremony, risk, frequency of deployment, and completion of testing still impact the pipeline architecture.

Like the layered architecture, overall reliability rates medium (three stars) in this architecture style, mostly due to the lack of network traffic, bandwidth, and latency found in most distributed architectures. We only gave it three stars for reliability because of the nature of the monolithic deployment of this architecture style in conjunction with testability and deployability issues (such as having to test the entire monolith and deploy the entire monolith for any given change).

Elasticity and scalability rate very low (one star) for the pipeline architecture, primarily due to monolithic deployments. Although it is possible to make certain functions within a monolith scale more than others, this effort usually requires very complex design techniques such as multithreading, internal messaging, and other parallel processing practices, techniques this architecture isn't well suited for. However, because the pipeline architecture is always a single system quantum due to the monolithic user interface, backend processing, and monolithic database, applications can only scale to a certain point based on the single architecture quantum.

Pipeline architectures don't support fault tolerance due to monolithic deployments and the lack of architectural modularity. If one small part of a pipeline architecture causes an out-of-memory condition to occur, the entire application unit is impacted and crashes. Furthermore, overall availability is impacted due to the high mean time to recovery (MTTR) usually experienced by most monolithic applications, with startup times ranging anywhere from 2 minutes for smaller applications, up to 15 minutes or more for most large applications.

CHAPTER 12

Microkernel Architecture Style

The *microkernel* architecture style (also referred to as the *plug-in* architecture) was coined several decades ago and is still widely used today. This architecture style is a natural fit for product-based applications (packaged and made available for download and installation as a single, monolithic deployment, typically installed on the customer's site as a third-party product) but is widely used in many nonproduct custom business applications as well.

Topology

The microkernel architecture style is a relatively simple monolithic architecture consisting of two architecture components: a core system and plug-in components. Application logic is divided between independent plug-in components and the basic core system, providing extensibility, adaptability, and isolation of application features and custom processing logic. Figure 12-1 illustrates the basic topology of the microkernel architecture style.

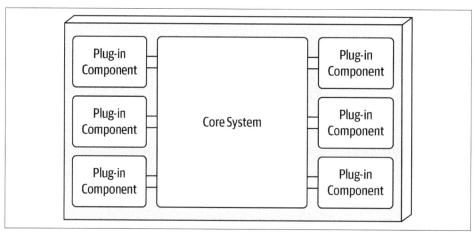

Figure 12-1. Basic components of the microkernel architecture style

Core System

The *core system* is formally defined as the minimal functionality required to run the system. The Eclipse IDE is a good example of this. The core system of Eclipse is just a basic text editor: open a file, change some text, and save the file. It's not until you add plug-ins that Eclipse starts becoming a usable product. However, another definition of the core system is the happy path (general processing flow) through the application, with little or no custom processing. Removing the cyclomatic complexity of the core system and placing it into separate plug-in components allows for better extensibility and maintainability, as well as increased testability. For example, suppose an electronic device recycling application must perform specific custom assessment rules for each electronic device received. The Java code for this sort of processing might look as follows:

```java
public void assessDevice(String deviceID) {
    if (deviceID.equals("iPhone6s")) {
        assessiPhone6s();
    } else if (deviceID.equals("iPad1"))
        assessiPad1();
    } else if (deviceID.equals("Galaxy5"))
        assessGalaxy5();
    } else ...
        ...
    }
}
```

Rather than placing all this client-specific customization in the core system with lots of cyclomatic complexity, it is much better to create a separate plug-in component for each electronic device being assessed. Not only do specific client plug-in components isolate independent device logic from the rest of the processing flow, but they also allow for expandability. Adding a new electronic device to assess is simply a matter of adding a new plug-in component and updating the registry. With the microkernel architecture style, assessing an electronic device only requires the core system to locate and invoke the corresponding device plug-ins as illustrated in this revised source code:

```
public void assessDevice(String deviceID) {
        String plugin = pluginRegistry.get(deviceID);
        Class<?> theClass = Class.forName(plugin);
        Constructor<?> constructor = theClass.getConstructor();
        DevicePlugin devicePlugin =
                (DevicePlugin)constructor.newInstance();
        DevicePlugin.assess();
}
```

In this example all of the complex rules and instructions for assessing a particular electronic device are self-contained in a standalone, independent plug-in component that can be generically executed from the core system.

Depending on the size and complexity, the core system can be implemented as a layered architecture or a modular monolith (as illustrated in Figure 12-2). In some cases, the core system can be split into separately deployed domain services, with each domain service containing specific plug-in components specific to that domain. For example, suppose Payment Processing is the domain service representing the core system. Each payment method (credit card, PayPal, store credit, gift card, and purchase order) would be separate plug-in components specific to the payment domain. In all of these cases, it is typical for the entire monolithic application to share a single database.

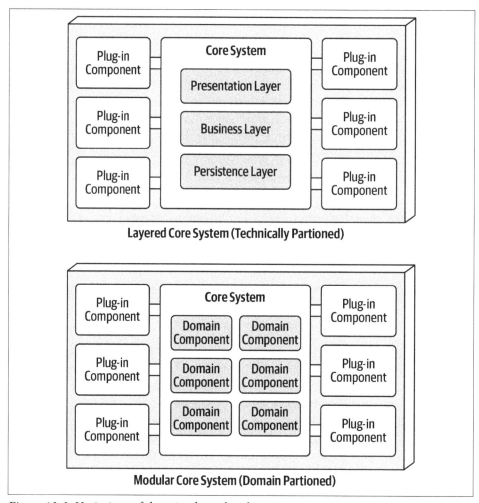

Figure 12-2. Variations of the microkernel architecture core system

The presentation layer of the core system can be embedded within the core system or implemented as a separate user interface, with the core system providing backend services. As a matter of fact, a separate user interface can also be implemented as a microkernel architecture style. Figure 12-3 illustrates these presentation layer variants in relation to the core system.

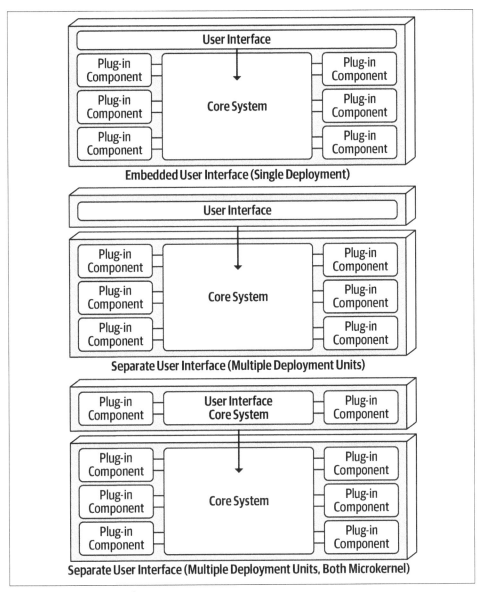

Figure 12-3. User interface variants

Plug-In Components

Plug-in components are standalone, independent components that contain special-ized processing, additional features, and custom code meant to enhance or extend the core system. Additionally, they can be used to isolate highly volatile code, creating better maintainability and testability within the application. Ideally, plug-in components should be independent of each other and have no dependencies between them.

The communication between the plug-in components and the core system is generally point-to-point, meaning the "pipe" that connects the plug-in to the core system is usually a method invocation or function call to the entry-point class of the plug-in component. In addition, the plug-in component can be either compile-based or runtime-based. Runtime plug-in components can be added or removed at runtime without having to redeploy the core system or other plug-ins, and they are usually managed through frameworks such as Open Service Gateway Initiative (OSGi) for Java (*https://www.osgi.org*), Penrose (Java) (*https://oreil.ly/J5XZw*), Jigsaw (Java) (*https://oreil.ly/wv9bW*), or Prism (.NET) (*https://oreil.ly/xmrtY*). Compile-based plug-in components are much simpler to manage but require the entire monolithic application to be redeployed when modified, added, or removed.

Point-to-point plug-in components can be implemented as shared libraries (such as a JAR, DLL, or Gem), package names in Java, or namespaces in C#. Continuing with the electronics recycling assessment application example, each electronic device plug-in can be written and implemented as a JAR, DLL, or Ruby Gem (or any other shared library), with the name of the device matching the name of the independent shared library, as illustrated in Figure 12-4.

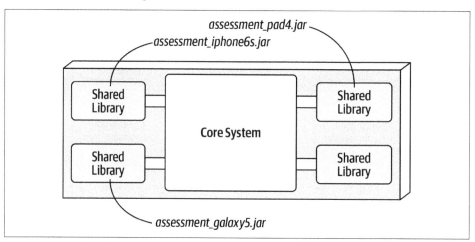

Figure 12-4. Shared library plug-in implementation

Alternatively, an easier approach shown in Figure 12-5 is to implement each plug-in component as a separate namespace or package name within the same code base or IDE project. When creating the namespace, we recommend the following semantics: app.plug-in.<domain>.<context>. For example, consider the namespace app.plugin.assessment.iphone6s. The second node (plugin) makes it clear this component is a plug-in and therefore should strictly adhere to the basic rules regarding plug-in components (namely, that they are self-contained and separate from other plug-ins). The third node describes the domain (in this case, `assessment`), thereby allowing plug-in components to be organized and grouped by a common purpose. The fourth node (`iphone6s`) describes the specific context for the plug-in, making it easy to locate the specific device plug-in for modification or testing.

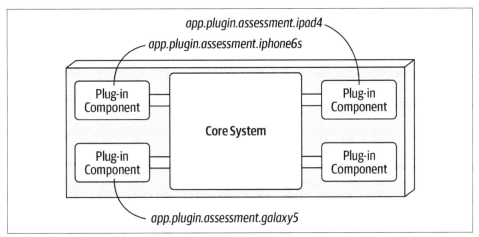

Figure 12-5. Package or namespace plug-in implementation

Plug-in components do not always have to be point-to-point communication with the core system. Other alternatives exist, including using REST or messaging as a means to invoke plug-in functionality, with each plug-in being a standalone service (or maybe even a microservice implemented using a container). Although this may sound like a good way to increase overall scalability, note that this topology (illustrated in Figure 12-6) is still only a single architecture quantum due to the monolithic core system. Every request must first go through the core system to get to the plug-in service.

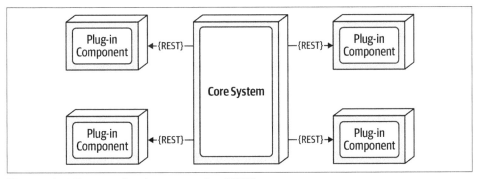

Figure 12-6. Remote plug-in access using REST

The benefits of the remote access approach to accessing plug-in components implemented as individual services is that it provides better overall component decoupling, allows for better scalability and throughput, and allows for runtime changes without any special frameworks like OSGi, Jigsaw, or Prism. It also allows for asynchronous communications to plug-ins, which, depending on the scenario, could significantly improve overall user responsiveness. Using the electronics recycling example, rather than having to wait for the electronic device assessment to run, the core system could make an asynchronous *request* to kick off an assessment for a particular device. When the assessment completes, the plug-in can notify the core system through another asynchronous messaging channel, which in turn would notify the user that the assessment is complete.

With these benefits comes trade-offs. Remote plug-in access turns the microkernel architecture into a distributed architecture rather than a monolithic one, making it difficult to implement and deploy for most third-party on-prem products. Furthermore, it creates more overall complexity and cost and complicates the overall deployment topology. If a plug-in becomes unresponsive or is not running, particularly when using REST, the request cannot be completed. This would not be the case with a monolithic deployment. The choice of whether to make the communication to plug-in components from the core system point-to-point or remote should be based on specific requirements and thus requires a careful trade-off analysis of the benefits and drawbacks of such an approach.

It is not a common practice for plug-in components to connect directly to a centrally shared database. Rather, the core system takes on this responsibility, passing whatever data is needed into each plug-in. The primary reason for this practice is decoupling. Making a database change should only impact the core system, not the plug-in components. That said, plug-ins can have their own separate data stores only accessible to that plug-in. For example, each electronic device assessment plug-in in the electronic recycling system example can have its own simple database or rules engine containing all of the specific assessment rules for each product. The data store owned by the plug-in component can be external (as shown in Figure 12-7), or it could be embedded as part of the plug-in component or monolithic deployment (as in the case of an in-memory or embedded database).

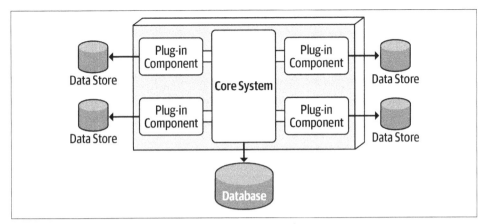

Figure 12-7. Plug-in components can own their own data store

Registry

The core system needs to know about which plug-in modules are available and how to get to them. One common way of implementing this is through a plug-in registry. This registry contains information about each plug-in module, including things like its name, data contract, and remote access protocol details (depending on how the plug-in is connected to the core system). For example, a plug-in for tax software that flags high-risk tax audit items might have a registry entry that contains the name of the service (AuditChecker), the data contract (input data and output data), and the contract format (XML).

The registry can be as simple as an internal map structure owned by the core system containing a key and the plug-in component reference, or it can be as complex as a registry and discovery tool either embedded within the core system or deployed externally (such as Apache ZooKeeper (*https://zookeeper.apache.org*) or Consul (*https://www.consul.io*)). Using the electronics recycling example, the following Java code implements a simple registry within the core system, showing a point-to-point entry, a messaging entry, and a RESTful entry example for assessing an iPhone 6S device:

```java
Map<String, String> registry = new HashMap<String, String>();
static {
  //point-to-point access example
  registry.put("iPhone6s", "Iphone6sPlugin");

  //messaging example
  registry.put("iPhone6s", "iphone6s.queue");

  //restful example
  registry.put("iPhone6s", "https://atlas:443/assess/iphone6s");
}
```

Contracts

The contracts between the plug-in components and the core system are usually standard across a domain of plug-in components and include behavior, input data, and output data returned from the plug-in component. Custom contracts are typically found in situations where plug-in components are developed by a third party where you have no control over the contract used by the plug-in. In such cases, it is common to create an adapter between the plug-in contract and your standard contract so that the core system doesn't need specialized code for each plug-in.

Plug-in contracts can be implemented in XML, JSON, or even objects passed back and forth between the plug-in and the core system. In keeping with the electronics recycling application, the following contract (implemented as a standard Java interface named AssessmentPlugin) defines the overall behavior (assess(), register(), and deregister()), along with the corresponding output data expected from the plug-in component (AssessmentOutput):

```
public interface AssessmentPlugin {
        public AssessmentOutput assess();
        public String register();
        public String deregister();
}

public class AssessmentOutput {
        public String assessmentReport;
        public Boolean resell;
        public Double value;
        public Double resellPrice;
}
```

In this contract example, the device assessment plug-in is expected to return the assessment report as a formatted string; a resell flag (true or false) indicating whether this device can be resold on a third-party market or safely disposed of; and finally, if it can be resold (another form of recycling), what the calculated value is of the item and what the recommended resell price should be.

Notice the roles and responsibility model between the core system and the plug-in component in this example, specifically with the assessmentReport field. It is not the responsibility of the core system to format and understand the details of the assessment report, only to either print it out or display it to the user.

Examples and Use Cases

Most of the tools used for developing and releasing software are implemented using the microkernel architecture. Some examples include the Eclipse IDE (*https://www.eclipse.org/ide*), PMD (*https://pmd.github.io*), Jira (*https://www.atlassian.com/software/jira*), and Jenkins (*https://jenkins.io*), to name a few). Internet web browsers such as Chrome and Firefox are another common product example using the micro-kernel architecture: viewers and other plug-ins add additional capabilities that are not otherwise found in the basic browser representing the core system. The examples are endless for product-based software, but what about large business applications? The microkernel architecture applies to these situations as well. To illustrate this point, consider an insurance company example involving insurance claims processing.

Claims processing is a very complicated process. Each jurisdiction has different rules and regulations for what is and isn't allowed in an insurance claim. For example, some jurisdictions (e.g., states) allow free windshield replacement if your windshield is damaged by a rock, whereas other states do not. This creates an almost infinite set of conditions for a standard claims process.

Most insurance claims applications leverage large and complex rules engines to han-dle much of this complexity. However, these rules engines can grow into a complex big ball of mud where changing one rule impacts other rules, or making a simple rule change requires an army of analysts, developers, and testers to make sure nothing is broken by a simple change. Using the microkernel architecture pattern can solve many of these issues.

The claims rules for each jurisdiction can be contained in separate standalone plug-in components (implemented as source code or a specific rules engine instance accessed by the plug-in component). This way, rules can be added, removed, or changed for a particular jurisdiction without impacting any other part of the system. Furthermore, new jurisdictions can be added and removed without impacting other parts of the system. The core system in this example would be the standard process for filing and processing a claim, something that doesn't change often.

Another example of a large and complex business application that can leverage the microkernel architecture is tax preparation software. For example, the United States has a basic two-page tax form called the 1040 form that contains a summary of all the information needed to calculate a person's tax liability. Each line in the 1040 tax form has a single number that requires many other forms and worksheets to arrive at that single number (such as gross income). Each of these additional forms and worksheets can be implemented as a plug-in component, with the 1040 summary tax form being the core system (the driver). This way, changes to tax law can be isolated to an inde-pendent plug-in component, making changes easier and less risky.

Architecture Characteristics Ratings

A one-star rating in the characteristics ratings in Figure 12-8 means the specific architecture characteristic isn't well supported in the architecture, whereas a five-star rating means the architecture characteristic is one of the strongest features in the architecture style. The definition for each characteristic identified in the scorecard can be found in Chapter 4.

Architecture characteristic	Star rating
Partitioning type	Domain and technical
Number of quanta	1
Deployability	☆☆☆
Elasticity	☆
Evolutionary	☆☆☆
Fault tolerance	☆
Modularity	☆☆☆
Overall cost	☆☆☆☆☆
Performance	☆☆☆
Reliability	☆☆☆
Scalability	☆
Simplicity	☆☆☆☆
Testability	☆☆☆

Figure 12-8. Microkernel architecture characteristics ratings

Similar to the layered architecture style, simplicity and overall cost are the main strengths of the microkernel architecture style, and scalability, fault tolerance, and extensibility its main weaknesses. These weaknesses are due to the typical monolithic deployments found with the microkernel architecture. Also, like the layered architecture style, the number of quanta is always singular (one) because all requests must go through the core system to get to independent plug-in components. That's where the similarities end.

The microkernel architecture style is unique in that it is the only architecture style that can be both domain partitioned *and* technically partitioned. While most microkernel architectures are technically partitioned, the domain partitioning aspect comes about mostly through a strong domain-to-architecture isomorphism. For example, problems that require different configurations for each location or client match extremely well with this architecture style. Another example is a product or application that places a strong emphasis on user customization and feature extensibility (such as Jira or an IDE like Eclipse).

Testability, deployability, and reliability rate a little above average (three stars), primarily because functionality can be isolated to independent plug-in components. If done right, this reduces the overall testing scope of changes and also reduces overall risk of deployment, particularly if plug-in components are deployed in a runtime fashion.

Modularity and extensibility also rate a little above average (three stars). With the microkernel architecture style, additional functionality can be added, removed, and changed through independent, self-contained plug-in components, thereby making it relatively easy to extend and enhance applications created using this architecture style and allowing teams to respond to changes much faster. Consider the tax preparation software example from the previous section. If the US tax law changes (which it does all the time), requiring a new tax form, that new tax form can be created as a plug-in component and added to the application without much effort. Similarly, if a tax form or worksheet is no longer needed, that plug-in can simply be removed from the application.

Performance is always an interesting characteristic to rate with the microkernel architecture style. We gave it three stars (a little above average) mostly because microkernel applications are generally small and don't grow as big as most layered architectures. Also, they don't suffer as much from the architecture sinkhole anti-pattern discussed in Chapter 10. Finally, microkernel architectures can be streamlined by unplugging unneeded functionality, therefore making the application run faster. A good example of this is Wildfly (*https://wildfly.org*) (previously the JBoss Application Server). By unplugging unnecessary functionality like clustering, caching, and messaging, the application server performs much faster than with these features in place.

CHAPTER 13

Service-Based Architecture Style

Service-based architecture is a hybrid of the microservices architecture style and is considered one of the most pragmatic architecture styles, mostly due to its architectural flexibility. Although service-based architecture is a distributed architecture, it doesn't have the same level of complexity and cost as other distributed architectures, such as microservices or event-driven architecture, making it a very popular choice for many business-related applications.

Topology

The basic topology of service-based architecture follows a distributed macro layered structure consisting of a separately deployed user interface, separately deployed remote coarse-grained services, and a monolithic database. This basic topology is illustrated in Figure 13-1.

Services within this architecture style are typically coarse-grained "portions of an application" (usually called *domain services*) that are independent and separately deployed. Services are typically deployed in the same manner as any monolithic application would be (such as an EAR file, WAR file, or assembly) and as such do not require containerization (although you could deploy a domain service in a container such as Docker). Because the services typically share a single monolithic database, the number of services within an application context generally range between 4 and 12 services, with the average being about 7 services.

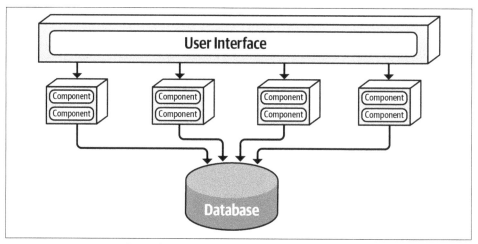

Figure 13-1. Basic topology of the service-based architecture style

In most cases there is only a single instance of each domain service within a service-based architecture. However, based on scalability, fault tolerance, and throughput needs, multiple instances of a domain service can certainly exist. Multiple instances of a service usually require some sort of load-balancing capability between the user interface and the domain service so that the user interface can be directed to a healthy and available service instance.

Services are accessed remotely from a user interface using a remote access protocol. While REST is typically used to access services from the user interface, messaging, remote procedure call (RPC), or even SOAP could be used as well. While an API layer consisting of a proxy or gateway can be used to access services from the user interface (or other external requests), in most cases the user interface accesses the services directly using a service locator pattern (*https://oreil.ly/wYLF2*) embedded within the user interface, API gateway, or proxy.

One important aspect of service-based architecture is that it typically uses a centrally shared database. This allows services to leverage SQL queries and joins in the same way a traditional monolithic layered architecture would. Because of the small number of services (4 to 12), database connections are not usually an issue in service-based architecture. Database changes, however, can be an issue. The section "Database Partitioning" on page 169 describes techniques for addressing and managing database change within a service-based architecture.

Topology Variants

Many topology variants exist within the service-based architecture style, making this perhaps one of the most flexible architecture styles. For example, the single monolithic user interface, as illustrated in Figure 13-1, can be broken apart into user interface domains, even to a level matching each domain service. These user interface variants are illustrated in Figure 13-2.

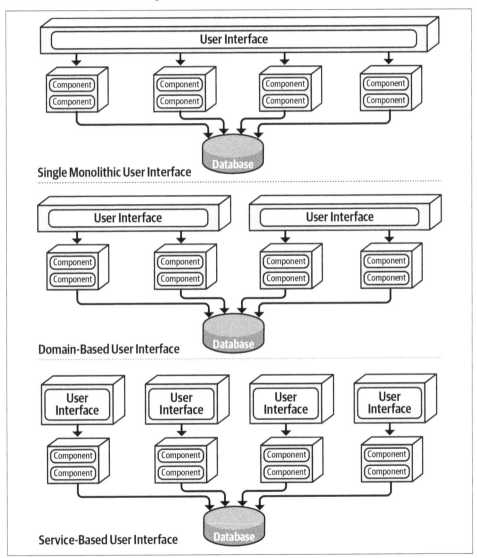

Figure 13-2. User interface variants

Similarly, opportunities may exist to break apart a single monolithic database into separate databases, even going as far as domain-scoped databases matching each domain service (similar to microservices). In these cases it is important to make sure the data in each separate database is not needed by another domain service. This avoids interservice communication between domain services (something to definitely avoid with service-based architecture) and also the duplication of data between databases. These database variants are illustrated in Figure 13-3.

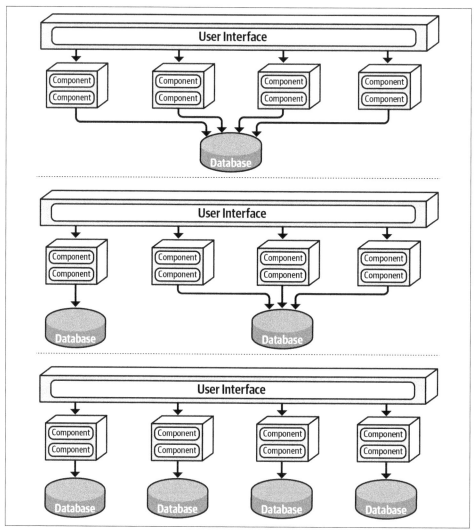

Figure 13-3. Database variants

Finally, it is also possible to add an API layer consisting of a reverse proxy or gateway between the user interface and services, as shown in Figure 13-4. This is a good practice when exposing domain service functionality to external systems or when consolidating shared cross-cutting concerns and moving them outside of the user interface (such as metrics, security, auditing requirements, and service discovery).

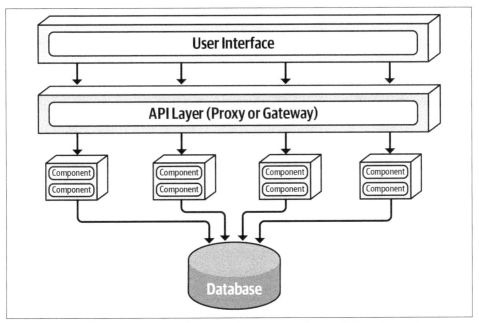

Figure 13-4. Adding an API layer between the user interface and domain services

Service Design and Granularity

Because domain services in a service-based architecture are generally coarse-grained, each domain service is typically designed using a layered architecture style consisting of an API facade layer, a business layer, and a persistence layer. Another popular design approach is to domain partition each domain service using sub-domains similar to the modular monolith architecture style. Each of these design approaches is illustrated in Figure 13-5.

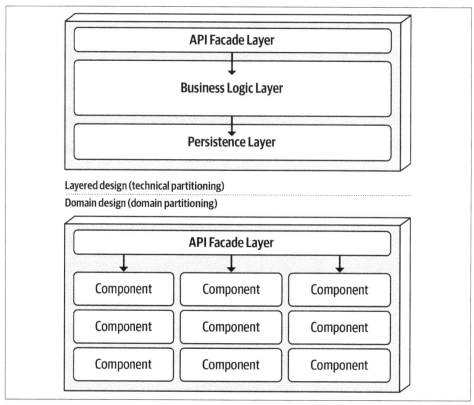

Figure 13-5. Domain service design variants

Regardless of the service design, a domain service must contain some sort of API access facade that the user interface interacts with to execute some sort of business functionality. The API access facade typically takes on the responsibility of orchestrating the business request from the user interface. For example, consider a business request from the user interface to place an order (also known as catalog checkout). This single request, received by the API access facade within the OrderService domain service, internally orchestrates the single business request: place the order, generate an order ID, apply the payment, and update the product inventory for each product ordered. In the microservices architecture style, this would likely involve the orchestration of many separately deployed remote single-purpose services to complete the request. This difference between internal class-level orchestration and external service orchestration points to one of the many significant differences between service-based architecture and microservices in terms of granularity.

Because domain services are coarse-grained, regular ACID (atomicity, consistency, isolation, durability) database transactions involving database commits and rollbacks are used to ensure database integrity within a single domain service. Highly distributed architectures like microservices, on the other hand, usually have fine-grained services and use a distributed transaction technique known as BASE transactions (basic availability, soft state, eventual consistency) that rely on eventual consistency and hence do not support the same level of database integrity as ACID transactions in a service-based architecture.

To illustrate this point, consider the example of a catalog checkout process within a service-based architecture. Suppose the customer places an order and the credit card used for payment has expired. Since this is an atomic transaction within the same service, everything added to the database can be removed using a rollback and a notice sent to the customer stating that the payment cannot be applied. Now consider this same process in a microservices architecture with smaller fine-grained services. First, the OrderPlacement service would accept the request, create the order, generate an order ID, and insert the order into the order tables. Once this is done, the order service would then make a remote call to the PaymentService, which would try to apply the payment. If the payment cannot be applied due to an expired credit card, then the order cannot be placed and the data is in an inconsistent state (the order information has already been inserted but has not been approved). In this case, what about the inventory for that order? Should it be marked as ordered and decremented? What if the inventory is low and another customer wishes to purchase the item? Should that new customer be allowed to buy it, or should the reserved inventory be reserved for the customer trying to place the order with an expired credit card? These are just a few of the questions that would need to be addressed when orchestrating a business process with multiple finer-grained services.

Domain services, being coarse-grained, allow for better data integrity and consistency, but there is a trade-off. With service-based architecture, a change made to the order placement functionality in the OrderService would require testing the entire coarse-grained service (including payment processing), whereas with microservices the same change would only impact a small OrderPlacement service (requiring no change to the PaymentService). Furthermore, because more code is being deployed, there is more risk with service-based architecture that something might break (including payment processing), whereas with microservices each service has a single responsibility, hence less chance of breaking other functionality when being changed.

Database Partitioning

Although not required, services within a service-based architecture usually share a single, monolithic database due to the small number of services (4 to 12) within a given application context. This database coupling can present an issue with respect to database table schema changes. If not done properly, a table schema change can potentially impact every service, making database changes a very costly task in terms of effort and coordination.

Within a service-based architecture, the shared class files representing the database table schemas (usually referred to as *entity objects*) reside in a custom shared library used by all the domain services (such as a JAR file or DLL). Shared libraries might also contain SQL code. The practice of creating a single shared library of entity objects is the least effective way of implementing service-based architecture. Any change to the database table structures would also require a change to the single shared library containing all of the corresponding entity objects, thus requiring a change and redeployment to every service, regardless of whether or not the services actually access the changed table. Shared library versioning can help address this issue, but nevertheless, with a single shared library it is difficult to know which services are actually impacted by the table change without manual, detailed analysis. This single shared library scenario is illustrated in Figure 13-6.

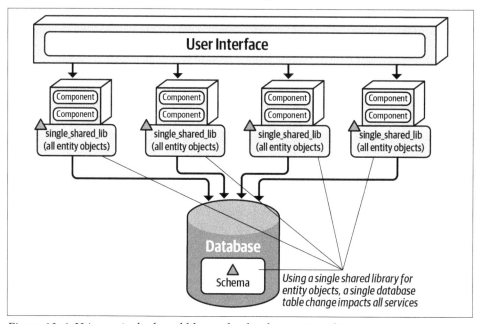

Figure 13-6. Using a single shared library for database entity objects

One way to mitigate the impact and risk of database changes is to logically partition the database and manifest the logical partitioning through federated shared libraries. Notice in Figure 13-7 that the database is logically partitioned into five separate domains (common, customer, invoicing, order, and tracking). Also notice that there are five corresponding shared libraries used by the domain services matching the logical partitions in the database. Using this technique, changes to a table within a particular logical domain (in this case, invoicing) match the corresponding shared library containing the entity objects (and possibly SQL as well), impacting only those services using that shared library, which in this case is the invoicing service. No other services are impacted by this change.

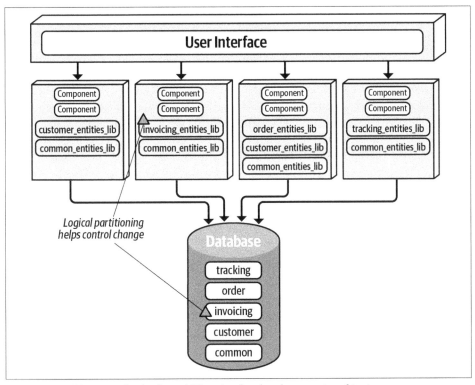

Figure 13-7. Using multiple shared libraries for database entity objects

Notice in Figure 13-7 the use of the *common* domain and the corresponding common_entities_lib shared library used by all services. This is a relatively common occurrence. These tables are common to all services, and as such, changes to these tables require coordination of all services accessing the shared database. One way to mitigate changes to these tables (and corresponding entity objects) is to lock the common entity objects in the version control system and restrict change access to only the database team. This helps control change and emphasizes the significance of changes to the common tables used by all services.

> Make the logical partitioning in the database as fine-grained as possible while still maintaining well-defined data domains to better control database changes within a service-based architecture.

Example Architecture

To illustrate the flexibility and power of the service-based architecture style, consider the real-world example of an electronic recycling system used to recycle old electronic devices (such as an iPhone or Galaxy cell phone). The processing flow of recycling old electronic devices works as follows: first, the customer asks the company (via a website or kiosk) how much money they can get for the old electronic device (called *quoting*). If satisfied, the customer will send the electronic device to the recycling company, which in turn will receive the physical device (called *receiving*). Once received, the recycling company will then assess the device to determine if the device is in good working condition or not (called *assessment*). If the device is in good working condition, the company will send the customer the money promised for the device (called *accounting*). Through this process, the customer can go to the website at any time to check on the status of the item (called *item status*). Based on the assessment, the device is then recycled by either safely destroying it or reselling it (called *recycling*). Finally, the company periodically runs ad hoc and scheduled financial and operational reports based on recycling activity (called *reporting*).

Figure 13-8 illustrates this system using a service-based architecture. Notice how each domain area identified in the prior description is implemented as a separately deployed independent domain service. Scalability can be achieved by only scaling those services needing higher throughput (in this case, the customer-facing `Quoting` service and `ItemStatus` service). The other services do not need to scale, and as such only require a single service instance.

Also notice in how the user interface applications are federated into their respective domains: *Customer Facing*, *Receiving*, and *Recycling and Accounting*. This federation allows for fault tolerance of the user interface, scalability, and security (external customers have no network path to internal functionality). Finally, notice in this example that there are two separate physical databases: one for external customer-facing operations, and one for internal operations. This allows the internal data and operations to reside in a separate network zone from the external operations (denoted by the vertical line), providing much better security access restrictions and data protection. One-way access through the firewall allows internal services to access and update the customer-facing information, but not vice versa. Alternatively, depending on the database being used, internal table mirroring and table synchronization could also be used.

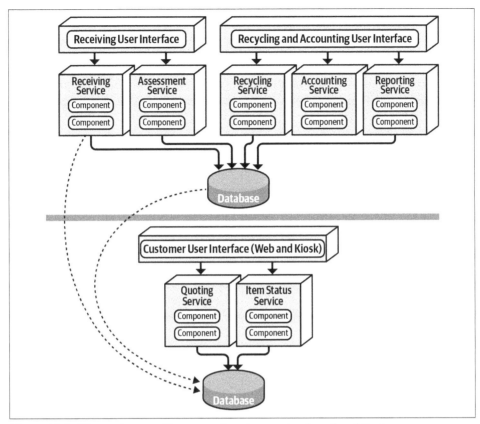

Figure 13-8. Electronics recycling example using service-based architecture

This example illustrates many of the benefits of the service-based architecture approach: scalability, fault tolerance, and security (data and functionality protection and access), in addition to agility, testability, and deployability. For example, the Assessment service is changed constantly to add assessment rules as new products are received. This frequent change is isolated to a single domain service, providing agility (the ability to respond quickly to change), as well as testability (the ease of and completeness of testing) and deployability (the ease, frequency, and risk of deployment).

Architecture Characteristics Ratings

A one-star rating in the characteristics ratings table in Figure 13-9 means the specific architecture characteristic isn't well supported in the architecture, whereas a five-star rating means the architecture characteristic is one of the strongest features in the architecture style. The definition for each characteristic identified in the scorecard can be found in Chapter 4.

Architecture characteristic	Star rating
Partitioning type	Domain
Number of quanta	1 to many
Deployability	☆☆☆☆
Elasticity	☆☆
Evolutionary	☆☆☆
Fault tolerance	☆☆☆☆
Modularity	☆☆☆☆
Overall cost	☆☆☆☆
Performance	☆☆☆
Reliability	☆☆☆☆
Scalability	☆☆☆
Simplicity	☆☆☆
Testability	☆☆☆☆

Figure 13-9. Service-based architecture characteristics ratings

Service-based architecture is a *domain-partitioned* architecture, meaning that the structure is driven by the domain rather than a technical consideration (such as presentation logic or persistence logic). Consider the prior example of the electronic recycling application. Each service, being a separately deployed unit of software, is scoped to a specific domain (such as item assessment). Changes made within this domain only impact the specific service, the corresponding user interface, and the corresponding database. Nothing else needs to be modified to support a specific assessment change.

Being a distributed architecture, the number of quanta can be greater than or equal to one. Even though there may be anywhere from 4 to 12 separately deployed services, if those services all share the same database or user interface, that entire system would be only a single quantum. However, as illustrated in "Topology Variants" on page 165, both the user interface and database can be federated, resulting in multiple quanta within the overall system. In the electronics recycling example, the system contains two quanta, as illustrated in Figure 13-10: one for the customer-facing portion of the application containing a separate customer user interface, database, and set of services (Quoting and Item Status); and one for the internal operations of receiving, assessing, and recycling the electronic device. Notice that even though the internal operations quantum contains separately deployed services and two separate user interfaces, they all share the same database, making the internal operations portion of the application a single quantum.

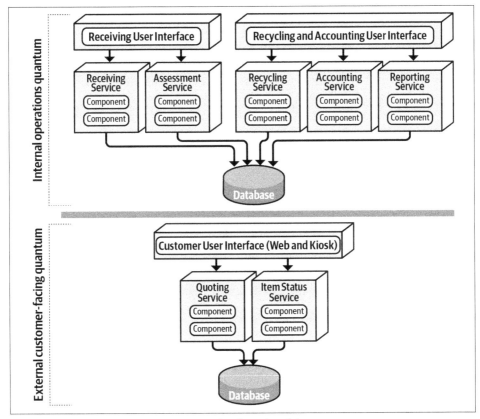

Figure 13-10. Separate quanta in a service-based architecture

Although service-based architecture doesn't contain any five-star ratings, it nevertheless rates high (four stars) in many important and vital areas. Breaking apart an application into separately deployed domain services using this architecture style allows for faster change (agility), better test coverage due to the limited scope of the domain (testability), and the ability for more frequent deployments carrying less risk than a large monolith (deployability). These three characteristics lead to better time-to-market, allowing an organization to deliver new features and bug fixes at a relatively high rate.

Fault tolerance and overall application availability also rate high for service-based architecture. Even though domain services tend to be coarse-grained, the four-star rating comes from the fact that with this architecture style, services are usually self-contained and do not leverage interservice communication due to database sharing and code sharing. As a result, if one domain service goes down (e.g., the Receiving service in the electronic recycling application example), it doesn't impact any of the other six services.

Scalability only rates three stars due to the coarse-grained nature of the services, and correspondingly, elasticity only two stars. Although programmatic scalability and elasticity are certainly possible with this architecture style, more functionality is replicated than with finer-grained services (such as microservices) and as such is not as efficient in terms of machine resources and not as cost-effective. Typically there are only single service instances with service-based architecture unless there is a need for better throughput or failover. A good example of this is the electronics recycling application example—only the Quoting and Item Status services need to scale to support high customer volumes, but the other operational services only require single instances, making it easier to support such things as single in-memory caching and database connection pooling.

Simplicity and overall cost are two other drivers that differentiate this architecture style from other, more expensive and complex distributed architectures, such as microservices, event-driven architecture, or even space-based architecture. This makes service-based one of the easiest and cost-effective distributed architectures to implement. While this is an attractive proposition, there is a trade-off to this cost savings and simplicity in all of the characteristics containing four-star ratings. The higher the cost and complexity, the better these ratings become.

Service-based architectures tend to be more reliable than other distributed architectures due to the coarse-grained nature of the domain services. Larger services mean less network traffic to and between services, fewer distributed transactions, and less bandwidth used, therefore increasing overall reliability with respect to the network.

When to Use This Architecture Style

The flexibility of this architecture style (see "Topology Variants" on page 165) combined with the number of three-star and four-star architecture characteristics ratings make service-based architecture one of the most pragmatic architecture styles available. While there are certainly other distributed architecture styles that are much more powerful, some companies find that power comes at too steep of a price, while others find that they quite simply don't need that much power. It's like having the power, speed, and agility of a Ferrari used only for driving back and forth to work in rush-hour traffic at 50 kilometers per hour—sure it looks cool, but what a waste of resources and money!

Service-based architecture is also a natural fit when doing domain-driven design. Because services are coarse-grained and domain-scoped, each domain fits nicely into a separately deployed domain service. Each service in service-based architecture encompasses a particular domain (such as recycling in the electronic recycling application), therefore compartmentalizing that functionality into a single unit of software, making it easier to apply changes to that domain.

Maintaining and coordinating database transactions is always an issue with distributed architectures in that they typically rely on eventual consistency rather than traditional ACID (atomicity, consistency, isolation, and durability) transactions. However, service-based architecture preserves ACID transactions better than any other distributed architecture due to the coarse-grained nature of the domain services. There are cases where the user interface or API gateway might orchestrate two or more domain services, and in these cases the transaction would need to rely on sagas and BASE transactions. However, in most cases the transaction is scoped to a particular domain service, allowing for the traditional commit and rollback transaction functionality found in most monolithic applications.

Lastly, service-based architecture is a good choice for achieving a good level of architectural modularity without having to get tangled up in the complexities and pitfalls of granularity. As services become more fine-grained, issues surrounding orchestration and choreography start to appear. Both orchestration and choreography are required when multiple services must be coordinated to complete a certain business transaction. Orchestration is the coordination of multiple services through the use of a separate mediator service that controls and manages the workflow of the transaction (like a conductor in an orchestra). Choreography, on the other hand, is the coordination of multiple services by which each service talks to one another without the use of a central mediator (like dancers in a dance). As services become more fine-grained, both orchestration and choreography are necessary to tie the services together to complete the business transaction. However, because services within a service-based architecture tend to be more coarse-grained, they don't require coordination nearly as much as other distributed architectures.

CHAPTER 14

Event-Driven Architecture Style

The *event-driven* architecture style is a popular distributed asynchronous architecture style used to produce highly scalable and high-performance applications. It is also highly adaptable and can be used for small applications and as well as large, complex ones. Event-driven architecture is made up of decoupled event processing components that asynchronously receive and process events. It can be used as a standalone architecture style or embedded within other architecture styles (such as an event-driven microservices architecture).

Most applications follow what is called a *request-based* model (illustrated in Figure 14-1). In this model, requests made to the system to perform some sort of action are send to a *request orchestrator*. The request orchestrator is typically a user interface, but it can also be implemented through an API layer or enterprise service bus. The role of the request orchestrator is to deterministically and synchronously direct the request to various *request processors*. The request processors handle the request, either retrieving or updating information in a database.

A good example of the request-based model is a request from a customer to retrieve their order history for the past six months. Retrieving order history information is a data-driven, deterministic request made to the system for data within a specific context, not an event happening that the system must react to.

An event-based model, on the other hand, reacts to a particular situation and takes action based on that event. An example of an event-based model is submitting a bid for a particular item within an online auction. Submitting the bid is not a request made to the system, but rather an event that happens after the current asking price is announced. The system must respond to this event by comparing the bid to others received at the same time to determine who is the current highest bidder.

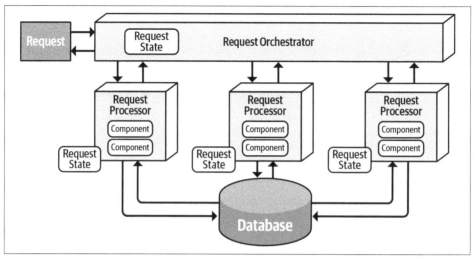

Figure 14-1. Request-based model

Topology

There are two primary topologies within event-driven architecture: the *mediator topology* and the *broker topology*. The mediator topology is commonly used when you require control over the workflow of an event process, whereas the broker topology is used when you require a high degree of responsiveness and dynamic control over the processing of an event. Because the architecture characteristics and implementation strategies differ between these two topologies, it is important to understand each one to know which is best suited for a particular situation.

Broker Topology

The broker topology differs from the mediator topology in that there is no central event mediator. Rather, the message flow is distributed across the event processor components in a chain-like broadcasting fashion through a lightweight message broker (such as RabbitMQ, ActiveMQ, HornetQ, and so on). This topology is useful when you have a relatively simple event processing flow and you do not need central event orchestration and coordination.

There are four primary architecture components within the broker topology: an initiating event, the event broker, an event processor, and a processing event. The *initiating event* is the initial event that starts the entire event flow, whether it be a simple event like placing a bid in an online auction or more complex events in a health benefits system like changing a job or getting married. The initiating event is sent to an event channel in the *event broker* for processing. Since there is no mediator component in the broker topology managing and controlling the event, a single *event processor* accepts the initiating event from the event broker and begins the processing of that event. The event processor that accepted the initiating event performs a specific task associated with the processing of that event, then asynchronously advertises what it did to the rest of the system by creating what is called a *processing event*. This processing event is then asynchronously sent to the event broker for further processing, if needed. Other event processors listen to the processing event, react to that event by doing something, then advertise through a new processing event what they did. This process continues until no one is interested in what a final event processor did. Figure 14-2 illustrates this event processing flow.

The event broker component is usually federated (meaning multiple domain-based clustered instances), where each federated broker contains all of the event channels used within the event flow for that particular domain. Because of the decoupled asynchronous fire-and-forget broadcasting nature of the broker topology, topics (or topic exchanges in the case of AMQP) are usually used in the broker topology using a publish-and-subscribe messaging model.

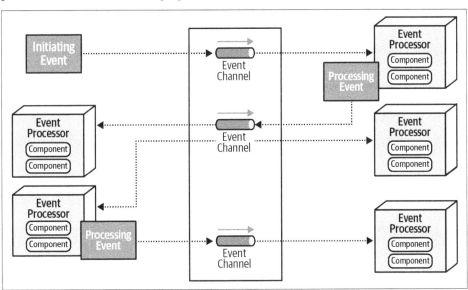

Figure 14-2. Broker topology

It is always a good practice within the broker topology for each event processor to advertise what it did to the rest of the system, regardless of whether or not any other event processor cares about what that action was. This practice provides architectural extensibility if additional functionality is required for the processing of that event. For example, suppose as part of a complex event process, as illustrated in Figure 14-3, an email is generated and sent to a customer notifying them of a particular action taken. The Notification event processor would generate and send the email, then advertise that action to the rest of the system through a new processing event sent to a topic. However, in this case, no other event processors are listening for events on that topic, and as such the message simply goes away.

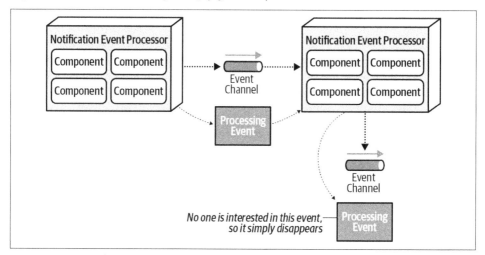

Figure 14-3. Notification event is sent but ignored

This is a good example of *architectural extensibility*. While it may seem like a waste of resources sending messages that are ignored, it is not. Suppose a new requirement comes along to analyze emails that have been sent to customers. This new event processor can be added to the overall system with minimal effort because the email information is available via the email topic to the new analyzer without having to add any additional infrastructure or apply any changes to other event processors.

To illustrate how the broker topology works, consider the processing flow in a typical retail order entry system, as illustrated in Figure 14-4, where an order is placed for an item (say, a book like this one). In this example, the OrderPlacement event processor receives the initiating event (PlaceOrder), inserts the order in a database table, and returns an order ID to the customer. It then advertises to the rest of the system that it created an order through an order-created processing event. Notice that three event processors are interested in that event: the Notification event processor, the Payment event processor, and the Inventory event processor. All three of these event processors perform their tasks in parallel.

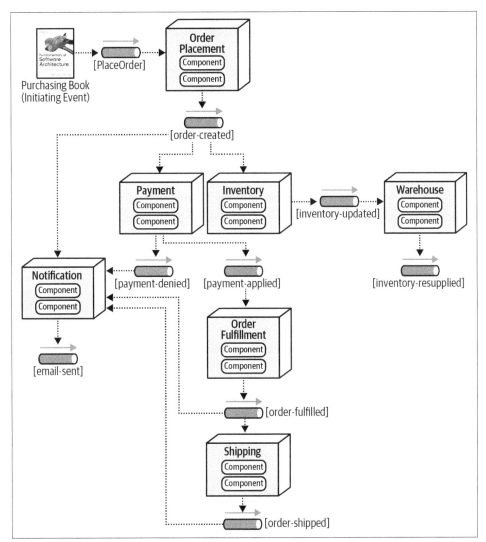

Figure 14-4. Example of the broker topology

The Notification event processor receives the order-created processing event and emails the customer. It then generates another processing event (email-sent). Notice that no other event processors are listening to that event. This is normal and illustrates the previous example describing architectural extensibility—an in-place hook so that other event processors can eventually tap into that event feed, if needed.

The `Inventory` event processor also listens for the `order-created` processing event and decrements the corresponding inventory for that book. It then advertises this action through an `inventory-updated` processing event, which is in turn picked up by the `Warehouse` event processor to manage the corresponding inventory between warehouses, reordering items if supplies get too low.

The `Payment` event processor also receives the `order-created` processing event and charges the customer's credit card for the order that was just created. Notice in Figure 14-4 that two events are generated as a result of the actions taken by the `Payment` event processor: one to notify the rest of the system that the payment was applied (`payment-applied`) and one processing event to notify the rest of the system that the payment was denied (`payment-denied`). Notice that the `Notification` event processor is interested in the `payment-denied` processing event, because it must, in turn, send an email to the customer informing them that they must update their credit card information or choose a different payment method.

The `OrderFulfillment` event processor listens to the `payment-applied` processing event and does order picking and packing. Once completed, it then advertises to the rest of the system that it fulfilled the order via an `order-fulfilled` processing event. Notice that both the `Notification` processing unit and the `Shipping` processing unit listen to this processing event. Concurrently, the `Notification` event processor notifies the customer that the order has been fulfilled and is ready for shipment, and at the same time the `Shipping` event processor selects a shipping method. The `Shipping` event processor ships the order and sends out an `order-shipped` processing event, which the `Notification` event processor also listens for to notify the customer of the order status change.

In analyzing the prior example, notice that all of the event processors are highly decoupled and independent of each other. The best way to understand the broker topology is to think about it as a relay race. In a relay race, runners hold a baton (a wooden stick) and run for a certain distance (say 1.5 kilometers), then hand off the baton to the next runner, and so on down the chain until the last runner crosses the finish line. In relay races, once a runner hands off the baton, that runner is done with the race and moves on to other things. This is also true with the broker topology. Once an event processor hands off the event, it is no longer involved with the processing of that specific event and is available to react to other initiating or processing events. In addition, each event processor can scale independently from one other to handle varying load conditions or backups in the processing within that event. The topics provide the back pressure point if an event processor comes down or slows down due to some environment issue.

While performance, responsiveness, and scalability are all great benefits of the broker topology, there are also some negatives about it. First of all, there is no control over the overall workflow associated with the initiating event (in this case, the PlaceOrder event). It is very dynamic based on various conditions, and no one in the system really knows when the business transaction of placing an order is actually complete. Error handling is also a big challenge with the broker topology. Because there is no mediator monitoring or controlling the business transaction, if a failure occurs (such as the Payment event processor crashing and not completing its assigned task), no one in the system is aware of that crash. The business process gets stuck and is unable to move without some sort of automated or manual intervention. Furthermore, all other processes are moving along without regard for the error. For example, the Inventory event processor still decrements the inventory, and all other event processors react as though everything is fine.

The ability to restart a business transaction (recoverability) is also something not supported with the broker topology. Because other actions have asynchronously been taken through the initial processing of the initiating event, it is not possible to resubmit the initiating event. No component in the broker topology is aware of the state or even owns the state of the original business request, and therefore no one is responsible in this topology for restarting the business transaction (the initiating event) and knowing where it left off. The advantages and disadvantages of the broker topology are summarized in Table 14-1.

Table 14-1. Trade-offs of the broker topology

Advantages	Disadvantages
Highly decoupled event processors	Workflow control
High scalability	Error handling
High responsiveness	Recoverability
High performance	Restart capabilities
High fault tolerance	Data inconsistency

Mediator Topology

The mediator topology of event-driven architecture addresses some of the shortcomings of the broker topology described in the previous section. Central to this topology is an event mediator, which manages and controls the workflow for initiating events that require the coordination of multiple event processors. The architecture components that make up the mediator topology are an initiating event, an event queue, an event mediator, event channels, and event processors.

Like in the broker topology, the initiating event is the event that starts the whole eventing process. Unlike the broker topology, the initiating event is sent to an initiating event queue, which is accepted by the event mediator. The event mediator only knows the steps involved in processing the event and therefore generates corresponding processing events that are sent to dedicated event channels (usually queues) in a point-to-point messaging fashion. Event processors then listen to dedicated event channels, process the event, and usually respond back to the mediator that they have completed their work. Unlike the broker topology, event processors within the mediator topology do not advertise what they did to the rest of the system. The mediator topology is illustrated in Figure 14-5.

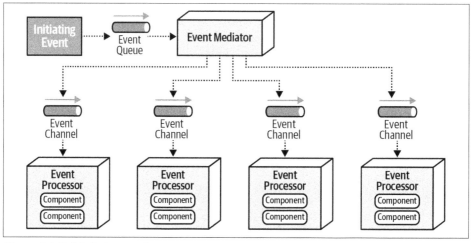

Figure 14-5. Mediator topology

In most implementations of the mediator topology, there are multiple mediators, usually associated with a particular domain or grouping of events. This reduces the single point of failure issue associated with this topology and also increases overall throughput and performance. For example, there might be a customer mediator that handles all customer-related events (such as new customer registration and profile update), and another mediator that handles order-related activities (such as adding an item to a shopping cart and checking out).

The event mediator can be implemented in a variety of ways, depending on the nature and complexity of the events it is processing. For example, for events requiring simple error handling and orchestration, a mediator such as Apache Camel (*https:// camel.apache.org*), Mule ESB (*https://www.mulesoft.com*), or Spring Integration (*https://oreil.ly/r2e4r*) will usually suffice. Message flows and message routes within these types of mediators are typically custom written in programming code (such as Java or C#) to control the workflow of the event processing.

However, if the event workflow requires lots of conditional processing and multiple dynamic paths with complex error handling directives, then a mediator such as Apache ODE (*https://ode.apache.org*) or the Oracle BPEL Process Manager (*https://oreil.ly/jMtta*) would be a good choice. These mediators are based on Business Process Execution Language (BPEL) (*https://oreil.ly/Uu-Fo*), an XML-like structure that describes the steps involved in processing an event. BPEL artifacts also contain structured elements used for error handling, redirection, multicasting, and so on. BPEL is a powerful but relatively complex language to learn, and as such is usually created using graphical interface tools provided in the product's BPEL engine suite.

BPEL is good for complex and dynamic workflows, but it does not work well for those event workflows requiring long-running transactions involving human intervention throughout the event process. For example, suppose a trade is being placed through a `place-trade` initiating event. The event mediator accepts this event, but during the processing finds that a manual approval is required because the trade is over a certain amount of shares. In this case the event mediator would have to stop the event processing, send a notification to a senior trader for the manual approval, and wait for that approval to occur. In these cases a Business Process Management (BPM) engine such as jBPM (*https://www.jbpm.org*) would be required.

It is important to know the types of events that will be processed through the mediator in order to make the correct choice for the implementation of the event mediator. Choosing Apache Camel for complex and long-running events involving human interaction would be extremely difficult to write and maintain. By the same token, using a BPM engine for simple event flows would take months of wasted effort when the same thing could be accomplished in Apache Camel in a matter of days.

Given that it's rare to have all events of one class of complexity, we recommend classifying events as simple, hard, or complex and having every event always go through a simple mediator (such as Apache Camel or Mule). The simple mediator can then interrogate the classification of the event, and based on that classification, handle the event itself or forward it to another, more complex, event mediator. In this manner, all types of events can be effectively processed by the type of mediator needed for that event. This mediator delegation model is illustrated in Figure 14-6.

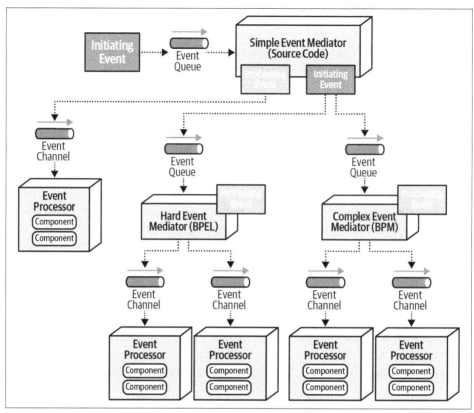

Figure 14-6. Delegating the event to the appropriate type of event mediator

Notice in Figure 14-6 that the Simple Event Mediator generates and sends a pro‐
cessing event when the event workflow is simple and can be handled by the simple
mediator. However, notice that when the initiating event coming into the Simple
Event Mediator is classified as either hard or complex, it forwards the original ini‐
tiating event to the corresponding mediators (BPEL or BMP). The Simple Event
Mediator, having intercepted the original event, may still be responsible for knowing
when that event is complete, or it simply delegates the entire workflow (including cli‐
ent notification) to the other mediators.

To illustrate how the mediator topology works, consider the same retail order entry
system example described in the prior broker topology section, but this time using
the mediator topology. In this example, the mediator knows the steps required to pro‐
cess this particular event. This event flow (internal to the mediator component) is
illustrated in Figure 14-7.

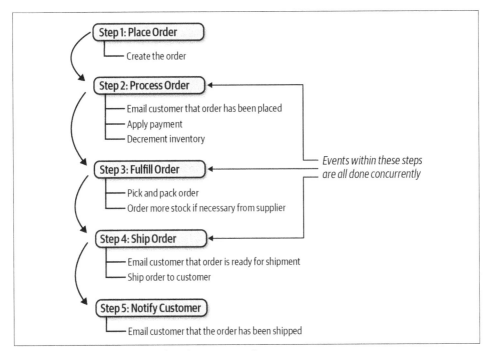

Figure 14-7. Mediator steps for placing an order

In keeping with the prior example, the same initiating event (PlaceOrder) is sent to the customer-event-queue for processing. The Customer mediator picks up this initiating event and begins generating processing events based on the flow in Figure 14-7. Notice that the multiple events shown in steps 2, 3, and 4 are all done concurrently and serially between steps. In other words, step 3 (fulfill order) must be completed and acknowledged before the customer can be notified that the order is ready to be shipped in step 4 (ship order).

Once the initiating event has been received, the Customer mediator generates a create-order processing event and sends this message to the order-placement-queue (see Figure 14-8). The OrderPlacement event processor accepts this event and validates and creates the order, returning to the mediator an acknowledgement along with the order ID. At this point the mediator might send that order ID back to the customer, indicating that the order was placed, or it might have to continue until all the steps are complete (this would be based on specific business rules about order placement).

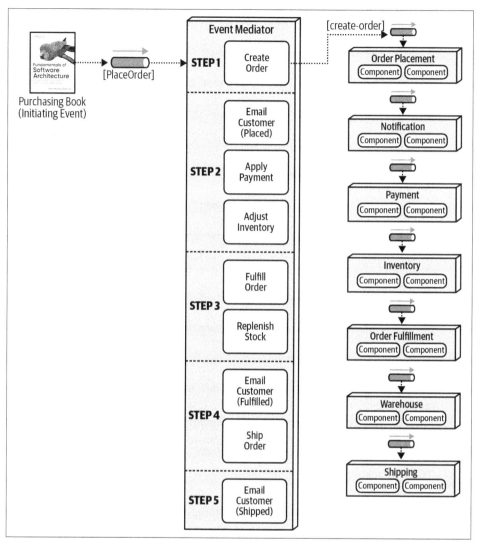

Figure 14-8. Step 1 of the mediator example

Now that step 1 is complete, the mediator now moves to step 2 (see Figure 14-9) and generates three messages at the same time: `email-customer`, `apply-payment`, and `adjust-inventory`. These processing events are all sent to their respective queues. All three event processors receive these messages, perform their respective tasks, and notify the mediator that the processing has been completed. Notice that the mediator must wait until it receives acknowledgement from all three parallel processes before moving on to step 3. At this point, if an error occurs in one of the parallel event processors, the mediator can take corrective action to fix the problem (this is discussed later in this section in more detail).

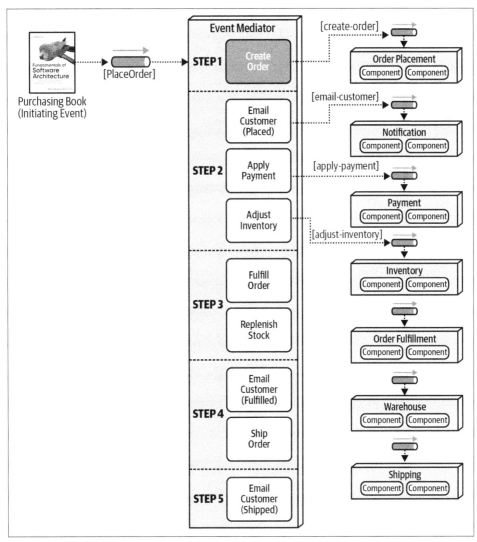

Figure 14-9. Step 2 of the mediator example

Once the mediator gets a successful acknowledgment from all of the event processors in step 2, it can move on to step 3 to fulfill the order (see Figure 14-10). Notice once again that both of these events (`fulfill-order` and `order-stock`) can occur simultaneously. The `OrderFulfillment` and `Warehouse` event processors accept these events, perform their work, and return an acknowledgement to the mediator.

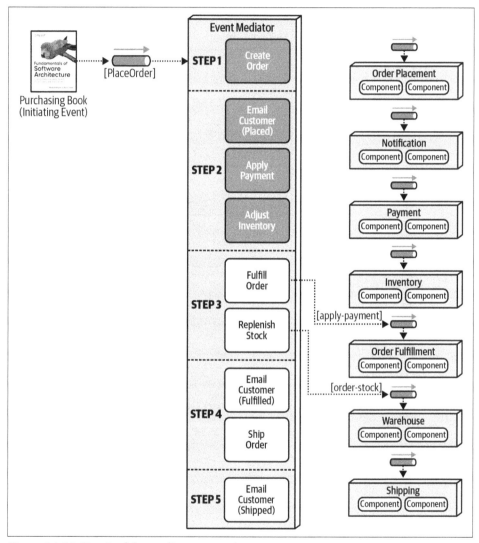

Figure 14-10. Step 3 of the mediator example

Once these events are complete, the mediator then moves on to step 4 (see Figure 14-11) to ship the order. This step generates another `email-customer` processing event with specific information about what to do (in this case, notify the customer that the order is ready to be shipped), as well as a `ship-order` event.

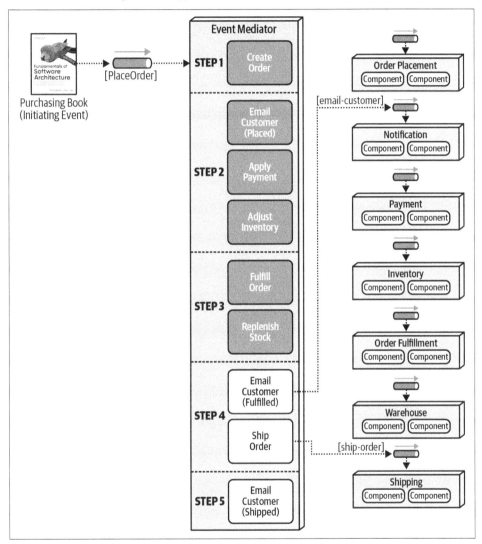

Figure 14-11. Step 4 of the mediator example

Finally, the mediator moves to step 5 (see Figure 14-12) and generates another contextual `email-customer` event to notify the customer that the order has been shipped. At this point the workflow is done, and the mediator marks the initiating event flow complete and removes all state associated with the initiating event.

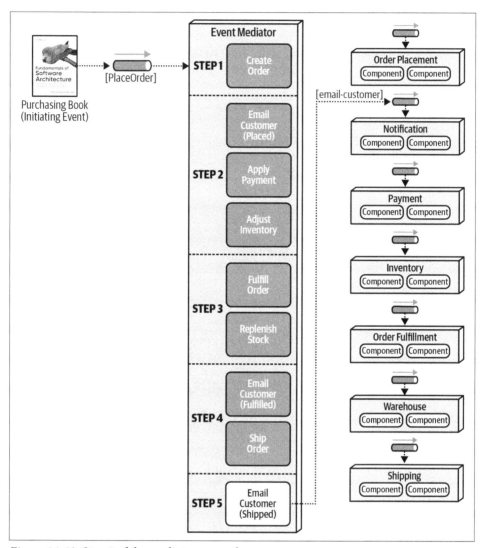

Figure 14-12. Step 5 of the mediator example

The mediator component has knowledge and control over the workflow, something the broker topology does not have. Because the mediator controls the workflow, it can maintain event state and manage error handling, recoverability, and restart capabilities. For example, suppose in the prior example the payment was not applied due to the credit card being expired. In this case the mediator receives this error condition, and knowing the order cannot be fulfilled (step 3) until payment is applied, stops the workflow and records the state of the request in its own persistent datastore. Once payment is eventually applied, the workflow can be restarted from where it left off (in this case, the beginning of step 3).

Another inherent difference between the broker and mediator topology is how the processing events differ in terms of their meaning and how they are used. In the broker topology example in the previous section, the processing events were published as events that had occurred in the system (such as order-created, payment-applied, and email-sent). The event processors took some action, and other event processors react to that action. However, in the mediator topology, processing occurrences such as place-order, send-email, and fulfill-order are *commands* (things that need to happen) as opposed to *events* (things that have already happened). Also, in the mediator topology, a command must be processed, whereas an event can be ignored in the broker topology.

While the mediator topology addresses the issues associated with the broker topology, there are some negatives associated with the mediator topology. First of all, it is very difficult to declaratively model the dynamic processing that occurs within a complex event flow. As a result, many workflows within the mediator only handle the general processing, and a hybrid model combining both the mediator and broker topologies is used to address the dynamic nature of complex event processing (such as out-of-stock conditions or other nontypical errors). Furthermore, although the event processors can easily scale in the same manner as the broker topology, the mediator must scale as well, something that occasionally produces a bottleneck in the overall event processing flow. Finally, event processors are not as highly decoupled in the mediator topology as with the broker topology, and performance is not as good due to the mediator controlling the processing of the event. These trade-offs are summarized in Table 14-2.

Table 14-2. Trade-offs of the mediator topology

Advantages	Disadvantages
Workflow control	More coupling of event processors
Error handling	Lower scalability
Recoverability	Lower performance
Restart capabilities	Lower fault tolerance
Better data consistency	Modeling complex workflows

The choice between the broker and mediator topology essentially comes down to a trade-off between workflow control and error handling capability versus high performance and scalability. Although performance and scalability are still good within the mediator topology, they are not as high as with the broker topology.

Asynchronous Capabilities

The event-driven architecture style offers a unique characteristic over other architecture styles in that it relies solely on asynchronous communication for both fire-and-forget processing (no response required) as well as request/reply processing (response required from the event consumer). Asynchronous communication can be a powerful technique for increasing the overall responsiveness of a system.

Consider the example illustrated in Figure 14-13 where a user is posting a comment on a website for a particular product review. Assume the comment service in this example takes 3,000 milliseconds to post the comment because it goes through several parsing engines: a bad word checker to check for unacceptable words, a grammar checker to make sure that the sentence structures are not saying something abusive, and finally a context checker to make sure the comment is about a particular product and not just a political rant. Notice in Figure 14-13 that the top path utilizes a synchronous RESTful call to post the comment: 50 milliseconds in latency for the service to receive the post, 3,000 milliseconds to post the comment, and 50 milliseconds in network latency to respond back to the user that the comment was posted. This creates a response time for the user of 3,100 milliseconds to post a comment. Now look at the bottom path and notice that with the use of asynchronous messaging, the response time from the end user's perspective for posting a comment on the website is only 25 milliseconds (as opposed to 3,100 milliseconds). It still takes 3,025 milliseconds to post the comment (25 milliseconds to receive the message and 3,000 milliseconds to post the comment), but from the end user's perspective it's already been done.

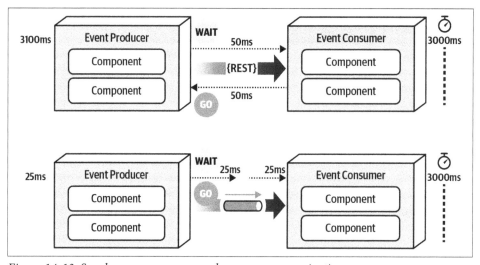

Figure 14-13. Synchronous versus asynchronous communication

This is a good example of the difference between *responsiveness* and *performance*. When the user does not need any information back (other than an acknowledgement or a thank you message), why make the user wait? Responsiveness is all about notifying the user that the action has been accepted and will be processed momentarily, whereas performance is about making the end-to-end process faster. Notice that nothing was done to optimize the way the comment service processes the text—in both cases it is still taking 3,000 milliseconds. Addressing *performance* would have been optimizing the comment service to run all of the text and grammar parsing engines in parallel with the use of caching and other similar techniques. The bottom example in Figure 14-13 addresses the overall responsiveness of the system but not the performance of the system.

The difference in response time between the two examples in Figure 14-13 from 3,100 milliseconds to 25 milliseconds is staggering. There is one caveat. On the synchronous path shown on the top of the diagram, the end user is guaranteed that the comment has been posted. However, on the bottom path there is only the acknowledgement of the post, with a future promise that eventually the comment will get posted. From the end user's perspective, the comment has been posted. But what happens if the user had typed a bad word in the comment? In this case the comment would be rejected, but there is no way to get back to the end user. Or is there? In this example, assuming the user is registered with the website (which to post a comment they would have to be), a message could be sent to the user indicating a problem with the comment and some suggestions on how to repair it. This is a simple example. What about a more complicated example where the purchase of some stock is taking place asynchronously (called a stock trade) and there is no way to get back to the user?

The main issue with asynchronous communications is error handling. While responsiveness is significantly improved, it is difficult to address error conditions, adding to the complexity of the event-driven system. The next section addresses this issue with a pattern of reactive architecture called the *workflow event* pattern.

Error Handling

The workflow event pattern of reactive architecture is one way of addressing the issues associated with error handling in an asynchronous workflow. This pattern is a reactive architecture pattern that addresses both resiliency and responsiveness. In other words, the system can be resilient in terms of error handling without an impact to responsiveness.

The workflow event pattern leverages delegation, containment, and repair through the use of a *workflow delegate*, as illustrated in Figure 14-14. The event producer asynchronously passes data through a message channel to the event consumer. If the event consumer experiences an error while processing the data, it immediately delegates that error to the *workflow processor* and moves on to the next message in the event queue. In this way, overall responsiveness is not impacted because the next message is immediately processed. If the event consumer were to spend the time trying to figure out the error, then it is not reading the next message in the queue, therefore impacting the responsiveness not only of the next message, but all other messages waiting in the queue to be processed.

Once the workflow processor receives an error, it tries to figure out what is wrong with the message. This could be a static, deterministic error, or it could leverage some machine learning algorithms to analyze the message to see some anomaly in the data. Either way, the workflow processor programmatically (without human intervention) makes changes to the original data to try and repair it, and then sends it back to the originating queue. The event consumer sees this message as a new one and tries to process it again, hopefully this time with some success. Of course, there are many times when the workflow processor cannot determine what is wrong with the message. In these cases the workflow processor sends the message off to another queue, which is then received in what is usually called a "dashboard," an application that looks similar to the Microsoft's Outlook or Apple's Mail. This dashboard usually resides on the desktop of a person of importance, who then looks at the message, applies manual fixes to it, and then resubmits it to the original queue (usually through a reply-to message header variable).

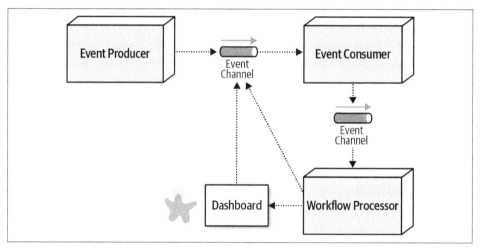

Figure 14-14. Workflow event pattern of reactive architecture

To illustrate the workflow event pattern, suppose a trading advisor in one part of the country accepts trade orders (instructions on what stock to buy and for how many shares) on behalf of a large trading firm in another part of the country. The advisor batches up the trade orders (what is usually called a basket) and asynchronously sends those to the large trading firm to be placed with a broker so the stock can be purchased. To simplify the example, suppose the contract for the trade instructions must adhere to the following:

```
ACCOUNT(String),SIDE(String),SYMBOL(String),SHARES(Long)
```

Suppose the large trading firm receives the following basket of Apple (AAPL) trade orders from the trading advisor:

```
12654A87FR4,BUY,AAPL,1254
87R54E3068U,BUY,AAPL,3122
6R4NB7609JJ,BUY,AAPL,5433
2WE35HF6DHF,BUY,AAPL,8756 SHARES
764980974R2,BUY,AAPL,1211
1533G658HD8,BUY,AAPL,2654
```

Notice the forth trade instruction (2WE35HF6DHF,BUY,AAPL,8756 SHARES) has the word SHARES after the number of shares for the trade. When these asynchronous trade orders are processed by the large trading firm without any error handling capabilities, the following error occurs within the trade placement service:

```
Exception in thread "main" java.lang.NumberFormatException:
        For input string: "8756 SHARES"
        at java.lang.NumberFormatException.forInputString
        (NumberFormatException.java:65)
        at java.lang.Long.parseLong(Long.java:589)
        at java.lang.Long.<init>(Long.java:965)
        at trading.TradePlacement.execute(TradePlacement.java:23)
        at trading.TradePlacement.main(TradePlacement.java:29)
```

When this exception occurs, there is nothing that the trade placement service can do, because this was an asynchronous request, except to possibly log the error condition. In other words, there is no user to synchronously respond to and fix the error.

Applying the workflow event pattern can programmatically fix this error. Because the large trading firm has no control over the trading advisor and the corresponding trade order data it sends, it must react to fix the error itself (as illustrated in Figure 14-15). When the same error occurs (2WE35HF6DHF,BUY,AAPL,8756 SHARES), the Trade Placement service immediately delegates the error via asynchronous messaging to the Trade Placement Error service for error handling, passing with the error information about the exception:

```
Trade Placed: 12654A87FR4,BUY,AAPL,1254
Trade Placed: 87R54E3068U,BUY,AAPL,3122
Trade Placed: 6R4NB7609JJ,BUY,AAPL,5433
Error Placing Trade: "2WE35HF6DHF,BUY,AAPL,8756 SHARES"
Sending to trade error processor  <-- delegate the error fixing and move on
Trade Placed: 764980974R2,BUY,AAPL,1211
...
```

The `Trade Placement Error` service (acting as the workflow delegate) receives the error and inspects the exception. Seeing that it is an issue with the word SHARES in the number of shares field, the `Trade Placement Error` service strips off the word SHARES and resubmits the trade for reprocessing:

```
Received Trade Order Error: 2WE35HF6DHF,BUY,AAPL,8756 SHARES
Trade fixed: 2WE35HF6DHF,BUY,AAPL,8756
Resubmitting Trade For Re-Processing
```

The fixed trade is then processed successfully by the trade placement service:

```
...
trade placed: 1533G658HD8,BUY,AAPL,2654
trade placed: 2WE35HF6DHF,BUY,AAPL,8756 <-- this was the original trade in error
```

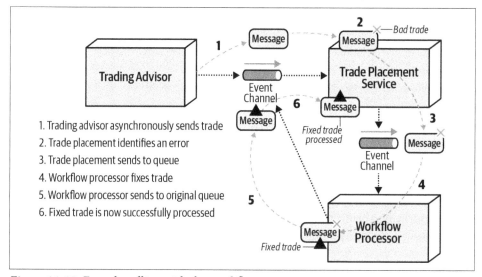

Figure 14-15. Error handling with the workflow event pattern

One of the consequences of the workflow event pattern is that messages in error are processed out of sequence when they are resubmitted. In our trading example, the order of messages matters, because all trades within a given account must be processed in order (for example, a SELL for IBM must occur before a BUY for AAPL within the same brokerage account). Although not impossible, it is a complex task to maintain message order within a given context (in this case the brokerage account number). One way this can be addressed is by the `Trade Placement` service queueing and storing the account number of the trade in error. Any trade with that same account number would be stored in a temporary queue for later processing (in FIFO order). Once the trade originally in error is fixed and processed, the `Trade Placement` service then de-queues the remaining trades for that same account and processes them in order.

Preventing Data Loss

Data loss is always a primary concern when dealing with asynchronous communications. Unfortunately, there are many places for data loss to occur within an event-driven architecture. By data loss we mean a message getting dropped or never making it to its final destination. Fortunately, there are basic out-of-the-box techniques that can be leveraged to prevent data loss when using asynchronous messaging.

To illustrate the issues associated with data loss within event-driven architecture, suppose Event Processor A asynchronously sends a message to a queue. Event Processor B accepts the message and inserts the data within the message into a database. As illustrated in Figure 14-16, three areas of data loss can occur within this typical scenario:

1. The message never makes it to the queue from Event Processor A; or even if it does, the broker goes down before the next event processor can retrieve the message.

2. Event Processor B de-queues the next available message and crashes before it can process the event.

3. Event Processor B is unable to persist the message to the database due to some data error.

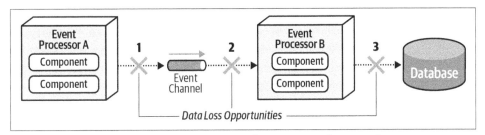

Figure 14-16. Where data loss can happen within an event-driven architecture

Each of these areas of data loss can be mitigated through basic messaging techniques. Issue 1 (the message never makes it to the queue) is easily solved by leveraging persistent message queues, along with something called *synchronous send*. Persisted message queues support what is known as guaranteed delivery. When the message broker receives the message, it not only stores it in memory for fast retrieval, but also persists the message in some sort of physical data store (such as a filesystem or database). If the message broker goes down, the message is physically stored on disk so that when the message broker comes back up, the message is available for processing. Synchronous send does a blocking wait in the message producer until the broker has acknowledged that the message has been persisted. With these two basic techniques there is no way to lose a message between the event producer and the queue because the message is either still with the message producer or persisted within the queue.

Issue 2 (Event Processor B de-queues the next available message and crashes before it can process the event) can also be solved using a basic technique of messaging called *client acknowledge mode*. By default, when a message is de-queued, it is immediately removed from the queue (something called *auto acknowledge* mode). Client acknowledge mode keeps the message in the queue and attaches the client ID to the message so that no other consumers can read the message. With this mode, if Event Processor B crashes, the message is still preserved in the queue, preventing message loss in this part of the message flow.

Issue 3 (Event Processor B is unable to persist the message to the database due to some data error) is addressed through leveraging ACID (atomicity, consistency, isolation, durability) transactions via a database commit. Once the database commit happens, the data is guaranteed to be persisted in the database. Leveraging something called *last participant support* (LPS) removes the message from the persisted queue by acknowledging that processing has been completed and that the message has been persisted. This guarantees the message is not lost during the transit from Event Processor A all the way to the database. These techniques are illustrated in Figure 14-17.

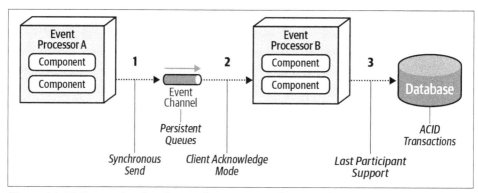

Figure 14-17. Preventing data loss within an event-driven architecture

Broadcast Capabilities

One of the other unique characteristics of event-driven architecture is the capability to broadcast events without knowledge of who (if anyone) is receiving the message and what they do with it. This technique, which is illustrated in Figure 14-18, shows that when a producer publishes a message, that same message is received by multiple subscribers.

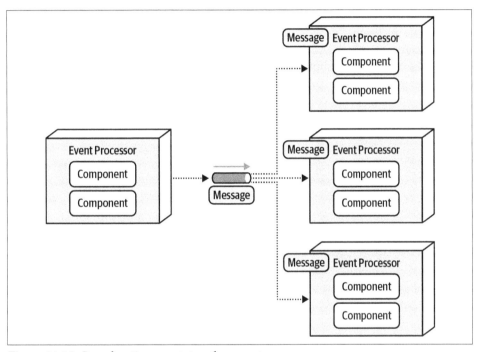

Figure 14-18. Broadcasting events to other event processors

Broadcasting is perhaps the highest level of decoupling between event processors because the producer of the broadcast message usually does not know which event processors will be receiving the broadcast message and more importantly, what they will do with the message. Broadcast capabilities are an essential part of patterns for eventual consistency, complex event processing (CEP), and a host of other situations. Consider frequent changes in stock prices for instruments traded on the stock market. Every ticker (the current price of a particular stock) might influence a number of things. However, the service publishing the latest price simply broadcasts it with no knowledge of how that information will be used.

Request-Reply

So far in this chapter we've dealt with asynchronous requests that don't need an immediate response from the event consumer. But what if an order ID is needed when ordering a book? What if a confirmation number is needed when booking a flight? These are examples of communication between services or event processors that require some sort of synchronous communication.

In event-driven architecture, synchronous communication is accomplished through *request-reply* messaging (sometimes referred to as *pseudosynchronous communications*). Each event channel within request-reply messaging consists of two queues: a request queue and a reply queue. The initial request for information is asynchronously sent to the request queue, and then control is returned to the message producer. The message producer then does a blocking wait on the reply queue, waiting for the response. The message consumer receives and processes the message and then sends the response to the reply queue. The event producer then receives the message with the response data. This basic flow is illustrated in Figure 14-19.

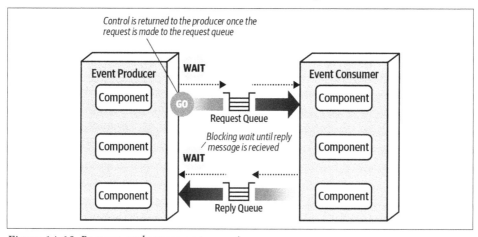

Figure 14-19. Request-reply message processing

There are two primary techniques for implementing request-reply messaging. The first (and most common) technique is to use a *correlation ID* contained in the message header. A correlation ID is a field in the reply message that is usually set to the message ID of the original request message. This technique, as illustrated in Figure 14-20, works as follows, with the message ID indicated with ID, and the correlation ID indicated with CID:

1. The event producer sends a message to the request queue and records the unique message ID (in this case ID 124). Notice that the correlation ID (CID) in this case is null.

---

2. The event producer now does a blocking wait on the reply queue with a message filter (also called a message selector), where the correlation ID in the message header equals the original message ID (in this case 124). Notice there are two messages in the reply queue: message ID 855 with correlation ID 120, and message ID 856 with correlation ID 122. Neither of these messages will be picked up because the correlation ID does not match what the event consumer is looking for (CID 124).

3. The event consumer receives the message (ID 124) and processes the request.

4. The event consumer creates the reply message containing the response and sets the correlation ID (CID) in the message header to the original message ID (124).

5. The event consumer sends the new message (ID 857) to the reply queue.

6. The event producer receives the message because the correlation ID (124) matches the message selector from step 2.

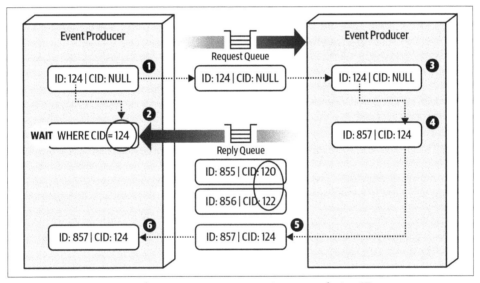

Figure 14-20. Request-reply message processing using a correlation ID

The other technique used to implement request-reply messaging is to use a *temporary queue* for the reply queue. A temporary queue is dedicated to the specific request, created when the request is made and deleted when the request ends. This technique, as illustrated in Figure 14-21, does not require a correlation ID because the temporary queue is a dedicated queue only known to the event producer for the specific request. The temporary queue technique works as follows:

1. The event producer creates a temporary queue (or one is automatically created, depending on the message broker) and sends a message to the request queue,

passing the name of the temporary queue in the reply-to header (or some other agreed-upon custom attribute in the message header).

2. The event producer does a blocking wait on the temporary reply queue. No message selector is needed because any message sent to this queue belongs solely to the event producer that originally sent to the message.

3. The event consumer receives the message, processes the request, and sends a response message to the reply queue named in the reply-to header.

4. The event processor receives the message and deletes the temporary queue.

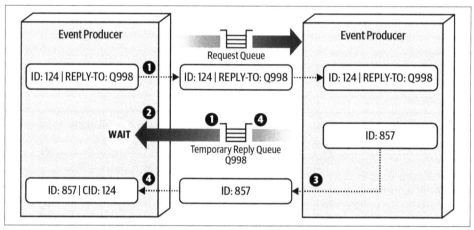

Figure 14-21. Request-reply message processing using a temporary queue

While the temporary queue technique is much simpler, the message broker must create a temporary queue for each request made and then delete it immediately afterward. Large messaging volumes can significantly slow down the message broker and impact overall performance and responsiveness. For this reason we usually recommend using the correlation ID technique.

Choosing Between Request-Based and Event-Based

The request-based model and event-based model are both viable approaches for designing software systems. However, choosing the right model is essential to the overall success of the system. We recommend choosing the request-based model for well-structured, data-driven requests (such as retrieving customer profile data) when certainty and control over the workflow is needed. We recommend choosing the event-based model for flexible, action-based events that require high levels of responsiveness and scale, with complex and dynamic user processing.

Understanding the trade-offs with the event-based model also helps decide which one is the best fit. Table 14-3 lists the advantages and disadvantages of the event-based model of event-driven architecture.

Table 14-3. Trade-offs of the event-driven model

Advantages over request-based	Trade-offs
Better response to dynamic user content	Only supports eventual consistency
Better scalability and elasticity	Less control over processing flow
Better agility and change management	Less certainty over outcome of event flow
Better adaptability and extensibility	Difficult to test and debug
Better responsiveness and performance	
Better real-time decision making	
Better reaction to situational awareness	

Hybrid Event-Driven Architectures

While many applications leverage the event-driven architecture style as the primary overarching architecture, in many cases event-driven architecture is used in conjunction with other architecture styles, forming what is known as a hybrid architecture. Some common architecture styles that leverage event-driven architecture as part of another architecture style include microservices and space-based architecture. Other hybrids that are possible include an event-driven microkernel architecture and an event-driven pipeline architecture.

Adding event-driven architecture to any architecture style helps remove bottlenecks, provides a back pressure point in the event requests get backed up, and provides a level of user responsiveness not found in other architecture styles. Both microservices and space-based architecture leverage messaging for data pumps, asynchronously sending data to another processor that in turn updates data in a database. Both also leverage event-driven architecture to provide a level of programmatic scalability to services in a microservices architecture and processing units in a space-based architecture when using messaging for interservice communication.

Architecture Characteristics Ratings

A one-star rating in the characteristics ratings table in Figure 14-22 means the specific architecture characteristic isn't well supported in the architecture, whereas a five-star rating means the architecture characteristic is one of the strongest features in the architecture style. The definition for each characteristic identified in the scorecard can be found in Chapter 4.

Event-driven architecture is primarily a technically partitioned architecture in that any particular domain is spread across multiple event processors and tied together through mediators, queues, and topics. Changes to a particular domain usually impact many event processors, mediators, and other messaging artifacts, hence why event-driven architecture is not domain partitioned.

Architecture characteristic	Star rating
Partitioning type	Technical
Number of quanta	1 to many
Deployability	★★☆
Elasticity	★★☆
Evolutionary	★★★★☆
Fault tolerance	★★★★☆
Modularity	★★★★
Overall cost	★★☆
Performance	★★★★☆
Reliability	★★☆
Scalability	★★★★☆
Simplicity	★
Testability	★☆

Figure 14-22. Event-driven architecture characteristics ratings

The number of quanta within event-driven architecture can vary from one to many quanta, which is usually based on the database interactions within each event processor and request-reply processing. Even though all communication in an event-driven architecture is asynchronous, if multiple event processors share a single database instance, they would all be contained within the same architectural quantum. The same is true for request-reply processing: even though the communication is still asynchronous between the event processors, if a request is needed right away from the event consumer, it ties those event processors together synchronously; hence they belong to the same quantum.

To illustrate this point, consider the example where one event processor sends a request to another event processor to place an order. The first event processor must wait for an order ID from the other event processor to continue. If the second event processor that places the order and generates an order ID is down, the first event processor cannot continue. Therefore, they are part of the same architecture quantum and share the same architectural characteristics, even though they are both sending and receiving asynchronous messages.

Event-driven architecture gains five stars for performance, scalability, and fault tolerance, the primary strengths of this architecture style. High performance is achieved through asynchronous communications combined with highly parallel processing. High scalability is realized through the programmatic load balancing of event processors (also called *competing consumers*). As the request load increases, additional event processors can be programmatically added to handle the additional requests. Fault tolerance is achieved through highly decoupled and asynchronous event processors that provide eventual consistency and eventual processing of event workflows. Providing the user interface or an event processor making a request does not need an immediate response, promises and futures can be leveraged to process the event at a later time if other downstream processors are not available.

Overall *simplicity* and *testability* rate relatively low with event-driven architecture, mostly due to the nondeterministic and dynamic event flows typically found within this architecture style. While deterministic flows within the request-based model are relatively easy to test because the paths and outcomes are generally known, such is not the case with the event-driven model. Sometimes it is not known how event processors will react to dynamic events, and what messages they might produce. These "event tree diagrams" can be extremely complex, generating hundreds to even thousands of scenarios, making it very difficult to govern and test.

Finally, event-driven architectures are highly evolutionary, hence the five-star rating. Adding new features through existing or new event processors is relatively straightforward, particularly in the broker topology. By providing hooks via published messages in the broker topology, the data is already made available, hence no changes are required in the infrastructure or existing event processors to add that new functionality.

CHAPTER 15

Space-Based Architecture Style

Most web-based business applications follow the same general request flow: a request from a browser hits the web server, then an application server, then finally the database server. While this pattern works great for a small set of users, bottlenecks start appearing as the user load increases, first at the web-server layer, then at the application-server layer, and finally at the database-server layer. The usual response to bottlenecks based on an increase in user load is to scale out the web servers. This is relatively easy and inexpensive, and it sometimes works to address the bottleneck issues. However, in most cases of high user load, scaling out the web-server layer just moves the bottleneck down to the application server. Scaling application servers can be more complex and expensive than web servers and usually just moves the bottleneck down to the database server, which is even more difficult and expensive to scale. Even if you can scale the database, what you eventually end up with is a triangle-shaped topology, with the widest part of the triangle being the web servers (easiest to scale) and the smallest part being the database (hardest to scale), as illustrated in Figure 15-1.

In any high-volume application with a large concurrent user load, the database will usually be the final limiting factor in how many transactions you can process concurrently. While various caching technologies and database scaling products help to address these issues, the fact remains that scaling out a normal application for extreme loads is a very difficult proposition.

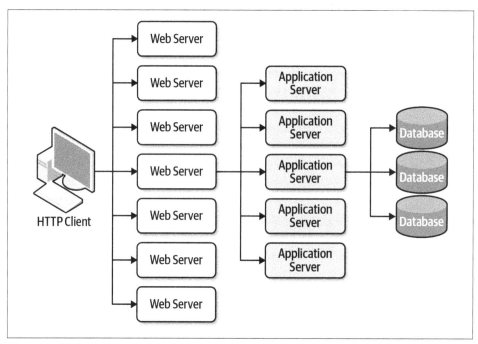

Figure 15-1. Scalability limits within a traditional web-based topology

The *space-based* architecture style is specifically designed to address problems involving high scalability, elasticity, and high concurrency issues. It is also a useful architecture style for applications that have variable and unpredictable concurrent user volumes. Solving the extreme and variable scalability issue architecturally is often a better approach than trying to scale out a database or retrofit caching technologies into a nonscalable architecture.

General Topology

Space-based architecture gets its name from the concept of *tuple space* (*https://oreil.ly/XVJ_D*), the technique of using multiple parallel processors communicating through shared memory. High scalability, high elasticity, and high performance are achieved by removing the central database as a synchronous constraint in the system and instead leveraging replicated in-memory data grids. Application data is kept in-memory and replicated among all the active processing units. When a processing unit updates data, it asynchronously sends that data to the database, usually via messaging with persistent queues. Processing units start up and shut down dynamically as user load increases and decreases, thereby addressing variable scalability. Because there is no central database involved in the standard transactional processing of the application, the database bottleneck is removed, thus providing near-infinite scalability within the application.

There are several architecture components that make up a space-based architecture: a *processing unit* containing the application code, *virtualized middleware* used to manage and coordinate the processing units, *data pumps* to asynchronously send updated data to the database, *data writers* that perform the updates from the data pumps, and *data readers* that read database data and deliver it to processing units upon startup. Figure 15-2 illustrates these primary architecture components.

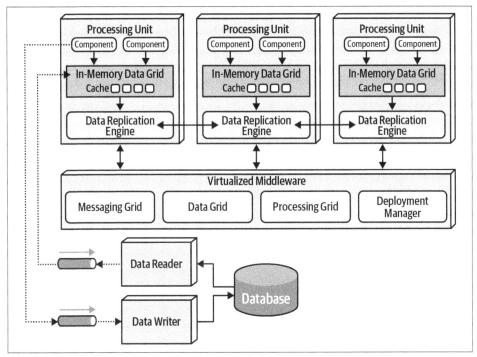

Figure 15-2. Space-based architecture basic topology

Processing Unit

The processing unit (illustrated in Figure 15-3) contains the application logic (or portions of the application logic). This usually includes web-based components as well as backend business logic. The contents of the processing unit vary based on the type of application. Smaller web-based applications would likely be deployed into a single processing unit, whereas larger applications may split the application functionality into multiple processing units based on the functional areas of the application. The processing unit can also contain small, single-purpose services (as with microservices). In addition to the application logic, the processing unit also contains an in-memory data grid and replication engine usually implemented through such products as Hazelcast (*https://hazelcast.com*), Apache Ignite (*https://ignite.apache.org*), and Oracle Coherence (*https://oreil.ly/XOUJL*).

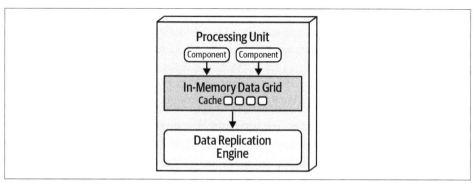

Figure 15-3. Processing unit

Virtualized Middleware

The virtualized middleware handles the infrastructure concerns within the architecture that control various aspects of data synchronization and request handling. The components that make up the virtualized middleware include a *messaging grid*, *data grid*, *processing grid*, and *deployment manager*. These components, which are described in detail in the next sections, can be custom written or purchased as third-party products.

Messaging grid

The messaging grid, shown in Figure 15-4, manages input request and session state. When a request comes into the virtualized middleware, the messaging grid component determines which active processing components are available to receive the request and forwards the request to one of those processing units. The complexity of the messaging grid can range from a simple round-robin algorithm to a more complex next-available algorithm that keeps track of which request is being processed by which processing unit. This component is usually implemented using a typical web server with load-balancing capabilities (such as HA Proxy and Nginx).

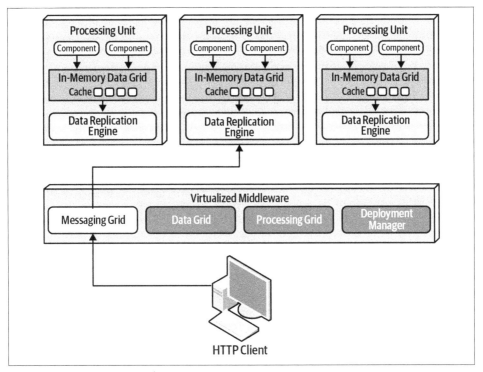

Figure 15-4. Messaging grid

Data grid

The data grid component is perhaps the most important and crucial component in this architecture style. In most modern implementations the data grid is implemented solely within the processing units as a replicated cache. However, for those replicated caching implementations that require an external controller, or when using a distributed cache, this functionality would reside in both the processing units as well as in the data grid component within the virtualized middleware. Since the messaging grid can forward a request to any of the processing units available, it is essential that each processing unit contains exactly the same data in its in-memory data grid. Although Figure 15-5 shows a synchronous data replication between processing units, in reality this is done asynchronously and very quickly, usually completing the data synchronization in less than 100 milliseconds.

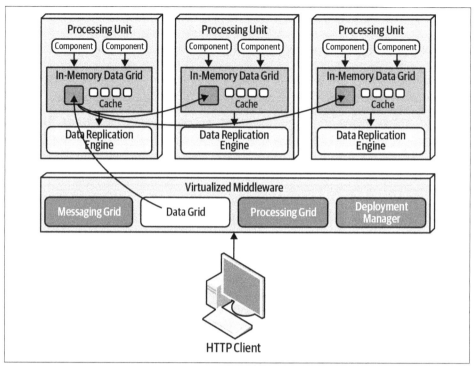

Figure 15-5. Data grid

Data is synchronized between processing units that contain the same named data grid. To illustrate this point, consider the following code in Java using Hazelcast that creates an internal replicated data grid for processing units containing customer profile information:

```
HazelcastInstance hz = Hazelcast.newHazelcastInstance();
Map<String, CustomerProfile> profileCache =
        hz.getReplicatedMap("CustomerProfile");
```

All processing units needing access to the customer profile information would contain this code. Changes made to the `CustomerProfile` named cache from any of the processing units would have that change replicated to all other processing units containing that same named cache. A processing unit can contain as many replicated caches as needed to complete its work. Alternatively, one processing unit can make a remote call to another processing unit to ask for data (choreography) or leverage the processing grid (described in the next section) to orchestrate the request.

Data replication within the processing units also allows service instances to come up and down without having to read data from the database, providing there is at least one instance containing the named replicated cache. When a processing unit instance comes up, it connects to the cache provider (such as Hazelcast) and makes a request to get the named cache. Once the connection is made to the other processing units, the cache will be loaded from one of the other instances.

Each processing unit knows about all other processing unit instances through the use of a *member list*. The member list contains the IP address and ports of all other processing units using that same named cache. For example, suppose there is a single processing instance containing code and replicated cached data for the customer profile. In this case there is only one instance, so the member list for that instance only contains itself, as illustrated in the following logging statements generated using Hazelcast:

```
Instance 1:
Members {size:1, ver:1} [
        Member [172.19.248.89]:5701 - 04a6f863-dfce-41e5-9d51-9f4e356ef268 this
]
```

When another processing unit starts up with the same named cache, the member list of both services is updated to reflect the IP address and port of each processing unit:

```
Instance 1:
Members {size:2, ver:2} [
        Member [172.19.248.89]:5701 - 04a6f863-dfce-41e5-9d51-9f4e356ef268 this
        Member [172.19.248.90]:5702 - ea9e4dd5-5cb3-4b27-8fe8-db5cc62c7316
]

Instance 2:
Members {size:2, ver:2} [
        Member [172.19.248.89]:5701 - 04a6f863-dfce-41e5-9d51-9f4e356ef268
        Member [172.19.248.90]:5702 - ea9e4dd5-5cb3-4b27-8fe8-db5cc62c7316 this
]
```

When a third processing unit starts up, the member list of instance 1 and instance 2 are both updated to reflect the new third instance:

```
Instance 1:
Members {size:3, ver:3} [
        Member [172.19.248.89]:5701 - 04a6f863-dfce-41e5-9d51-9f4e356ef268 this
        Member [172.19.248.90]:5702 - ea9e4dd5-5cb3-4b27-8fe8-db5cc62c7316
        Member [172.19.248.91]:5703 - 1623eadf-9cfb-4b83-9983-d80520cef753
]

Instance 2:
Members {size:3, ver:3} [
        Member [172.19.248.89]:5701 - 04a6f863-dfce-41e5-9d51-9f4e356ef268
        Member [172.19.248.90]:5702 - ea9e4dd5-5cb3-4b27-8fe8-db5cc62c7316 this
        Member [172.19.248.91]:5703 - 1623eadf-9cfb-4b83-9983-d80520cef753
]
```

```
Instance 3:
Members {size:3, ver:3} [
        Member [172.19.248.89]:5701 - 04a6f863-dfce-41e5-9d51-9f4e356ef268
        Member [172.19.248.90]:5702 - ea9e4dd5-5cb3-4b27-8fe8-db5cc62c7316
        Member [172.19.248.91]:5703 - 1623eadf-9cfb-4b83-9983-d80520cef753 this
]
```

Notice that all three instances know about each other (including themselves). Suppose instance 1 receives a request to update the customer profile information. When instance 1 updates the cache with a `cache.put()` or similar cache update method, the data grid (such as Hazelcast) will asynchronously update the other replicated caches with the same update, ensuring all three customer profile caches always remain in sync with one another.

When processing unit instances go down, all other processing units are automatically updated to reflect the lost member. For example, if instance 2 goes down, the member lists of instance 1 and 3 are updated as follows:

```
Instance 1:
Members {size:2, ver:4} [
        Member [172.19.248.89]:5701 - 04a6f863-dfce-41e5-9d51-9f4e356ef268 this
        Member [172.19.248.91]:5703 - 1623eadf-9cfb-4b83-9983-d80520cef753
]

Instance 3:
Members {size:2, ver:4} [
        Member [172.19.248.89]:5701 - 04a6f863-dfce-41e5-9d51-9f4e356ef268
        Member [172.19.248.91]:5703 - 1623eadf-9cfb-4b83-9983-d80520cef753 this
]
```

Processing grid

The processing grid, illustrated in Figure 15-6, is an optional component within the virtualized middleware that manages orchestrated request processing when there are multiple processing units involved in a single business request. If a request comes in that requires coordination between processing unit types (e.g., an order processing unit and a payment processing unit), it is the processing grid that mediates and orchestrates the request between those two processing units.

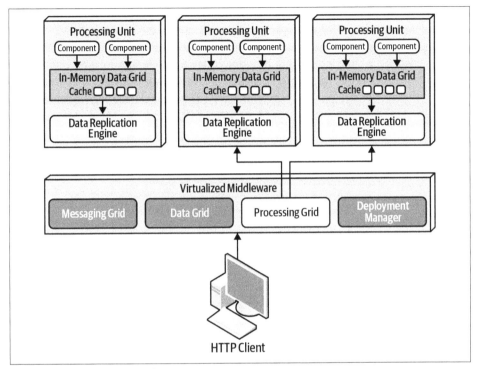

Figure 15-6. Processing grid

Deployment manager

The deployment manager component manages the dynamic startup and shutdown of processing unit instances based on load conditions. This component continually monitors response times and user loads, starts up new processing units when load increases, and shuts down processing units when the load decreases. It is a critical component to achieving variable scalability (elasticity) needs within an application.

Data Pumps

A *data pump* is a way of sending data to another processor which then updates data in a database. Data pumps are a necessary component within space-based architecture, as processing units do not directly read from and write to a database. Data pumps within a space-based architecture are always asynchronous, providing eventual consistency with the in-memory cache and the database. When a processing unit instance receives a request and updates its cache, that processing unit becomes the owner of the update and is therefore responsible for sending that update through the data pump so that the database can be updated eventually.

Data pumps are usually implemented using messaging, as shown in Figure 15-7. Messaging is a good choice for data pumps when using a space-based architecture. Not only does messaging support asynchronous communication, but it also supports guaranteed delivery and preserving message order through first-in, first-out (FIFO) queueing. Furthermore, messaging provides a decoupling between the processing unit and the data writer so that if the data writer is not available, uninterrupted processing can still take place within the processing units.

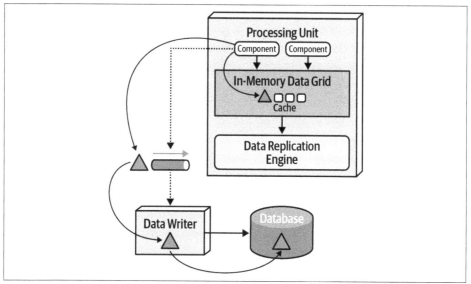

Figure 15-7. Data pump used to send data to a database

In most cases there are multiple data pumps, each one usually dedicated to a particular domain or subdomain (such as customer or inventory). Data pumps can be dedicated to each type of cache (such as `CustomerProfile`, `CustomerWishlist`, and so on), or they can be dedicated to a processing unit domain (such as `Customer`) containing a much larger and general cache.

Data pumps usually have associated contracts, including an action associated with the contract data (add, delete, or update). The contract can be a JSON schema, XML schema, an object, or even a *value-driven message* (map message containing name-value pairs). For updates, the data contained in the message of the data pump usually only contains the new data values. For example, if a customer changes a phone number on their profile, only the new phone number would be sent, along with the customer ID and an action to update the data.

Alternatively, each class of processing unit can have its own dedicated data writer component, as illustrated in Figure 15-9. In this model the data writer is dedicated to each corresponding data pump and contains only the database processing logic for that particular processing unit (such as Wallet). While this model tends to produce too many data writer components, it does provide better scalability and agility due to the alignment of processing unit, data pump, and data writer.

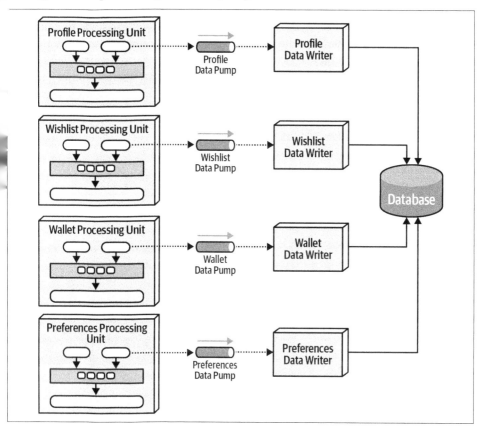

Figure 15-9. Dedicated data writers for each data pump

Data Readers

Whereas data writers take on the responsibility for updating the database, data readers take on the responsibility for reading data from the database and sending it to the processing units via a reverse data pump. In space-based architecture, data readers are only invoked under one of three situations: a crash of all processing unit instances of the same named cache, a redeployment of all processing units within the same named cache, or retrieving archive data not contained in the replicated cache.

Data Writers

The data writer component accepts messages from a data pump and base with the information contained in the message of the Figure 15-7). Data writers can be implemented as services, applicati (such as Ab Initio (*https://www.abinitio.com/en*)). The granularity o can vary based on the scope of the data pumps and processing units.

A domain-based data writer contains all of the necessary database l the updates within a particular domain (such as customer), regardle of data pumps it is accepting. Notice in Figure 15-8 that there are fc cessing units and four different data pumps representing the cu (Profile, WishList, Wallet, and Preferences) but only one data v customer data writer listens to all four data pumps and contains the base logic (such as SQL) to update the customer-related data in the da

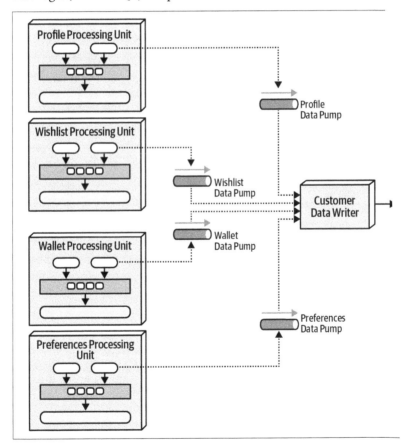

Figure 15-8. Domain-based data writer

In the event where all instances come down (due to a system-wide crash or redeployment of all instances), data must be read from the database (something that is generally avoided in space-based architecture). When instances of a class of processing unit start coming up, each one tries to grab a lock on the cache. The first one to get the lock becomes the temporary cache owner; the others go into a wait state until the lock is released (this might vary based on the type of cache implementation being used, but regardless, there is one primary owner of the cache in this scenario). To load the cache, the instance that gained temporary cache owner status sends a message to a queue requesting data. The data reader component accepts the read request and then performs the necessary database query logic to retrieve the data needed by the processing unit. As the data reader queries data from the database, it sends that data to a different queue (called a reverse data pump). The temporary cache owner processing unit receives the data from the reverse data pump and loads the cache. Once all the data is loaded, the temporary owner releases the lock on the cache, all other instances are then synchronized, and processing can begin. This processing flow is illustrated in Figure 15-10.

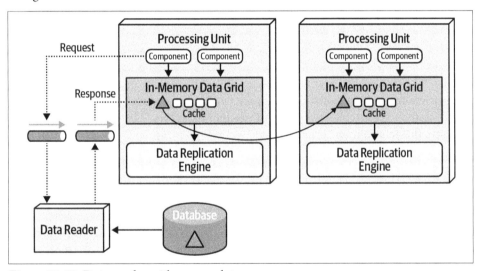

Figure 15-10. Data reader with reverse data pump

Like data writers, data readers can also be domain-based or dedicated to a specific class of processing unit (which is usually the case). The implementation is also the same as the data writers—either service, application, or data hub.

The data writers and data readers essentially form what is usually known as a *data abstraction layer* (or *data access layer* in some cases). The difference between the two is in the amount of detailed knowledge the processing units have with regard to the structure of the tables (or schema) in the database. A data access layer means that the processing units are coupled to the underlying data structures in the database, and only use the data readers and writers to indirectly access the database. A data abstraction layer, on the other hand, means that the processing unit is decoupled from the underlying database table structures through separate contracts. Space-based architecture generally relies on a data abstraction layer model so that the replicated cache schema in each processing unit can be different than the underlying database table structures. This allows for incremental changes to the database without necessarily impacting the processing units. To facilitate this incremental change, the data writers and data readers contain transformation logic so that if a column type changes or a column or table is dropped, the data readers and data writers can buffer the database change until the necessary changes can be made to the processing unit caches.

Data Collisions

When using replicated caching in an active/active state where updates can occur to any service instance containing the same named cache, there is the possibility of a *data collision* due to replication latency. A data collision occurs when data is updated in one cache instance (cache A), and during replication to another cache instance (cache B), the same data is updated by that cache (cache B). In this scenario, the local update to cache B will be overridden through replication by the old data from cache A, and through replication the same data in cache A will be overridden by the update from cache B.

To illustrate this problem, assume there are two service instances (Service A and Service B) containing a replicated cache of product inventory. The following flow demonstrates the data collision problem:

- The current inventory count for blue widgets is 500 units
- Service A updates the inventory cache for blue widgets to 490 units (10 sold)
- During replication, Service B updates the inventory cache for blue widgets to 495 units (5 sold)
- The Service B cache gets updated to 490 units due to replication from Service A update
- The Service A cache gets updates to 495 units due to replication from Service B update
- Both caches in Service A and B are incorrect and out of sync (inventory should be 485 units)

There are several factors that influence how many data collisions might occur: the number of processing unit instances containing the same cache, the update rate of the cache, the cache size, and finally the replication latency of the caching product. The formula used to determine probabilistically how many potential data collisions might occur based on these factors is as follows:

$$CollisionRate = N * \frac{UR^2}{S} * RL$$

where N represents the number of service instances using the same named cache, UR represents the update rate in milliseconds (squared), S the cache size (in terms of number of rows), and RL the replication latency of the caching product.

This formula is useful for determining the percentage of data collisions that will likely occur and hence the feasibility of the use of replicated caching. For example, consider the following values for the factors involved in this calculation:

Update rate (UR):	20 updates/second
Number of instances (N):	5
Cache size (S):	50,000 rows
Replication latency (RL):	100 milliseconds
Updates:	72,000 per hour
Collision rate:	14.4 per hour
Percentage:	0.02%

Applying these factors to the formula yields 72,000 updates and hour, with a high probability that 14 updates to the same data may collide. Given the low percentage (0.02%), replication would be a viable option.

Varying the replication latency has a significant impact on the consistency of data. Replication latency depends on many factors, including the type of network and the physical distance between processing units. For this reason replication latency values are rarely published and must be calculated and derived from actual measurements in a production environment. The value used in the prior example (100 milliseconds) is a good planning number if the actual replication latency, a value we frequently use to determine the number of data collisions, is not available. For example, changing the replication latency from 100 milliseconds to 1 millisecond yields the same number of updates (72,000 per hour) but produces only the probability of 0.1 collisions per hour! This scenario is shown in the following table:

Update rate (UR):	20 updates/second
Number of instances (N):	5
Cache size (S):	50,000 rows
Replication latency (RL):	1 millisecond (changed from 100)
Updates:	72,000 per hour
Collision rate:	0.1 per hour
Percentage:	0.0002%

The number of processing units containing the same named cache (as represented through the *number of instances* factor) also has a direct proportional relationship to the number of data collisions possible. For example, reducing the number of processing units from 5 instances to 2 instances yields a data collision rate of only 6 per hour out of 72,000 updates per hour:

Update rate (UR):	20 updates/second
Number of instances (N):	2 (changed from 5)
Cache size (S):	50,000 rows
Replication latency (RL):	100 milliseconds
Updates:	72,000 per hour
Collision rate:	5.8 per hour
Percentage:	0.008%

The cache size is the only factor that is inversely proportional to the collision rate. As the cache size decreases, collision rates increase. In our example, reducing the cache size from 50,000 rows to 10,000 rows (and keeping everything the same as in the first example) yields a collision rate of 72 per hour, significantly higher than with 50,000 rows:

Update rate (UR):	20 updates/second
Number of instances (N):	5
Cache size (S):	10,000 rows (changed from 50,000)
Replication latency (RL):	100 milliseconds
Updates:	72,000 per hour
Collision rate:	72.0 per hour
Percentage:	0.1%

Under normal circumstances, most systems do not have consistent update rates over such a long period of time. As such, when using this calculation it is helpful to understand the maximum update rate during peak usage and calculate minimum, normal, and peak collision rates.

Cloud Versus On-Premises Implementations

Space-based architecture offers some unique options when it comes to the environments in which it is deployed. The entire topology, including the processing units, virtualized middleware, data pumps, data readers and writers, and the database, can be deployed within cloud-based environments on-premises ("on-prem"). However, this architecture style can also be deployed between these environments, offering a unique feature not found in other architecture styles.

A powerful feature of this architecture style (as illustrated in Figure 15-11) is to deploy applications via processing units and virtualized middleware in managed cloud-based environments while keeping the physical databases and corresponding data on-prem. This topology supports very effective cloud-based data synchronization due to the asynchronous data pumps and eventual consistency model of this architecture style. Transactional processing can occur on dynamic and elastic cloud-based environments while preserving physical data management, reporting, and data analytics within secure and local on-prem environments.

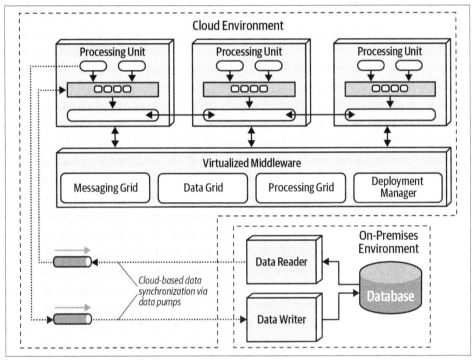

Figure 15-11. Hybrid cloud-based and on-prem topology

Replicated Versus Distributed Caching

Space-based architecture relies on caching for the transactional processing of an application. Removing the need for direct reads and writes to a database is how space-based architecture is able to support high scalability, high elasticity, and high performance. Space-based architecture mostly relies on replicated caching, although distributed caching can be used as well.

With replicated caching, as illustrated in Figure 15-12, each processing unit contains its own in-memory data grid that is synchronized between all processing units using that same named cache. When an update occurs to a cache within any of the processing units, the other processing units are automatically updated with the new information.

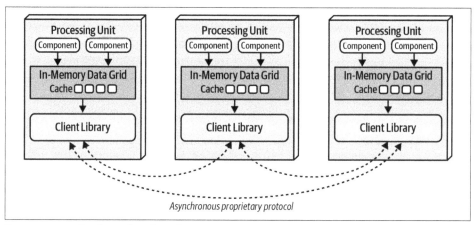

Figure 15-12. Replicated caching between processing units

Replicated caching is not only extremely fast, but it also supports high levels of fault tolerance. Since there is no central server holding the cache, replicated caching does not have a single point of failure. There may be exceptions to this rule, however, based on the implementation of the caching product used. Some caching products require the presence of an external controller to monitor and control the replication of data between processing units, but most product companies are moving away from this model.

While replicated caching is the standard caching model for space-based architecture, there are some cases where it is not possible to use replicated caching. These situations include high data volumes (size of the cache) and high update rates to the cache data. Internal memory caches in excess of 100 MB might start to cause issues with regard to elasticity and high scalability due to the amount of memory used by each processing unit. Processing units are generally deployed within a virtual machine (or in some cases represent the virtual machine). Each virtual machine only has a certain amount of memory available for internal cache usage, limiting the number of processing unit instances that can be started to process high-throughput situations. Furthermore, as shown in "Data Collisions" on page 224, if the update rate of the cache data is too high, the data grid might be unable to keep up with that high update rate to ensure data consistency across all processing unit instances. When these situations occur, distributed caching can be used.

Distributed caching, as illustrated in Figure 15-13, requires an external server or service dedicated to holding a centralized cache. In this model the processing units do not store data in internal memory, but rather use a proprietary protocol to access the data from the central cache server. Distributed caching supports high levels of data consistency because the data is all in one place and does not need to be replicated. However, this model has less performance than replicated caching because the cache data must be accessed remotely, adding to the overall latency of the system. Fault tolerance is also an issue with distributed caching. If the cache server containing the data goes down, no data can be accessed or updated from any of the processing units, rendering them nonoperational. Fault tolerance can be mitigated by mirroring the distributed cache, but this could present consistency issues if the primary cache server goes down unexpectedly and the data does not make it to the mirrored cache server.

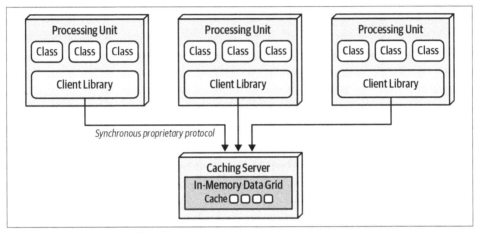

Figure 15-13. Distributed caching between processing units

When the size of the cache is relatively small (under 100 MB) and the update rate of the cache is low enough that the replication engine of the caching product can keep up with the cache updates, the decision between using a replicated cache and a distributed cache becomes one of data consistency versus performance and fault tolerance. A distributed cache will always offer better data consistency over a replicated cache because the cache of data is in a single place (as opposed to being spread across multiple processing units). However, performance and fault tolerance will always be better when using a replicated cache. Many times this decision comes down to the type of data being cached in the processing units. The need for highly consistent data (such as inventory counts of the available products) usually warrants a distributed cache, whereas data that does not change often (such as reference data like name/ value pairs, product codes, and product descriptions) usually warrants a replicated cache for quick lookup. Some of the selection criteria that can be used as a guide for choosing when to use a distributed cache versus a replicated cache are listed in Table 15-1.

Table 15-1. Distributed versus replicated caching

Decision criteria	Replicated cache	Distributed cache
Optimization	Performance	Consistency
Cache size	Small (<100 MB)	Large (>500 MB)
Type of data	Relatively static	Highly dynamic
Update frequency	Relatively low	High update rate
Fault tolerance	High	Low

When choosing the type of caching model to use with space-based architecture, remember that in most cases *both* models will be applicable within any given application context. In other words, neither replicated caching nor distributed caching solve every problem. Rather than trying to seek compromises through a single consistent caching model across the application, leverage each for its strengths. For example, for a processing unit that maintains the current inventory, choose a distributed caching model for data consistency; for a processing unit that maintains the customer profile, choose a replicated cache for performance and fault tolerance.

Near-Cache Considerations

A *near-cache* is a type of caching hybrid model bridging in-memory data grids with a distributed cache. In this model (illustrated in Figure 15-14) the distributed cache is referred to as the *full backing cache*, and each in-memory data grid contained within each processing unit is referred to as the *front cache*. The front cache always contains a smaller subset of the full backing cache, and it leverages an *eviction policy* to remove older items so that newer ones can be added. The front cache can be what is known as a most recently used (MRU) cache containing the most recently used items or a most frequently used (MFU) cache containing the most frequently used items. Alternatively, a *random replacement* eviction policy can be used in the front cache so that items are removed in a random manner when space is needed to add a new item. Random replacement (RR) is a good eviction policy when there is no clear analysis of the data with regard to keeping either the latest used versus the most frequently used.

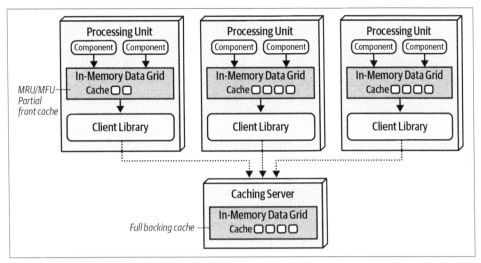

Figure 15-14. Near-cache topology

While the front caches are always kept in sync with the full backing cache, the front caches contained within each processing unit are not synchronized between other processing units sharing the same data. This means that multiple processing units sharing the same data context (such as a customer profile) will likely all have different data in their front cache. This creates inconsistencies in performance and responsiveness between processing units because each processing unit contains different data in the front cache. For this reason we do not recommended using a near-cache model for space-based architecture.

Implementation Examples

Space-based architecture is well suited for applications that experience high spikes in user or request volume and applications that have throughput in excess of 10,000 concurrent users. Examples of space-based architecture include applications like online concert ticketing systems and online auction systems. Both of these examples require high performance, high scalability, and high levels of elasticity.

Concert Ticketing System

Concert ticketing systems have a unique problem domain in that concurrent user volume is relatively low until a popular concert is announced. Once concert tickets go on sale, user volumes usually spike from several hundred concurrent users to several thousand (possibly in the tens of thousands, depending on the concert), all trying to acquire a ticket for the concert (hopefully, good seats!). Tickets usually sell out in a matter of minutes, requiring the kind of architecture characteristics supported by space-based architecture.

There are many challenges associated with this sort of system. First, there are only a certain number of tickets available, regardless of the seating preferences. Seating availability must continually be updated and made available as fast as possible given the high number of concurrent requests. Also, assuming assigned seats are an option, seating availability must also be updated as fast as possible. Continually accessing a central database synchronously for this sort of system would likely not work—it would be very difficult for a typical database to handle tens of thousands of concurrent requests through standard database transactions at this level of scale and update frequency.

Space-based architecture would be a good fit for a concert ticketing system due to the high elasticity requirements required of this type of application. An instantaneous increase in the number of concurrent users wanting to purchase concert tickets would be immediately recognized by the *deployment manager*, which in turn would start up a large number of processing units to handle the large volume of requests. Optimally, the deployment manager would be configured to start up the necessary number of processing units shortly *before* the tickets went on sale, therefore having those instances on standby right before the significant increase in user load.

Online Auction System

Online auction systems (bidding on items within an auction) share the same sort of characteristics as the online concert ticketing systems described previously—both require high levels of performance and elasticity, and both have unpredictable spikes in user and request load. When an auction starts, there is no way of determining how many people will be joining the auction, and of those people, how many concurrent bids will occur for each asking price.

Space-based architecture is well suited for this type of problem domain in that multiple processing units can be started as the load increases; and as the auction winds down, unused processing units could be destroyed. Individual processing units can be devoted to each auction, ensuring consistency with bidding data. Also, due to the asynchronous nature of the data pumps, bidding data can be sent to other processing (such as bid history, bid analytics, and auditing) without much latency, therefore increasing the overall performance of the bidding process.

Architecture Characteristics Ratings

A one-star rating in the characteristics ratings table in Figure 15-15 means the specific architecture characteristic isn't well supported in the architecture, whereas a five-star rating means the architecture characteristic is one of the strongest features in the architecture style. The definition for each characteristic identified in the scorecard can be found in Chapter 4.

Architecture characteristic	Star rating
Partitioning type	Domain and technical
Number of quanta	1 to many
Deployability	☆☆☆
Elasticity	☆☆☆☆☆
Evolutionary	☆☆☆
Fault tolerance	☆☆☆
Modularity	☆☆☆
Overall cost	☆☆
Performance	☆☆☆☆☆
Reliability	☆☆☆☆
Scalability	☆☆☆☆☆
Simplicity	☆
Testability	☆

Figure 15-15. Space-based architecture characteristics ratings

Notice that space-based architecture maximizes elasticity, scalability, and performance (all five-star ratings). These are the driving attributes and main advantages of this architecture style. High levels of all three of these architecture characteristics are achieved by leveraging in-memory data caching and removing the database as a constraint. As a result, processing millions of concurrent users is possible using this architecture style.

While high levels of elasticity, scalability, and performance are advantages in this architecture style, there is a trade-off for this advantage, specifically with regard to overall simplicity and testability. Space-based architecture is a very complicated architecture style due to the use of caching and eventual consistency of the primary data store, which is the ultimate system of record. Care must be taken to ensure no data is lost in the event of a crash in any of the numerous moving parts of this architecture style (see "Preventing Data Loss" on page 201 in Chapter 14).

Testing gets a one-star rating due to the complexity involved with simulating the high levels of scalability and elasticity supported in this architecture style. Testing hundreds of thousands of concurrent users at peak load is a very complicated and expensive task, and as a result most high-volume testing occurs within production environments with actual extreme load. This produces significant risk for normal operations within a production environment.

Cost is another factor when choosing this architecture style. Space-based architecture is relatively expensive, mostly due to licensing fees for caching products and high resource utilization within cloud and on-prem systems due to high scalability and elasticity.

It is difficult to identify the partitioning type of space-based architecture, and as a result we have identified it as both domain partitioned as well as technically partitioned. Space-based architecture is domain partitioned not only because it aligns itself with a specific type of domain (highly elastic and scalable systems), but also because of the flexibility of the processing units. Processing units can act as domain services in the same way services are defined in a service-based architecture or microservices architecture. At the same time, space-based architecture is technically partitioned in the way it separates the concerns about transactional processing using caching from the actual storage of the data in the database via data pumps. The processing units, data pumps, data readers and writers, and the database all form a technical layering in terms of how requests are processed, very similar with regard to how a monolithic n-tiered layered architecture is structured.

The number of quanta within space-based architecture can vary based on how the user interface is designed and how communication happens between processing units. Because the processing units do not communicate synchronously with the database, the database itself is not part of the quantum equation. As a result, quanta within a space-based architecture are typically delineated through the association between the various user interfaces and the processing units. Processing units that synchronously communicate with each other (or synchronously through the processing grid for orchestration) would all be part of the same architectural quantum.

CHAPTER 16

Orchestration-Driven Service-Oriented Architecture

Architecture styles, like art movements, must be understood in the context of the era in which they evolved, and this architecture exemplifies this rule more than any other. The combination of external forces that often influence architecture decisions, combined with a logical but ultimately disastrous organizational philosophy, doomed this architecture to irrelevance. However, it provides a great example of how a particular organizational idea can make logical sense yet hinder most important parts of the development process.

History and Philosophy

This style of service-oriented architecture appeared just as companies were becoming enterprises in the late 1990s: merging with smaller companies, growing at a breakneck pace, and requiring more sophisticated IT to accommodate this growth. However, computing resources were scarce, precious, and commercial. Distributed computing had just become possible and necessary, and many companies needed the variable scalability and other beneficial characteristics.

Many external drivers forced architects in this era toward distributed architectures with significant constraints. Before open source operating systems were thought reliable enough for serious work, operating systems were expensive and licensed per machine. Similarly, commercial database servers came with Byzantine licensing schemes, which caused application server vendors (which offered database connection pooling) to battle with database vendors. Thus, architects were expected to reuse as much as possible. In fact, *reuse* in all forms became the dominant philosophy in this architecture, the side effects of which we cover in "Reuse...and Coupling" on page 239.

This style of architecture also exemplifies how far architects can push the idea of technical partitioning, which had good motivations but bad consequences.

Topology

The topology of this type of service-oriented architecture is shown in Figure 16-1.

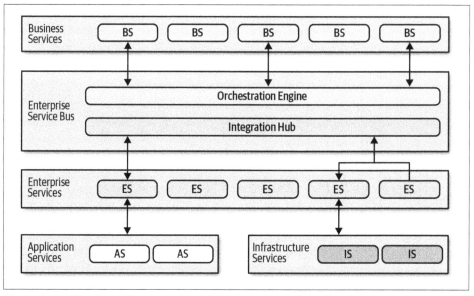

Figure 16-1. Topology of orchestration-driven service-oriented architecture

Not all examples of this style of architecture had the exact layers illustrated in Figure 16-1, but they all followed the same idea of establishing a taxonomy of services within the architecture, each layer with a specific responsibility.

Service-oriented architecture is a distributed architecture; the exact demarcation of boundaries isn't shown in Figure 16-1 because it varied based on organization.

Taxonomy

The architect's driving philosophy in this architecture centered around enterprise-level reuse. Many large companies were annoyed at how much they had to continue to rewrite software, and they struck on a strategy to gradually solve that problem. Each layer of the taxonomy supported this goal.

Business Services

Business services sit at the top of this architecture and provide the entry point. For example, services like `ExecuteTrade` or `PlaceOrder` represent domain behavior. One litmus test common at the time—could an architect answer affirmatively to the question "Are we in the business of…" for each of these services?

These service definitions contained no code—just input, output, and sometimes schema information. They were usually defined by business users, hence the name business services.

Enterprise Services

The *enterprise services* contain fine-grained, shared implementations. Typically, a team of developers is tasked with building atomic behavior around particular business domains: `CreateCustomer`, `CalculateQuote`, and so on. These services are the building blocks that make up the coarse-grained business services, tied together via the orchestration engine.

This separation of responsibility flows from the reuse goal in this architecture. If developers can build fine-grained enterprise services at just the correct level of granularity, the business won't have to rewrite that part of the business workflow again. Gradually, the business will build up a collection of reusable assets in the form of reusable enterprise services.

Unfortunately, the dynamic nature of reality defies these attempts. Business components aren't like construction materials, where solutions last decades. Markets, technology changes, engineering practices, and a host of other factors confound attempts to impose stability on the software world.

Application Services

Not all services in the architecture require the same level of granularity or reuse as the enterprise services. *Application services* are one-off, single-implementation services. For example, perhaps one application needs geo-location, but the organization doesn't want to take the time or effort to make that a reusable service. An application service, typically owned by a single application team, solves these problems.

Infrastructure Services

Infrastructure services supply the operational concerns, such as monitoring, logging, authentication, and authorization. These services tend to be concrete implementations, owned by a shared infrastructure team that works closely with operations.

Orchestration Engine

The *orchestration engine* forms the heart of this distributed architecture, stitching together the business service implementations using orchestration, including features like transactional coordination and message transformation. This architecture is typically tied to a single relational database, or a few, rather than a database per service as in microservices architectures. Thus, transactional behavior is handled declaratively in the orchestration engine rather than in the database.

The orchestration engine defines the relationship between the business and enterprise services, how they map together, and where transaction boundaries lie. It also acts as an integration hub, allowing architects to integrate custom code with package and legacy software systems.

Because this mechanism forms the heart of the architecture, Conway's law (see "Conway's Law" on page 103) correctly predicts that the team of integration architects responsible for this engine become a political force within an organization, and eventually a bureaucratic bottleneck.

While this approach might sound appealing, in practice it was mostly a disaster. Offloading transaction behavior to an orchestration tool sounded good, but finding the correct level of granularity of transactions became more and more difficult. While building a few services wrapped in a distributed transaction is possible, the architecture becomes increasingly complex as developers must figure out where the appropriate transaction boundaries lie between services.

Message Flow

All requests go through the orchestration engine—it is the location within this architecture where logic resides. Thus, message flow goes through the engine even for internal calls, as shown in Figure 16-2.

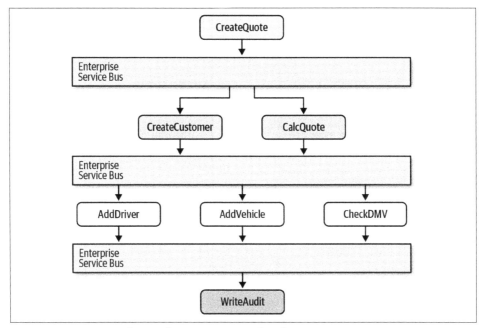

Figure 16-2. Message flow with service-oriented architecture

In Figure 16-2, the `CreateQuote` business-level service calls the service bus, which defines the workflow that consists of calls to `CreateCustomer` and `CalculateQuote`, each of which also has calls to application services. The service bus acts as the intermediary for all calls within this architecture, serving as both an integration hub and orchestration engine.

Reuse…and Coupling

A major goal of this architecture is reuse at the service level—the ability to gradually build business behavior that can be incrementally reused over time. Architects in this architecture were instructed to find reuse opportunities as aggressively as possible. For example, consider the situation illustrated in Figure 16-3.

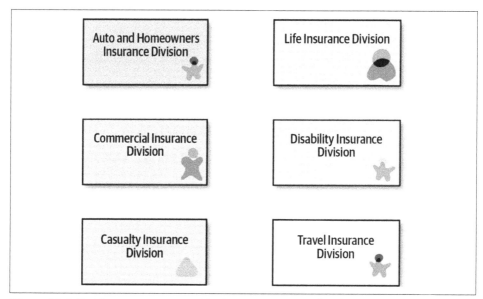

Figure 16-3. Seeking reuse opportunities in service-oriented architecture

In Figure 16-3, an architect realizes that each of these divisions within an insurance company all contain a notion of Customer. Therefore, the proper strategy for service-oriented architecture entails extracting the customer parts into a reusable service and allowing the original services to reference the canonical Customer service, shown in Figure 16-4.

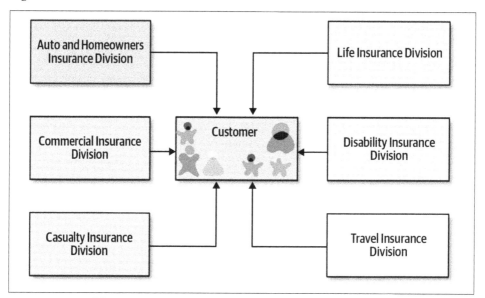

Figure 16-4. Building canonical representations in service-oriented architecture

In Figure 16-4, the architect has isolated all customer behavior into a single `Customer` service, achieving obvious reuse goals.

However, architects only slowly realized the negative trade-offs of this design. First, when a team builds a system primarily around reuse, they also incur a huge amount of coupling between components. For example, in Figure 16-4, a change to the `Customer` service ripples out to all the other services, making change risky. Thus, in service-oriented architecture, architects struggled with making incremental change—each change had a potential huge ripple effect. That in turn led to the need for coordinated deployments, holistic testing, and other drags on engineering efficiency.

Another negative side effect of consolidating behavior into a single place: consider the case of auto and disability insurance in Figure 16-4. To support a single `Customer` service, it must include all the details the organization knows about customers. Auto insurance requires a driver's license, which is a property of the person, not the vehicle. Therefore, the `Customer` service will have to include details about driver's licenses that the *disability insurance division* cares nothing about. Yet, the team that deals with disability must deal with the extra complexity of a single customer definition.

Perhaps the most damaging revelation from this architecture came with the realization of the impractically of building an architecture so focused on technical partitioning. While it makes sense from a separation and reuse philosophy standpoint, it was a practical nightmare. Domain concepts like `CatalogCheckout` were spread so thinly throughout this architecture that they were virtually ground to dust. Developers commonly work on tasks like "add a new address line to `CatalogCheckout`." In a service-oriented architecture, that could entail dozens of services in several different tiers, plus changes to a single database schema. And, if the current enterprise services aren't defined at the correct transactional granularity, the developers will either have to change their design or build a new, near-identical service to change transactional behavior. So much for reuse.

Architecture Characteristics Ratings

Many of the modern criteria we use to evaluate architecture now were not priorities when this architecture was popular. In fact, the Agile software movement had just started and had not penetrated into the size of organizations likely to use this architecture.

A one-star rating in the characteristics ratings table in Figure 16-5 means the specific architecture characteristic isn't well supported in the architecture, whereas a five-star rating means the architecture characteristic is one of the strongest features in the architecture style. The definition for each characteristic identified in the scorecard can be found in Chapter 4.

Service-oriented architecture is perhaps the most technically partitioned general-purpose architecture ever attempted! In fact, the backlash against the disadvantages of this structure lead to more modern architectures such as microservices. It has a single quantum even though it is a distributed architecture for two reasons. First, it generally uses a single database or just a few databases, creating coupling points within the architecture across many different concerns. Second, and more importantly, the orchestration engine acts as a giant coupling point—no part of the architecture can have different architecture characteristics than the mediator that orchestrates all behavior. Thus, this architecture manages to find the disadvantages of both monolithic *and* distributed architectures.

Architecture characteristic	Star rating
Partitioning type	Technical
Number of quanta	1
Deployability	☆
Elasticity	☆☆☆
Evolutionary	☆
Fault tolerance	☆☆☆
Modularity	☆☆☆
Overall cost	☆
Performance	☆☆
Reliability	☆☆
Scalability	☆☆☆☆
Simplicity	☆
Testability	☆

Figure 16-5. Ratings for service-oriented architecture

Modern engineering goals such as deployability and testability score disastrously in this architecture, both because they were poorly supported and because those were not important (or even aspirational) goals during that era.

This architecture did support some goals such as elasticity and scalability, despite the difficulties in implementing those behaviors, because tool vendors poured enormous effort into making these systems scalable by building session replication across application servers and other techniques. However, being a distributed architecture, performance was never a highlight of this architecture style and was extremely poor because each business request was split across so much of the architecture.

Because of all these factors, simplicity and cost have the inverse relationship most architects would prefer. This architecture was an important milestone because it taught architects how difficult distributed transactions can be in the real world and the practical limits of technical partitioning.

CHAPTER 17

Microservices Architecture

Microservices is an extremely popular architecture style that has gained significant momentum in recent years. In this chapter, we provide an overview of the important characteristics that set this architecture apart, both topologically and philosophically.

History

Most architecture styles are named after the fact by architects who notice a particular pattern that keeps reappearing—there is no secret group of architects who decide what the next big movement will be. Rather, it turns out that many architects end up making common decisions as the software development ecosystem shifts and changes. The common best ways of dealing with and profiting from those shifts become architecture styles that others emulate.

Microservices differs in this regard—it was named fairly early in its usage and popularized by a famous blog entry by Martin Fowler and James Lewis entitled "Microservices," (*https://oreil.ly/Px3Wk*) published in March 2014. They recognized many common characteristics in this relatively new architectural style and delineated them. Their blog post helped define the architecture for curious architects and helped them understand the underlying philosophy.

Microservices is heavily inspired by the ideas in domain-driven design (DDD), a logical design process for software projects. One concept in particular from DDD, *bounded context*, decidedly inspired microservices. The concept of bounded context represents a decoupling style. When a developer defines a domain, that domain includes many entities and behaviors, identified in artifacts such as code and database schemas. For example, an application might have a domain called `CatalogCheckout`, which includes notions such as catalog items, customers, and payment. In a traditional monolithic architecture, developers would share many of these concepts, building reusable classes and linked databases. Within a bounded context, the internal parts, such as code and data schemas, are coupled together to produce work; but they are never coupled to anything outside the bounded context, such as a database or class definition from another bounded context. This allows each context to define only what it needs rather than accommodating other constituents.

While reuse is beneficial, remember the First Law of Software Architecture regarding trade-offs. The negative trade-off of reuse is coupling. When an architect designs a system that favors reuse, they also favor coupling to achieve that reuse, either by inheritance or composition.

However, if the architect's goal requires high degrees of decoupling, then they favor duplication over reuse. The primary goal of microservices is high decoupling, physically modeling the logical notion of bounded context.

Topology

The topology of microservices is shown in Figure 17-1.

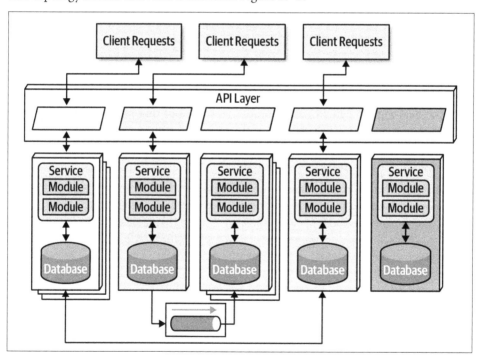

Figure 17-1. The topology of the microservices architecture style

As illustrated in Figure 17-1, due to its single-purpose nature, the service size in microservices is much smaller than other distributed architectures, such as the orchestration-driven service-oriented architecture. Architects expect each service to include all necessary parts to operate independently, including databases and other dependent components. The different characteristics appear in the following sections.

Distributed

Microservices form a *distributed architecture*: each service runs in its own process, which originally implied a physical computer but quickly evolved to virtual machines and containers. Decoupling the services to this degree allows for a simple solution to a common problem in architectures that heavily feature multitenant infrastructure for hosting applications. For example, when using an application server to manage multiple running applications, it allows operational reuse of network bandwidth, memory, disk space, and a host of other benefits. However, if all the supported applications continue to grow, eventually some resource becomes constrained on the shared infrastructure. Another problem concerns improper isolation between shared applications.

Separating each service into its own process solves all the problems brought on by sharing. Before the evolutionary development of freely available open source operating systems, combined with automated machine provisioning, it was impractical for each domain to have its own infrastructure. Now, however, with cloud resources and container technology, teams can reap the benefits of extreme decoupling, both at the domain and operational level.

Performance is often the negative side effect of the distributed nature of microservices. Network calls take much longer than method calls, and security verification at every endpoint adds additional processing time, requiring architects to think carefully about the implications of granularity when designing the system.

Because microservices is a distributed architecture, experienced architects advise against the use of transactions across service boundaries, making determining the granularity of services the key to success in this architecture.

Bounded Context

The driving philosophy of microservices is the notion of *bounded context*: each service models a domain or workflow. Thus, each service includes everything necessary to operate within the application, including classes, other subcomponents, and database schemas. This philosophy drives many of the decisions architects make within this architecture. For example, in a monolith, it is common for developers to share common classes, such as `Address`, between disparate parts of the application. However, microservices try to avoid coupling, and thus an architect building this architecture style prefers duplication to coupling.

Microservices take the concept of a domain-partitioned architecture to the extreme. Each service is meant to represent a domain or subdomain; in many ways, microservices is the physical embodiment of the logical concepts in domain-driven design.

Granularity

Architects struggle to find the correct granularity for services in microservices, and often make the mistake of making their services too small, which requires them to build communication links back between the services to do useful work.

> The term "microservice" is a *label*, not a *description*.
>
> —Martin Fowler

In other words, the originators of the term needed to call this new style *something*, and they chose "microservices" to contrast it with the dominant architecture style at the time, service-oriented architecture, which could have been called "gigantic services". However, many developers take the term "microservices" as a commandment, not a description, and create services that are too fine-grained.

The purpose of service boundaries in microservices is to capture a domain or workflow. In some applications, those natural boundaries might be large for some parts of the system—some business processes are more coupled than others. Here are some guidelines architects can use to help find the appropriate boundaries:

Purpose
   The most obvious boundary relies on the inspiration for the architecture style, a domain. Ideally, each microservice should be extremely functionally cohesive, contributing one significant behavior on behalf of the overall application.

Transactions
   Bounded contexts are business workflows, and often the entities that need to cooperate in a transaction show architects a good service boundary. Because transactions cause issues in distributed architectures, if architects can design their system to avoid them, they generate better designs.

Choreography
   If an architect builds a set of services that offer excellent domain isolation yet require extensive communication to function, the architect may consider bundling these services back into a larger service to avoid the communication overhead.

Iteration is the only way to ensure good service design. Architects rarely discover the perfect granularity, data dependencies, and communication styles on their first pass. However, after iterating over the options, an architect has a good chance of refining their design.

Data Isolation

Another requirement of microservices, driven by the bounded context concept, is data isolation. Many other architecture styles use a single database for persistence. However, microservices tries to avoid all kinds of coupling, including shared schemas and databases used as integration points.

Data isolation is another factor an architect must consider when looking at service granularity. Architects must be wary of the entity trap (discussed in "Entity trap" on page 110) and not simply model their services to resemble single entities in a database.

Architects are accustomed to using relational databases to unify values within a system, creating a single source of truth, which is no longer an option when distributing data across the architecture. Thus, architects must decide how they want to handle this problem: either identifying one domain as the source of truth for some fact and coordinating with it to retrieve values or using database replication or caching to distribute information.

While this level of data isolation creates headaches, it also provides opportunities. Now that teams aren't forced to unify around a single database, each service can choose the most appropriate tool, based on price, type of storage, or a host of other factors. Teams have the advantage in a highly decoupled system to change their mind and choose a more suitable database (or other dependency) without affecting other teams, which aren't allowed to couple to implementation details.

API Layer

Most pictures of microservices include an API layer sitting between the consumers of the system (either user interfaces or calls from other systems), but it is optional. It is common because it offers a good location within the architecture to perform useful tasks, either via indirection as a proxy or a tie into operational facilities, such as a naming service (covered in "Operational Reuse" on page 250).

While an API layer may be used for variety of things, it should not be used as a mediator or orchestration tool if the architect wants to stay true to the underlying philosophy of this architecture: all interesting logic in this architecture should occur inside a bounded context, and putting orchestration or other logic in a mediator violates that rule. This also illustrates the difference between technical and domain partitioning in architecture: architects typically use mediators in technically partitioned architectures, whereas microservices is firmly domain partitioned.

Operational Reuse

Given that microservices prefers duplication to coupling, how do architects handle the parts of architecture that really do benefit from coupling, such as operational concerns like monitoring, logging, and circuit breakers? One of the philosophies in the traditional service-oriented architecture was to reuse as much functionality as possible, domain and operational alike. In microservices, architects try to split these two concerns.

Once a team has built several microservices, they realize that each has common elements that benefit from similarity. For example, if an organization allows each service team to implement monitoring themselves, how can they ensure that each team does so? And how do they handle concerns like upgrades? Does it become the responsibility of each team to handle upgrading to the new version of the monitoring tool, and how long will that take?

The *sidecar* pattern offers a solution to this problem, illustrated in Figure 17-2.

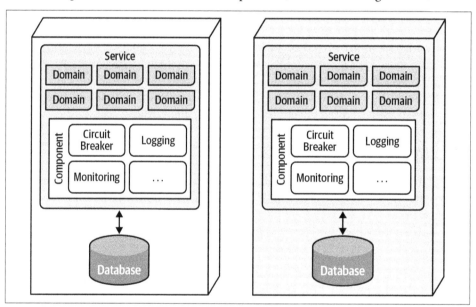

Figure 17-2. The sidecar pattern in microservices

In Figure 17-2, the common operational concerns appear within each service as a separate component, which can be owned by either individual teams or a shared infrastructure team. The sidecar component handles all the operational concerns that teams benefit from coupling together. Thus, when it comes time to upgrade the monitoring tool, the shared infrastructure team can update the sidecar, and each microservices receives that new functionality.

Once teams know that each service includes a common sidecar, they can build a *service mesh*, allowing unified control across the architecture for concerns like logging and monitoring. The common sidecar components connect to form a consistent operational interface across all microservices, as shown in Figure 17-3.

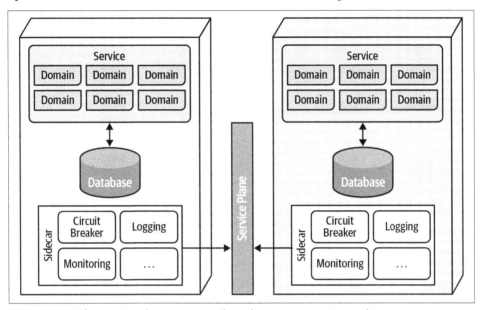

Figure 17-3. The service plane connects the sidecars in a service mesh

In Figure 17-3, each sidecar wires into the service plane, which forms the consistent interface to each service.

The service mesh itself forms a console that allows developers holistic access to services, which is shown in Figure 17-4.

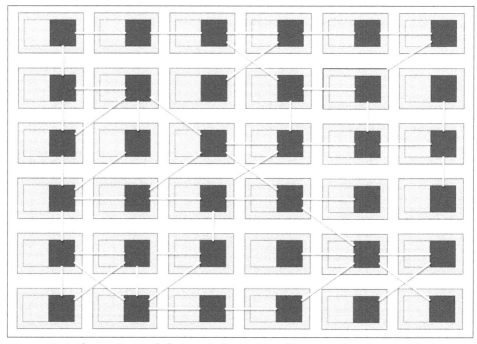

Figure 17-4. The service mesh forms a holistic view of the operational aspect of microservices

Each service forms a node in the overall mesh, as shown in Figure 17-4. The service mesh forms a console that allows teams to globally control operational coupling, such as monitoring levels, logging, and other cross-cutting operational concerns.

Architects use *service discovery* as a way to build elasticity into microservices architectures. Rather than invoke a single service, a request goes through a service discovery tool, which can monitor the number and frequency of requests, as well as spin up new instances of services to handle scale or elasticity concerns. Architects often include service discovery in the service mesh, making it part of every microservice. The API layer is often used to host service discovery, allowing a single place for user interfaces or other calling systems to find and create services in an elastic, consistent way.

Frontends

Microservices favors decoupling, which would ideally encompass the user interfaces as well as backend concerns. In fact, the original vision for microservices included the user interface as part of the bounded context, faithful to the principle in DDD. However, practicalities of the partitioning required by web applications and other external constraints make that goal difficult. Thus, two styles of user interfaces commonly appear for microservices architectures; the first appears in Figure 17-5.

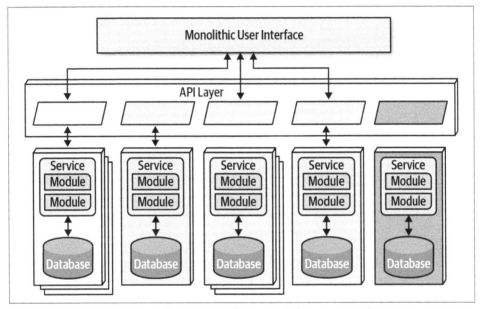

Figure 17-5. Microservices architecture with a monolithic user interface

In Figure 17-5, the monolithic frontend features a single user interface that calls through the API layer to satisfy user requests. The frontend could be a rich desktop, mobile, or web application. For example, many web applications now use a JavaScript web framework to build a single user interface.

The second option for user interfaces uses *microfrontends*, shown in Figure 17-6.

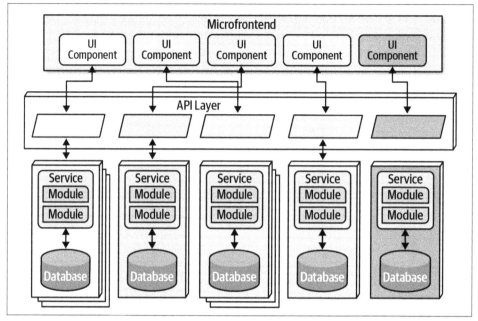

Figure 17-6. Microfrontend pattern in microservices

In Figure 17-6, this approach utilizes components at the user interface level to create a synchronous level of granularity and isolation in the user interface as the backend services. Each service emits the user interface for that service, which the frontend coordinates with the other emitted user interface components. Using this pattern, teams can isolate service boundaries from the user interface to the backend services, unifying the entire domain within a single team.

Developers can implement the microfrontend pattern in a variety of ways, either using a component-based web framework such as React (*https://reactjs.org*) or using one of several open source frameworks that support this pattern.

Communication

In microservices, architects and developers struggle with appropriate granularity, which affects both data isolation and communication. Finding the correct communication style helps teams keep services decoupled yet still coordinated in useful ways.

Fundamentally, architects must decide on *synchronous* or *asynchronous* communication. Synchronous communication requires the caller to wait for a response from the callee. Microservices architectures typically utilize *protocol-aware heterogeneous interoperability*. We'll break down that term for you:

Protocol-aware

Because microservices usually don't include a centralized integration hub to avoid operational coupling, each service should know how to call other services. Thus, architects commonly standardize on how particular services call each other: a certain level of REST, message queues, and so on. That means that services must know (or discover) which protocol to use to call other services.

Heterogeneous

Because microservices is a distributed architecture, each service may be written in a different technology stack. *Heterogeneous* suggests that microservices fully supports polyglot environments, where different services use different platforms.

Interoperability

Describes services calling one another. While architects in microservices try to discourage transactional method calls, services commonly call other services via the network to collaborate and send/receive information.

Enforced Heterogeneity

A well-known architect who was a pioneer in the microservices style was the chief architecture at a personal information manager startup for mobile devices. Because they had a fast-moving problem domain, the architect wanted to ensure that none of the development teams accidentally created coupling points between each other, hindering the teams' ability to move independently. It turned out that this architect had a wide mix of technical skills on the teams, thus mandating that each development team use a different technology stack. If one team was using Java and the other was using .NET, it was impossible to accidentally share classes!

This approach is the polar opposite of most enterprise governance policies, which insist on standardizing on a single technology stack. The goal in the microservices world isn't to create the most complex ecosystem possible, but rather to choose the correct scale technology for the narrow scope of the problem. Not every service needs an industrial-strength relational database, and forcing it on small teams slows them rather than benefitting them. This concept leverages the highly decoupled nature of microservices.

For asynchronous communication, architects often use events and messages, thus internally utilizing an event-driven architecture, covered in Chapter 14; the broker and mediator patterns manifest in microservices as *choreography* and *orchestration*.

Choreography and Orchestration

Choreography utilizes the same communication style as a broker event-driven architecture. In other words, no central coordinator exists in this architecture, respecting the bounded context philosophy. Thus, architects find it natural to implement decoupled events between services.

Domain/architecture isomorphism is one key characteristic that architects should look for when assessing how appropriate an architecture style is for a particular problem. This term describes how the shape of an architecture maps to a particular architecture style. For example, in Figure 8-7, the Silicon Sandwiches' technically partitioned architecture structurally supports customizability, and the microkernel architecture style offers the same general structure. Therefore, problems that require a high degree of customization become easier to implement in a microkernel.

Similarly, because the architect's goal in a microservices architecture favors decoupling, the shape of microservices resembles the broker EDA, making these two patterns symbiotic.

In choreography, each service calls other services as needed, without a central mediator. For example, consider the scenario shown in Figure 17-7.

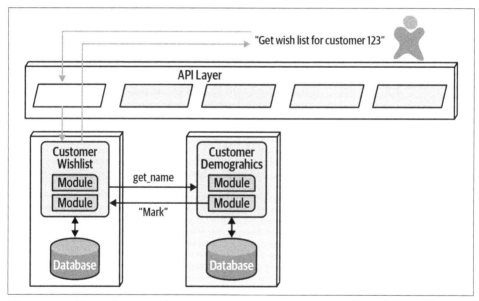

Figure 17-7. Using choreography in microservices to manage coordination

In Figure 17-7, the user requests details about a user's wish list. Because the `Customer WishList` service doesn't contain all the necessary information, it makes a call to `CustomerDemographics` to retrieve the missing information, returning the result to the user.

Because microservices architectures don't include a global mediator like other service-oriented architectures, if an architect needs to coordinate across several services, they can create their own localized mediator, as shown in Figure 17-8.

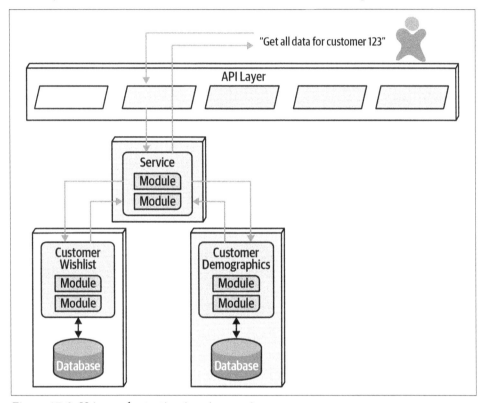

Figure 17-8. Using orchestration in microservices

In Figure 17-8, the developers create a service whose sole responsibility is coordinating the call to get all information for a particular customer. The user calls the `Report CustomerInformation` mediator, which calls the necessary other services.

The First Law of Software Architecture suggests that neither of these solutions is perfect—each has trade-offs. In choreography, the architect preserves the highly decoupled philosophy of the architecture style, thus reaping maximum benefits touted by the style. However, common problems like error handling and coordination become more complex in choreographed environments.

Consider an example with a more complex workflow, shown in Figure 17-9.

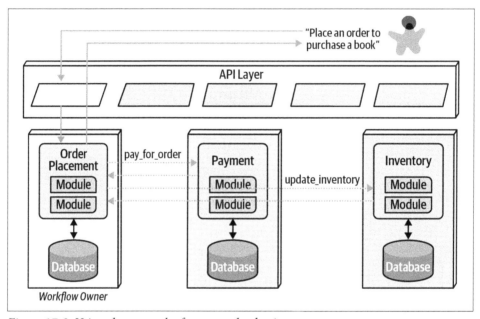

Figure 17-9. Using choreography for a complex business process

In Figure 17-9, the first service called must coordinate across a wide variety of other services, basically acting as a mediator in addition to its other domain responsibilities. This pattern is called the *front controller* pattern, where a nominally choreographed service becomes a more complex mediator for some problem. The downside to this pattern is added complexity in the service.

Alternatively, an architect may choose to use orchestration for complex business processes, illustrated in Figure 17-10.

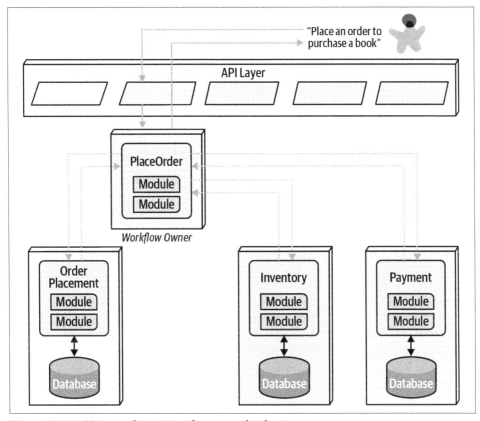

Figure 17-10. Using orchestration for a complex business process

In Figure 17-10, the architect builds a mediator to handle the complexity and coordination required for the business workflow. While this creates coupling between these services, it allows the architect to focus coordination into a single service, leaving the others less affected. Often, domain workflows are inherently coupled—the architect's job entails finding the best way to represent that coupling in ways that support both the domain and architectural goals.

Transactions and Sagas

Architects aspire to extreme decoupling in microservices, but then often encounter the problem of how to do transactional coordination across services. Because the decoupling in the architecture encourages the same level for the databases, atomicity that was trivial in monolithic applications becomes a problem in distributed ones.

Building transactions across service boundaries violates the core decoupling principle of the microservices architecture (and also creates the worst kind of dynamic connascence, connascence of value). The best advice for architects who want to do transactions across services is: *don't!* Fix the granularity components instead. Often, architects who build microservices architectures who then find a need to wire them together with transactions have gone too granular in their design. Transaction boundaries is one of the common indicators of service granularity.

 Don't do transactions in microservices—fix granularity instead!

Exceptions always exist. For example, a situation may arise where two different services need vastly different architecture characteristics, requiring distinct service boundaries, yet still need transactional coordination. In those situations, patterns exist to handle transaction orchestration, with serious trade-offs.

A popular distributed transactional pattern in microservices is the *saga* pattern, illustrated in Figure 17-11.

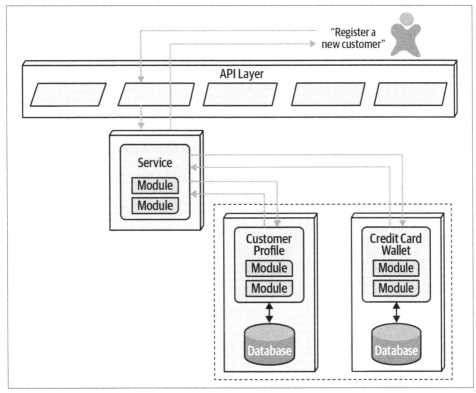

Figure 17-11. The saga pattern in microservices architecture

In Figure 17-11, a service acts a mediator across multiple service calls and coordinates the transaction. The mediator calls each part of the transaction, records success or failure, and coordinates results. If everything goes as planned, all the values in the services and their contained databases update synchronously.

In an error condition, the mediator must ensure that no part of the transaction succeeds if one part fails. Consider the situation shown in Figure 17-12.

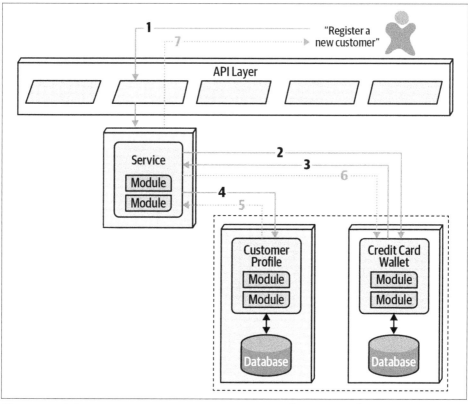

Figure 17-12. Saga pattern compensating transactions for error conditions

In Figure 17-12, if the first part of the transaction succeeds, yet the second part fails, the mediator must send a request to all the parts of the transaction that were successful and tell them to undo the previous request. This style of transactional coordination is called a *compensating transaction framework*. Developers implement this pattern by usually having each request from the mediator enter a pending state until the mediator indicates overall success. However, this design becomes complex if asynchronous requests must be juggled, especially if new requests appear that are contingent on pending transactional state. This also creates a lot of coordination traffic at the network level.

Another implementation of a compensating transaction framework has developers build *do* and *undo* for each potentially transactional operation. This allows less coordination during transactions, but the *undo* operations tend to be significantly more complex than the *do* operations, more than doubling the design, implementation, and debugging work.

While it is possible for architects to build transactional behavior across services, it goes against the reason for choosing the microservices pattern. Exceptions always exist, so the best advice for architects is to use the saga pattern sparingly.

 A few transactions across services is sometimes necessary; if it's the dominant feature of the architecture, mistakes were made!

Architecture Characteristics Ratings

The microservices architecture style offers several extremes on our standard ratings scale, shown in Figure 17-13. A one-star rating means the specific architecture characteristic isn't well supported in the architecture, whereas a five-star rating means the architecture characteristic is one of the strongest features in the architecture style. The definition for each characteristic identified in the scorecard can be found in Chapter 4.

Notable is the high support for modern engineering practices such as automated deployment, testability, and others not listed. Microservices couldn't exist without the DevOps revolution and the relentless march toward automating operational concerns.

As microservices is a distributed architecture, it suffers from many of the deficiencies inherent in architectures made from pieces wired together at runtime. Thus, fault tolerance and reliability are impacted when too much interservice communication is used. However, these ratings only point to tendencies in the architecture; developers fix many of these problems by redundancy and scaling via service discovery. Under normal circumstances, however, independent, single-purpose services generally lead to high fault tolerance, hence the high rating for this characteristic within a microservices architecture.

Architecture characteristic	Star rating
Partitioning type	Domain
Number of quanta	1 to many
Deployability	★★★★☆ (4 of 5)
Elasticity	★★★★★ (5 of 5)
Evolutionary	★★★★★ (5 of 5)
Fault tolerance	★★★★☆ (4 of 5)
Modularity	★★★★★ (5 of 5)
Overall cost	★ (1 of 5)
Performance	★★ (2 of 5)
Reliability	★★★★☆ (4 of 5)
Scalability	★★★★★ (5 of 5)
Simplicity	★ (1 of 5)
Testability	★★★★☆ (4 of 5)

Figure 17-13. Ratings for microservices

The high points of this architecture are scalability, elasticity, and evolutionary. Some of the most scalable systems yet written have utilized this style to great success. Similarly, because the architecture relies heavily on automation and intelligent integration with operations, developers can also build elasticity support into the architecture. Because the architecture favors high decoupling at an incremental level, it supports the modern business practice of evolutionary change, even at the architecture level. Modern business move fast, and software development has struggled to keep apace. By building an architecture that has extremely small deployment units that are highly decoupled, architects have a structure that can support a faster rate of change.

Performance is often an issue in microservices—distributed architectures must make many network calls to complete work, which has high performance overhead, and they must invoke security checks to verify identity and access for each endpoint. Many patterns exist in the microservices world to increase performance, including intelligent data caching and replication to prevent an excess of network calls.

Performance is another reason that microservices often use choreography rather than orchestration, as less coupling allows for faster communication and fewer bottlenecks.

Microservices is decidedly a domain-centered architecture, where each service boundary should correspond to domains. It also has the most distinct quanta of any modern architecture—in many ways, it exemplifies what the quantum measure evaluates. The driving philosophy of extreme decoupling creates many headaches in this architecture but yields tremendous benefits when done well. As in any architecture, architects must understand the rules to break them intelligently.

Additional References

While our goal in this chapter was to touch on some of the significant aspects of this architecture style, many excellent resources exist to get further and more detailed about this architecture style. Additional and more detailed information can be found about microservices in the following references:

- *Building Microservices* by Sam Newman (O'Reilly)
- *Microservices vs. Service-Oriented Architecture* by Mark Richards (O'Reilly)
- *Microservices AntiPatterns and Pitfalls* by Mark Richards (O'Reilly)

CHAPTER 18

Choosing the Appropriate Architecture Style

It depends! With all the choices available (and new ones arriving almost daily), we would like to tell you which one to use—but we cannot. Nothing is more contextual to a number of factors within an organization and what software it builds. Choosing an architecture style represents the culmination of analysis and thought about trade-offs for architecture characteristics, domain considerations, strategic goals, and a host of other things.

However contextual the decision is, some general advice exists around choosing an appropriate architecture style.

Shifting "Fashion" in Architecture

Preferred architecture styles shift over time, driven by a number of factors:

Observations from the past

New architecture styles generally arise from observations and pain points from past experiences. Architects have experience with systems in the past that influence their thoughts about future systems. Architects must rely on their past experience—it is that experience that allowed that person to become an architect in the first place. Often, new architecture designs reflect specific deficiencies from past architecture styles. For example, architects seriously rethought the implications of code reuse after building architectures that featured it and then realizing the negative trade-offs.

Changes in the ecosystem

Constant change is a reliable feature of the software development ecosystem—everything changes all the time. The change in our ecosystem is particularly chaotic, making even the type of change impossible to predict. For example, a few years ago, no one knew what *Kubernetes* was, and now there are multiple conferences around the world with thousands of developers. In a few more years, Kubernetes may be replaced with some other tool that hasn't been written yet.

New capabilities

When new capabilities arise, architecture may not merely replace one tool with another but rather shift to an entirely new paradigm. For example, few architects or developers anticipated the tectonic shift caused in the software development world by the advent of containers such as Docker. While it was an evolutionary step, the impact it had on architects, tools, engineering practices, and a host of other factors astounded most in the industry. The constant change in the ecosystem also delivers a new collection of tools and capabilities on a regular basis. Architects must keep a keen eye open to not only new tools but new paradigms. Something may just look like a new one-of-something-we-already-have, but it may include nuances or other changes that make it a game changer. New capabilities don't even have to rock the entire development world—the new features may be a minor change that aligns exactly with an architect's goals.

Acceleration

Not only does the ecosystem constantly change, but the rate of change also continues to rise. New tools create new engineering practices, which lead to new design and capabilities. Architects live in a constant state of flux because change is both pervasive and constant.

Domain changes

The domain that developers write software for constantly shifts and changes, either because the business continues to evolve or because of factors like mergers with other companies.

Technology changes

As technology continues to evolve, organizations try to keep up with at least some of these changes, especially those with obvious bottom-line benefits.

External factors

Many external factors only peripherally associated with software development may drive change within an organizations. For example, architects and developers might be perfectly happy with a particular tool, but the licensing cost has become prohibitive, forcing a migration to another option.

Regardless of where an organization stands in terms of current architecture fashion, an architect should understand current industry trends to make intelligent decisions about when to follow and when to make exceptions.

Decision Criteria

When choosing an architectural style, an architect must take into account all the various factors that contribute to the structure for the domain design. Fundamentally, an architect designs two things: whatever domain has been specified, and all the other structural elements required to make the system a success.

Architects should go into the design decision comfortable with the following things:

The domain

Architects should understand many important aspects of the domain, especially those that affect operational architecture characteristics. Architects don't have to be subject matter experts, but they must have at least a good general understanding of the major aspects of the domain under design.

Architecture characteristics that impact structure

Architects must discover and elucidate the architecture characteristics needed to support the domain and other external factors.

Data architecture

Architects and DBAs must collaborate on database, schema, and other data-related concerns. We don't cover much about data architecture in this book; it is its own specialization. However, architects must understand the impact that data design might have on their design, particularly if the new system must interact with an older and/or in-use data architecture.

Organizational factors

Many external factors may influence design. For example, the cost of a particular cloud vendor may prevent the ideal design. Or perhaps the company plans to engage in mergers and acquisitions, which encourages an architect to gravitate toward open solutions and integration architectures.

Knowledge of process, teams, and operational concerns

Many specific project factors influence an architect's design, such as the software development process, interaction (or lack of) with operations, and the QA process. For example, if an organization lacks maturity in Agile engineering practices, architecture styles that rely on those practices for success will present difficulties.

Domain/architecture isomorphism

Some problem domains match the topology of the architecture. For example, the microkernel architecture style is perfectly suited to a system that requires customizability—the architect can design customizations as plug-ins. Another example might be genome analysis, which requires a large number of discrete operations, and space-based architecture, which offers a large number of discrete processors.

Similarly, some problem domains may be particularly ill-suited for some architecture styles. For example, highly scalable systems struggle with large monolithic designs because architects find it difficult to support a large number of concurrent users in a highly coupled code base. A problem domain that includes a huge amount of semantic coupling matches poorly with a highly decoupled, distributed architecture. For instance, an insurance company application consisting of multipage forms, each of which is based on the context of previous pages, would be difficult to model in microservices. This is a highly coupled problem that will present architects with design challenges in a decoupled architecture; a less coupled architecture like service-based architecture would suit this problem better.

Taking all these things into account, the architect must make several determinations:

Monolith versus distributed

Using the quantum concepts discussed earlier, the architect must determine if a single set of architecture characteristics will suffice for the design, or do different parts of the system need differing architecture characteristics? A single set implies that a monolith is suitable (although other factors may drive an architect toward a distributed architecture), whereas different architecture characteristics imply a distributed architecture.

Where should data live?

If the architecture is monolithic, architects commonly assume a single relational databases or a few of them. In a distributed architecture, the architect must decide which services should persist data, which also implies thinking about how data must flow throughout the architecture to build workflows. Architects must consider both structure and behavior when designing architecture and not be fearful of iterating on the design to find better combinations.

What communication styles between services—synchronous or asynchronous?

Once the architect has determined data partitioning, their next design consideration is the communication between services—synchronous or asynchronous? Synchronous communication is more convenient in most cases, but it can lead to scalability, reliability, and other undesirable characteristics. Asynchronous communication can provide unique benefits in terms of performance and scale but can present a host of headaches: data synchronization, deadlocks, race conditions, debugging, and so on.

Because synchronous communication presents fewer design, implementation, and debugging challenges, architects should default to synchronous when possible and use asynchronous when necessary.

 Use synchronous by default, asynchronous when necessary.

The output of this design process is architecture topology, taking into account what architecture style (and hybridizations) the architect chose, architecture decision records about the parts of the design which required the most effort by the architect, and architecture fitness functions to protect important principles and operational architecture characteristics.

Monolith Case Study: Silicon Sandwiches

In the Silicon Sandwiches architecture kata, after investigating the architecture characteristics, we determined that a single quantum was sufficient to implement this system. Plus, this is a simple application without a huge budget, so the simplicity of a monolith appeals.

However, we created two different component designs for Silicon Sandwiches: one domain partitioned and another technically partitioned. Given the simplicity of the solution, we'll create designs for each and cover trade-offs.

Modular Monolith

A modular monolith builds domain-centric components with a single database, deployed as a single quantum; the modular monolith design for Silicon Sandwiches appears in Figure 18-1.

This is a monolith with a single relational database, implemented with a single web-based user interface (with careful design considerations for mobile devices) to keep overall cost down. Each of the domains the architect identified earlier appear as components. If time and resources are sufficient, the architect should consider creating the same separation of tables and other database assets as the domain components, allowing for this architecture to migrate to a distributed architecture more easily if future requirements warrant it.

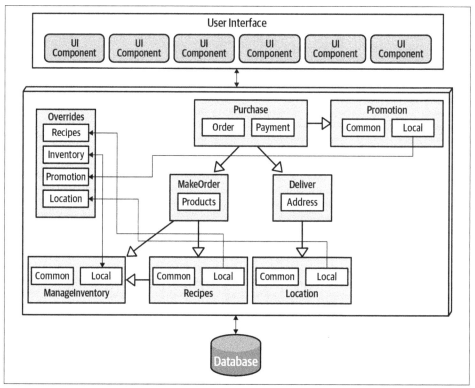

Figure 18-1. A modular monolith implementation of Silicon Sandwiches

Because the architecture style itself doesn't inherently handle customization, the architect must make sure that that feature becomes part of domain design. In this case, the architect designs an Override endpoint where developers can upload individual customizations. Correspondingly, the architect must ensure that each of the domain components references the Override component for each customizable characteristic—this would make a perfect fitness function.

Microkernel

One of the architecture characteristics the architect identified in Silicon Sandwiches was customizability. Looking at domain/architecture isomorphism, an architect may choose to implement it using a microkernel, as illustrated in Figure 18-2.

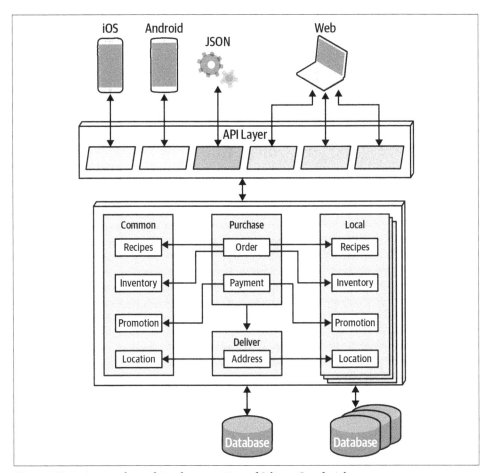

Figure 18-2. A microkernel implementation of Silicon Sandwiches

In Figure 18-2, the core system consists of the domain components and a single rela‐
tional database. As in the previous design, careful synchronization between domains
and data design will allow future migration of the core to a distributed architecture.
Each customization appears in a plug-in, the common ones in a single set of plug-ins
(with a corresponding database), and a series of local ones, each with their own data.
Because none of the plug-ins need to be coupled to the other plug-ins, they can each
maintain their data, leaving the plug-ins decoupled.

The other unique design element here utilizes the Backends for Frontends (BFF)
(*https://oreil.ly/i3Hsc*) pattern, making the API layer a thin microkernel adaptor. It
supplies general information from the backend, and the BFF adaptors translate the
generic information into the suitable format for the frontend device. For example, the
BFF for iOS will take the generic output from the backend and customize it for what
the iOS native application expects: the data format, pagination, latency, and other fac‐

tors. Building each BFF adaptor allows for the richest user interfaces and the ability to expand to support other devices in the future—one of the benefits of the microkernel style.

Communication within either Silicon Sandwich architecture can be synchronous—the architecture doesn't require extreme performance or elasticity requirements—and none of the operations will be lengthy.

Distributed Case Study: Going, Going, Gone

The Going, Going, Gone (GGG) kata presents more interesting architecture challenges. Based on the component analysis in "Case Study: Going, Going, Gone: Discovering Components" on page 112, this architecture needs differing architecture characteristics for different parts of the architecture. For example, architecture characteristics like availability and scalability will differ between roles like auctioneer and bidder.

The requirements for GGG also explicitly state certain ambitious levels of scale, elasticity, performance, and a host of other tricky operational architecture characteristics. The architect needs to choose a pattern that allows for a high degree of customization at a fine-grained level within the architecture. Of the candidate distributed architectures, either low-level event-driven or microservices match most of the architecture characteristics. Of the two, microservices better supports differing operational architecture characteristics—purely event-driven architectures typically don't separate pieces because of these operational architecture characteristics but are rather based on communication style, orchestrated versus choreographed.

Achieving the stated performance will provide a challenge in microservices, but architects can often address any weak point of an architecture by designing to accommodate it. For example, while microservices offers a high degrees of scalability naturally, architects commonly have to address specific performance issues caused by too much orchestration, too aggressive data separation, and so on.

An implementation of GGG using microservices is shown in Figure 18-3.

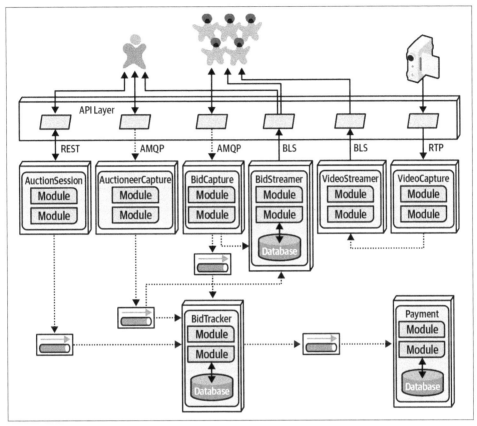

Figure 18-3. A microservices implementation of Going, Going, Gone

In Figure 18-3, each identified component became services in the architecture, matching component and service granularity. GGG has three distinct user interfaces:

Bidder
    The numerous bidders for the online auction.

Auctioneer
    One per auction.

Streamer
    Service responsible for streaming video and bid stream to the bidders. Note that this is a read-only stream, allowing optimizations not available if updates were necessary.

The following services appear in this design of the GGG architecture:

BidCapture

>   Captures online bidder entries and asynchronously sends them to `Bid Tracker`. This service needs no persistence because it acts as a conduit for the online bids.

BidStreamer

>   Streams the bids back to online participants in a high performance, read-only stream.

BidTracker

>   Tracks bids from both `Auctioneer Capture` and `Bid Capture`. This is the component that unifies the two different information streams, ordering the bids as close to real time as possible. Note that both inbound connections to this service are asynchronous, allowing the developers to use message queues as buffers to handle very different rates of message flow.

Auctioneer Capture

>   Captures bids for the auctioneer. The result of quanta analysis in "Case Study: Going, Going, Gone: Discovering Components" on page 112 led the architect to separate `Bid Capture` and `Auctioneer Capture` because they have quite different architecture characteristics.

Auction Session

>   This manages the workflow of individual auctions.

Payment

>   Third-party payment provider that handles payment information after the `Auction Session` has completed the auction.

Video Capture

>   Captures the video stream of the live auction.

Video Streamer

>   Streams the auction video to online bidders.

The architect was careful to identify both synchronous and asynchronous communication styles in this architecture. Their choice for asynchronous communication is primarily driven by accommodating differing operational architecture characteristics between services. For example, if the `Payment` service can only process a new payment every 500 ms and a large number of auctions end at the same time, synchronous communication between the services would cause time outs and other reliability headaches. By using message queues, the architect can add reliability to a critical part of the architecture that exhibits fragility.

In the final analysis, this design resolved to five quanta, identified in Figure 18-4.

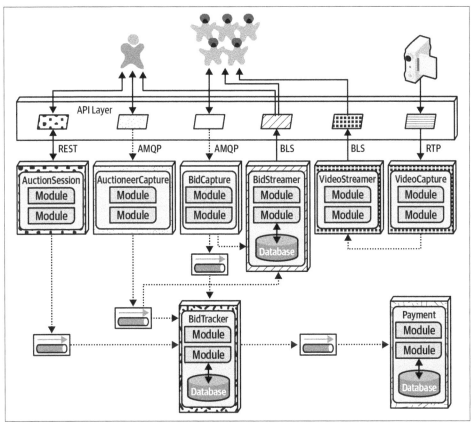

Figure 18-4. The quanta boundaries for GGG

In Figure 18-4, the design includes quanta for `Payment`, `Auctioneer`, `Bidder`, `Bidder Streams`, and `Bid Tracker`, roughly corresponding to the services. Multiple instances are indicated by stacks of containers in the diagram. Using quantum analysis at the component design stage allowed the architect to more easily identify service, data, and communication boundaries.

Note that this isn't the "correct" design for GGG, and it's certainly not the only one. We don't even suggest that it's the best possible design, but it seems to have the *least worst* set of trade-offs. Choosing microservices, then intelligently using events and messages, allows the architecture to leverage the most out of a generic architecture pattern while still building a foundation for future development and expansion.

PART III

Techniques and Soft Skills

An effective software architect must not only understand the technical aspects of software architecture, but also the primary techniques and soft skills necessary to think like an architect, guide development teams, and effectively communicate the architecture to various stakeholders. This section of the book addresses the key techniques and soft skills necessary to become an effective software architect.

CHAPTER 19

Architecture Decisions

One of the core expectations of an architect is to make architecture decisions. Architecture decisions usually involve the structure of the application or system, but they may involve technology decisions as well, particularly when those technology decisions impact architecture characteristics. Whatever the context, a good architecture decision is one that helps guide development teams in making the right technical choices. Making architecture decisions involves gathering enough relevant information, justifying the decision, documenting the decision, and effectively communicating that decision to the right stakeholders.

Architecture Decision Anti-Patterns

There is an art to making architecture decisions. Not surprisingly, several architecture anti-patterns emerge when making decisions as an architect. The programmer Andrew Koenig (*https://oreil.ly/p9i_Y*) defines an anti-pattern as something that seems like a good idea when you begin, but leads you into trouble. Another definition of an anti-pattern is a repeatable process that produces negative results. The three major architecture anti-patterns that can (and usually do) emerge when making architecture decisions are the *Covering Your Assets* anti-pattern, the *Groundhog Day* anti-pattern, and the *Email-Driven Architecture* anti-pattern. These three anti-patterns usually follow a progressive flow: overcoming the Covering Your Assets anti-pattern leads to the Groundhog Day anti-pattern, and overcoming this anti-pattern leads to the Email-Driven Architecture anti-pattern. Making effective and accurate architecture decisions requires an architect to overcome all three of these anti-patterns.

Covering Your Assets Anti-Pattern

The first anti-pattern to emerge when trying to make architecture decisions is the Covering Your Assets anti-pattern. This anti-pattern occurs when an architect avoids or defers making an architecture decision out of fear of making the wrong choice.

There are two ways to overcome this anti-pattern. The first is to wait until the *last responsible moment* to make an important architecture decision. The last responsible moment means waiting until you have enough information to justify and validate your decision, but not waiting so long that you hold up development teams or fall into the *Analysis Paralysis* anti-pattern. The second way to avoid this anti-pattern is to continually collaborate with development teams to ensure that the decision you made can be implemented as expected. This is vitally important because it is not feasible as an architect to possibly know every single detail about a particular technology and all the associated issues. By closely collaborating with development teams, the architect can respond quickly to a change in the architecture decision if issues occur.

To illustrate this point, suppose an architect makes the decision that all product-related reference data (product description, weight, and dimensions) be cached in all service instances needing that information using a read-only replicated cache, with the primary replica owned by the catalog service. A replicated cache means that if there are any changes to product information (or a new product is added), the catalog service would update its cache, which would then be replicated to all other services requiring that data through a replicated (in-memory) cache product. A good justification for this decision is to reduce coupling between the services and to effectively share data without having to make an interservice call. However, the development teams implementing this architecture decision find that due to certain scalability requirements of some of the services, this decision would require more in-process memory than is available. By closely collaborating with the development teams, the architect can quickly become aware of the issue and adjust the architecture decision to accommodate these situations.

Groundhog Day Anti-Pattern

Once an architect overcomes the Covering Your Assets anti-pattern and starts making decisions, a second anti-pattern emerges: the Groundhog Day anti-pattern. The Groundhog Day anti-pattern occurs when people don't know why a decision was made, so it keeps getting discussed over and over and over. The Groundhog Day anti-pattern gets it name from the Bill Murray movie *Groundhog Day*, where it was February 2 over and over every day.

The Groundhog Day anti-pattern occurs because once an architect makes an architecture decision, they fail to provide a justification for the decision (or a complete justification). When justifying architecture decisions it is important to provide both technical and business justifications for your decision. For example, an architect may make the decision to break apart a monolithic application into separate services to decouple the functional aspects of the application so that each part of the application uses fewer virtual machine resources and can be maintained and deployed separately. While this is a good example of a technical justification, what is missing is the business justification—in other words, why should the business pay for this architectural refactoring? A good business justification for this decision might be to deliver new business functionality faster, therefore improving time to market. Another might be to reduce the costs associated with the development and release of new features.

Providing the business value when justifying decisions is vitally important for any architecture decision. It is also a good litmus test for determining whether the architecture decision should be made in the first place. If a particular architecture decision does not provide any business value, then perhaps it is not a good decision and should be reconsidered.

Four of the most common business justifications include cost, time to market, user satisfaction, and strategic positioning. When focusing on these common business justifications, it is important to take into consideration what is important to the business stakeholders. Justifying a particular decision based on cost savings alone might not be the right decision if the business stakeholders are less concerned about cost and more concerned about time to market.

Email-Driven Architecture Anti-Pattern

Once an architect makes decisions and fully justifies those decisions, a third architecture anti-pattern emerges: *Email-Driven Architecture*. The Email-Driven Architecture anti-pattern is where people lose, forget, or don't even know an architecture decision has been made and therefore cannot possibly implement that architecture decision. This anti-pattern is all about effectively communicating your architecture decisions. Email is a great tool for communication, but it makes a poor document repository system.

There are many ways to increase the effectiveness of communicating architecture decisions, thereby avoiding the Email-Driven Architecture anti-pattern. The first rule of communicating architecture decisions is to not include the architecture decision in the body of an email. Including the architecture decision in the body of the email creates multiple systems of record for that decision. Many times important details (including the justification) are left out of the email, therefore creating the Groundhog Day anti-pattern all over again. Also, if that architecture decision is ever changed or superseded, how may people received the revised decision? A better approach is to mention only the nature and context of the decision in the body of the email and provide a link to the single system of record for the actual architecture decision and corresponding details (whether it be a link to a wiki page or a document in a filesystem).

The second rule of effectively communicating architecture decisions is to only notify those people who really care about the architecture decision. One effective technique is to write the body of the email as follows:

"Hi Sandra, I've made an important decision regarding communication between services that directly impacts you. Please see the decision using the following link…"

Notice the phrasing in the first sentence: "important decision regarding communication between services." Here, the context of the decision is mentioned, but not the actual decision itself. The second part of the first sentence is even more important: "that directly impacts you." If an architectural decision doesn't directly impact the person, then why bother that person with your architecture decision? This is a great litmus test for determining which stakeholders (including developers) should be notified directly of an architecture decision. The second sentence provides a link to the location of the architecture decision so it is located in only one place, hence a single system of record for the decision.

Architecturally Significant

Many architects believe that if the architecture decision involves any specific technology, then it's not an architecture decision, but rather a technical decision. This is not always true. If an architect makes a decision to use a particular technology because it directly supports a particular architecture characteristic (such as performance or scalability), then it's an architecture decision.

Michael Nygard (*https://www.michaelnygard.com*), a well-known software architect and author of *Release It!* (Pragmatic Bookshelf), addressed the problem of what decisions an architect should be responsible for (and hence what is an architecture decision) by coining the term *architecturally significant*. According to Michael, architecturally significant decisions are those decisions that affect the structure, nonfunctional characteristics, dependencies, interfaces, or construction techniques.

The *structure* refers to decisions that impact the patterns or styles of architecture being used. An example of this is the decision to share data between a set of microservices. This decision impacts the bounded context of the microservice, and as such affects the structure of the application.

The *nonfunctional characteristics* are the architecture characteristics ("-ilities") that are important for the application or system being developed or maintained. If a choice of technology impacts performance, and performance is an important aspect of the application, then it becomes an architecture decision.

Dependencies refer to coupling points between components and/or services within the system, which in turn impact overall scalability, modularity, agility, testability, reliability, and so on.

Interfaces refer to how services and components are accessed and orchestrated, usually through a gateway, integration hub, service bus, or API proxy. Interfaces usually involve defining contracts, including the versioning and deprecation strategy of those contracts. Interfaces impact others using the system and hence are architecturally significant.

Finally, *construction techniques* refer to decisions about platforms, frameworks, tools, and even processes that, although technical in nature, might impact some aspect of the architecture.

Architecture Decision Records

One of the most effective ways of documenting architecture decisions is through *Architecture Decision Records* (ADRs (*https://adr.github.io*)). ADRs were first evangelized by Michael Nygard in a blog post (*https://oreil.ly/yDcU2*) and later marked as "adopt" in the ThoughtWorks Technology Radar (*https://oreil.ly/0nwHw*). An ADR consists of a short text file (usually one to two pages long) describing a specific architecture decision. While ADRs can be written using plain text, they are usually written in some sort of text document format like AsciiDoc (*http://asciidoc.org*) or Markdown (*https://www.markdownguide.org*). Alternatively, an ADR can also be written using a wiki page template.

Tooling is also available for managing ADRs. Nat Pryce, coauthor of *Growing Object-Oriented Software Guided by Tests* (Addison-Wesley), has written an open source tool for ADRs called ADR-tools (*https://oreil.ly/6d8LN*). ADR-tools provides a command-line interface to manage ADRs, including the numbering schemes, locations, and superseded logic. Micha Kops, a software engineer from Germany, has written a blog post (*https://oreil.ly/OgBZK*) about using ADR-tools that provides some great examples on how they can be used to manage architecture decision records.

Basic Structure

The basic structure of an ADR consists of five main sections: *Title*, *Status*, *Context*, *Decision*, and *Consequences*. We usually add two additional sections as part of the basic structure: *Compliance* and *Notes*. This basic structure (as illustrated in Figure 19-1) can be extended to include any other section deemed needed, providing the template is kept both consistent and concise. A good example of this might be to add an *Alternatives* section if necessary to provide an analysis of all the other possible alternative solutions.

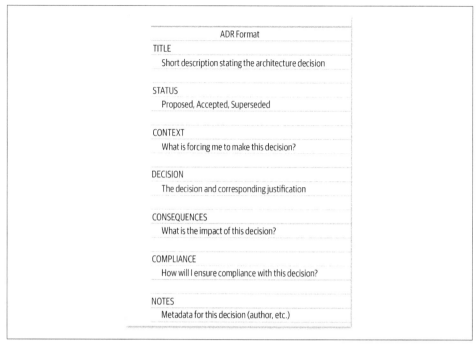

Figure 19-1. Basic ADR structure

Title

The title of an ADR is usually numbered sequentially and contains a short phrase describing the architecture decisions. For example, the decision to use asynchronous messaging between the Order Service and the Payment Service might read: "42. Use of Asynchronous Messaging Between Order and Payment Services." The title should be descriptive enough to remove any ambiguity about the nature and context of the decision but at the same time be short and concise.

Status

The status of an ADR can be marked as *Proposed*, *Accepted*, or *Superseded*. *Proposed* status means the decision must be approved by either a higher-level decision maker or some sort of architectural governance body (such as an architecture review board). *Accepted* status means the decision has been approved and is ready for implementation. A status of *Superseded* means the decision has been changed and superseded by another ADR. Superseded status always assumes the prior ADR status was accepted; in other words, a proposed ADR would never be superseded by another ADR, but rather continued to be modified until accepted.

The Superseded status is a powerful way of keeping a historical record of what decisions were made, why they were made at that time, and what the new decision is and why it was changed. Usually, when an ADR has been superseded, it is marked with the decision that superseded it. Similarly, the decision that supersedes another ADR is marked with the ADR it superseded. For example, assume ADR 42 ("Use of Asynchronous Messaging Between Order and Payment Services") was previously approved, but due to later changes to the implementation and location of the Payment Service, REST must now be used between the two services (ADR 68). The status would look as follows:

> ADR 42. *Use of Asynchronous Messaging Between Order and Payment Services*
>
> Status: Superseded by 68
>
> ADR 68. *Use of REST Between Order and Payment Services*
>
> Status: Accepted, supersedes 42

The link and history trail between ADRs 42 and 68 avoid the inevitable "what about using messaging?" question regarding ADR 68.

ADRs and Request for Comments (RFC)

If an architect wishes to send out a draft ADR for comments (which is sometimes a good idea when the architect wants to validate various assumptions and assertions with a larger audience of stakeholders), we recommend creating a new status named *Request for Comments* (or *RFC*) and specify a deadline date when that review would be complete. This practice avoids the inevitable Analysis Paralysis anti-pattern where the decision is forever discussed but never actually made. Once that date is reached, the architect can analyze all the comments made on the ADR, make any necessary adjustments to the decision, make the final decision, and set the status to Proposed (unless the architect is able to approve the decision themselves, in which case the status would then be set to Accepted). An example of an RFC status for an ADR would look as follows:

STATUS
Request For Comments, Deadline 09 JAN 2010

Another significant aspect of the Status section of an ADR is that it forces an architect to have necessary conversations with their boss or lead architect about the criteria with which they can approve an architecture decision on their own, or whether it must be approved through a higher-level architect, an architecture review board, or some other architecture governing body.

Three criteria that form a good start for these conversations are cost, cross-team impact, and security. Cost can include software purchase or licensing fees, additional hardware costs, as well as the overall level of effort to implement the architecture decision. Level of effort costs can be estimated by multiplying the estimated number of hours to implement the architecture decision by the company's standard *Full-Time Equivalency* (FTE) rate. The project owner or project manager usually has the FTE amount. If the cost of the architecture decision exceeds a certain amount, then it must be set to Proposed status and approved by someone else. If the architecture decision impacts other teams or systems or has any sort of security implication, then it cannot be self-approved by the architect and must be approved by a higher-level governing body or lead architect.

Once the criteria and corresponding limits have been established and agreed upon (such as "costs exceeding €5,000 must be approved by the architecture review board"), this criteria should be well documented so that all architects creating ADRs know when they can and cannot approve their own architecture decisions.

Context

The context section of an ADR specifies the forces at play. In other words, "what situation is forcing me to make this decision?" This section of the ADR allows the architect to describe the specific situation or issue and concisely elaborate on the possible alternatives. If an architect is required to document the analysis of each alternative in detail, then an additional Alternatives section can be added to the ADR rather than adding that analysis to the Context section.

The Context section also provides a way to document the architecture. By describing the context, the architect is also describing the architecture. This is an effective way of documenting a specific area of the architecture in a clear and concise manner. Continuing with the example from the prior section, the context might read as follows: "The order service must pass information to the payment service to pay for an order currently being placed. This could be done using REST or asynchronous messaging." Notice that this concise statement not only specified the scenario, but also the alternatives.

Decision

The Decision section of the ADR contains the architecture decision, along with a full justification for the decision. Michael Nygard introduced a great way of stating an architecture decision by using a very affirmative, commanding voice rather than a passive one. For example, the decision to use asynchronous messaging between services would read "*we will use* asynchronous messaging between services." This is a much better way of stating a decision as opposed to "*I think* asynchronous messaging between services would be the best choice." Notice here it is not clear what the decision is or even if a decision has even been made—only the opinion of the architect is stated.

Perhaps one of the most powerful aspects of the Decision section of ADRs is that it allows an architect to place more emphasis on the *why* rather than the *how*. Understanding why a decision was made is far more important than understanding how something works. Most architects and developers can identify how things work by looking at context diagrams, but not why a decision was made. Knowing why a decision was made and the corresponding justification for the decision helps people better understand the context of the problem and avoids possible mistakes through refactoring to another solution that might produce issues.

To illustrate this point, consider an original architecture decision several years ago to use Google's Remote Procedure Call (gRPC (*https://www.grpc.io*)) as a means to communicate between two services. Without understanding why that decision was made, another architect several years later makes the choice to override that decision and use messaging instead to better decouple the services. However, implementing this refactoring suddenly causes a significant increase in latency, which in turn ultimately causes time outs to occur in upstream systems. Understanding that the original use of gRPC was to significantly reduce latency (at the cost of tightly coupled services) would have prevented the refactoring from happening in the first place.

Consequences

The Consequences section of an ADR is another very powerful section. This section documents the overall impact of an architecture decision. Every architecture decision an architect makes has some sort of impact, both good and bad. Having to specify the impact of an architecture decision forces the architect to think about whether those impacts outweigh the benefits of the decision.

Another good use of this section is to document the trade-off analysis associated with the architecture decision. These trade-offs could be cost-based or trade-offs against other architecture characteristics ("-ilities"). For example, consider the decision to use asynchronous (fire-and-forget) messaging to post a review on a website. The justification for this decision is to significantly increase the responsiveness of the post review request from 3,100 milliseconds to 25 milliseconds because users would not need to wait for the actual review to be posted (only for the message to be sent to a queue). While this is a good justification, someone else might argue that this is a bad idea due to the complexity of the error handling associated with an asynchronous request ("what happens if someone posts a review with some bad words?"). Unknown to the person challenging this decision, that issue was already discussed with the business stakeholders and other architects, and it was decided from a trade-off perspective that it was more important to have the increase in responsiveness and deal with the complex error handling rather than have the wait time to synchronously provide feedback to the user that the review was successfully posted. By leveraging ADRs, that trade-off analysis can be included in the Consequences section, providing a complete picture of the context (and trade-offs) of the architecture decision and thus avoiding these situations.

Compliance

The compliance section of an ADR is not one of the standard sections in an ADR, but it's one we highly recommend adding. The Compliance section forces the architect to think about how the architecture decision will be measured and governed from a compliance perspective. The architect must decide whether the compliance check for this decision must be manual or if it can be automated using a fitness function. If it can be automated using a fitness function, the architect can then specify in this section how that fitness function would be written and whether there are any other changes to the code base are needed to measure this architecture decision for compliance.

For example, consider the following architecture decision within a traditional n-tiered layered architecture as illustrated in Figure 19-2. All shared objects used by business objects in the business layer will reside in the shared services layer to isolate and contain shared functionality.

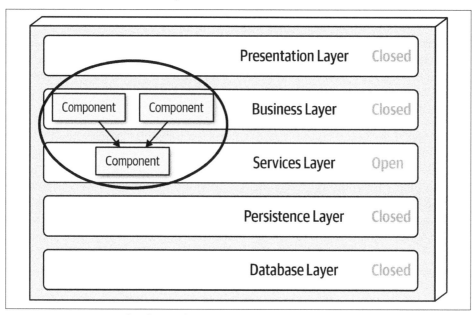

Figure 19-2. An example of an architecture decision

This architecture decision can be measured and governed automatically by using either ArchUnit (*https://www.archunit.org*) in Java or NetArchTest (*https://oreil.ly/0J5fN*) in C#. For example, using ArchUnit in Java, the automated fitness function test might look as follows:

```
@Test
public void shared_services_should_reside_in_services_layer() {
    classes().that().areAnnotatedWith(SharedService.class)
        .should().resideInAPackage("..services..")
        .because("All shared services classes used by business " +
                "objects in the business layer should reside in the services " +
                "layer to isolate and contain shared logic")
        .check(myClasses);
}
```

Notice that this automated fitness function would require new stories to be written to create a new Java annotation (`@SharedService`) and to then add this annotation to all shared classes. This section also specifies what the test is, where the test can be found, and how the test will be executed and when.

Notes

Another section that is not part of a standard ADR but that we highly recommend adding is the Notes section. This section includes various metadata about the ADR, such as the following:

- Original author
- Approval date
- Approved by
- Superseded date
- Last modified date
- Modified by
- Last modification

Even when storing ADRs in a version control system (such as Git), additional meta-information is useful beyond what the repository can support, so we recommend adding this section regardless of how and where ADRs are stored.

Storing ADRs

Once an architect creates an ADR, it must be stored somewhere. Regardless of where ADRs are stored, each architecture decision should have its own file or wiki page. Some architects like to keep ADRs in the Git repository with the source code. Keeping ADRs in a Git repository allows the ADR to be versioned and tracked as well. However, for larger organizations we caution against this practice for several reasons. First, everyone who needs to see the architecture decision may not have access to the Git repository. Second, this is not a good place to store ADRs that have a context outside of the application Git repository (such as integration architecture decisions, enterprise architecture decisions, or those decisions common to every application).

For these reasons we recommend storing ADRs either in a wiki (using a wiki template) or in a shared directory on a shared file server that can be accessed easily by a wiki or other document rendering software. Figure 19-3 shows an example of what this directory structure (or wiki page navigation structure) might look like.

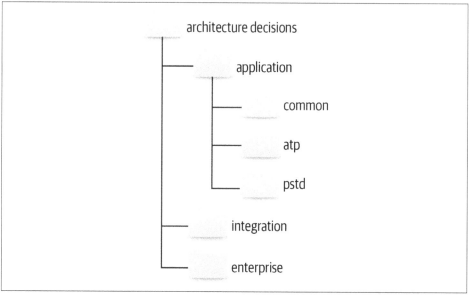

Figure 19-3. Example directory structure for storing ADRs

The *application* directory contains those architecture decisions that are specific to some sort of application context. This directory is subdivided into further directories. The *common* subdirectory is for architecture decisions that apply to all applications, such as "All framework-related classes will contain an annotation (@Framework in Java) or attribute ([Framework] in C#) identifying the class as belonging to the underlying framework code." Subdirectories under the *application* directory correspond to the specific application or system context and contain the architecture decisions specific to that application or system (in this example, the ATP and PSTD applications). The *integration* directory contains those ADRs that involve the communication between application, systems, or services. Enterprise architecture ADRs are contained within the *enterprise* directory, indicating that these are global architecture decisions impacting all systems and applications. An example of an enterprise architecture ADR would be "All access to a system database will only be from the owning system," thus preventing the sharing of databases across multiple systems.

When storing ADRs in a wiki (our recommendation), the same structure previously described applies, with each directory structure representing a navigational landing page. Each ADR would be represented as a single wiki page within each navigational landing page (Application, Integration, or Enterprise).

The directory or landing page names indicated in this section are only a recommendation. Each company can choose whatever names fit their situation, as long as those names are consistent across teams.

ADRs as Documentation

Documenting software architecture has always been a difficult topic. While some standards are emerging for diagramming architecture (such as software architect Simon Brown's C4 Model (*https://c4model.com*) or The Open Group ArchiMate (*https://oreil.ly/gbNQG*) standard), no such standard exists for documenting software architecture. That's where ADRs come in.

Architecture Decision Records can be used an an effective means to document a software architecture. The Context section of an ADR provides an excellent opportunity to describe the specific area of the system that requires an architecture decision to be made. This section also provides an opportunity to describe the alternatives. Perhaps more important is that the Decision section describes the reasons why a particular decision is made, which is by far the best form of architecture documentation. The Consequences section adds the final piece to the architecture documentation by describing additional aspects of a particular decision, such as the trade-off analysis of choosing performance over scalability.

Using ADRs for Standards

Very few people like standards. Most times standards seem to be in place more for controlling people and the way they do things than anything useful. Using ADRs for standards can change this bad practice. For example, the Context section of an ADR describes the situation that is forcing the particular standard. The Decision section of an ADR can be used to not only indicate what the standard is, but more importantly why the standard needs to exist. This is a wonderful way of being able to qualify whether the particular standard should even exist in the first place. If an architect cannot justify the standard, then perhaps it is not a good standard to make and enforce. Furthermore, the more developers understand why a particular standard exists, the more likely they are to follow it (and correspondingly not challenge it). The Consequences section of an ADR is another great place an architect can qualify whether a standard is valid and should be made. In this section the architect must think about and document what the implications and consequences are of a particular standard they are making. By analyzing the consequences, the architect might decide that the standard should not be applied after all.

Example

Many architecture decisions exist within our ongoing "Case Study: Going, Going, Gone" on page 95. The use of event-driven microservices, the splitting up of the bidder and auctioneer user interfaces, the use of the Real-time Transport Protocol (RTP) for video capture, the use of a single API layer, and the use of publish-and-subscribe messaging are just a few of the dozens of architecture decisions that are made for this auction system. Every architecture decision made in a system, no matter how obvious, should be documented and justified.

Figure 19-4 illustrates one of the architecture decisions within the Going, Going, Gone auction system, which is the use of publish-and-subscribe (pub/sub) messaging between the bid capture, bid streamer, and bid tracker services.

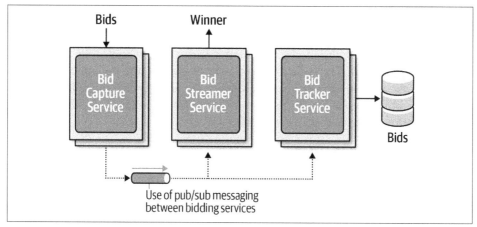

Figure 19-4. Use of pub/sub between services

The ADR for this architecture decision might look simliar to Figure 19-5:

ADR 76. Asynchronous Pub/Sub Messaging Between Bidding Services

STATUS
Accepted

CONTEXT
The Bid Capture Service, upon receiving a bid from an online bidder or from a live bidder via the auctioneer, must forward that bid onto the Bid Streamer Service and the Bidder Tracker Service. This could be done using asynchronous point-to-point (p2p) messaging, asynchronous publish-and-subscribe (pub/sub) messaging, or REST via the Online Auction API Layer.

DECISION
We will use asynchronous pub/sub messaging between the Bid Capture Service, Bid Streamer Service, and the Bidder Tracker Service.

The Bid Capture Service does not need any information back from the Bid Streamer Service or Bidder Tracker Service.

The Bid Streamer Service must receive bids in the exact order they were accepted by the Bid Capture Service. Using messaging and queues automatically guarantees the bid order for the stream.

Using async pub/sub messaging will increase the performance of the bidding process and allow for extensibility of bidding information.

CONSEQUENCES
We will require clustering and high availability of the message queues.

Internal bid events will be bypassing security checks done in the API layer.

UPDATE: Upon review at the April 14th, 2020 ARB meeting, the ARB decided that this was an acceptable trade-off and no additional security checks would be needed for bid events between these services.

COMPLIANCE
We will use periodic manual code and design reviews to ensure that asynchronous pub/sub messaging is being used between the Bid Capture Service, Bid Streamer Service, and the Bidder Tracker Service.

NOTES
Author: Subashini Nadella
Approved By: ARB Meeting Members, 14 APRIL 2020
Last Updated: 15 APRIL 2020 by Subashini Nadella

Figure 19-5. ADR 76. Asynchronous Pub/Sub Messaging Between Bidding Services

CHAPTER 20

Analyzing Architecture Risk

Every architecture has risk associated with it, whether it be risk involving availability, scalability, or data integrity. Analyzing architecture risk is one of the key activities of architecture. By continually analyzing risk, the architect can address deficiencies within the architecture and take corrective action to mitigate the risk. In this chapter we introduce some of the key techniques and practices for qualifying risk, creating risk assessments, and identifying risk through an activity called *risk storming*.

Risk Matrix

The first issue that arises when assessing architecture risk is determining whether the risk should be classified as low, medium, or high. Too much subjectiveness usually enters into this classification, creating confusion about which parts of the architecture are really high risk versus medium risk. Fortunately, there is a risk matrix architects can leverage to help reduce the level of subjectiveness and qualify the risk associated with a particular area of the architecture.

The architecture risk matrix (illustrated in Figure 20-1) uses two dimensions to qualify risk: the overall impact of the risk and the likelihood of that risk occurring. Each dimensions has a low (1), medium (2), and high (3) rating. These numbers are multiplied together within each grid of the matrix, providing an objective numerical number representing that risk. Numbers 1 and 2 are considered low risk (green), numbers 3 and 4 are considered medium risk (yellow), and numbers 6 through 9 are considered high risk (red).

	Likelihood of risk occurring		
	Low (1)	Medium (2)	High (3)
Overall impact of risk — Low (1)	1	2	3
Overall impact of risk — Medium (2)	2	4	6
Overall impact of risk — High (3)	3	6	9

Figure 20-1. Matrix for determining architecture risk

To see how the risk matrix can be used, suppose there is a concern about availability with regard to a primary central database used in the application. First, consider the impact dimension—what is the overall impact if the database goes down or becomes unavailable? Here, an architect might deem that high risk, making that risk either a 3 (medium), 6 (high), or 9 (high). However, after applying the second dimension (likelihood of risk occurring), the architect realizes that the database is on highly available servers in a clustered configuration, so the likelihood is low that the database would become unavailable. Therefore, the intersection between the high impact and low likelihood gives an overall risk rating of 3 (medium risk).

When leveraging the risk matrix to qualify the risk, consider the impact dimension first and the likelihood dimension second.

Risk Assessments

The risk matrix described in the previous section can be used to build what is called a *risk assessment*. A risk assessment is a summarized report of the overall risk of an architecture with respect to some sort of contextual and meaningful assessment criteria.

Risk assessments can vary greatly, but in general they contain the risk (qualified from the risk matrix) of some *assessment criteria* based on services or domain areas of an application. This basic risk assessment report format is illustrated in Figure 20-2, where light gray (1-2) is low risk, medium gray (3-4) is medium risk, and dark gray (6-9) is high risk. Usually these are color-coded as green (low), yellow (medium), and red (high), but shading can be useful for black-and-white rendering and for color blindness.

RISK CRITERIA	Customer registration	Catalog checkout	Order fulfillment	Order shipment	TOTAL RISK
Scalability	2	6	1	2	11
Availability	3	4	2	1	10
Performance	4	2	3	6	15
Security	6	3	1	1	11
Data integrity	9	6	1	1	17
TOTAL RISK	24	21	8	11	

Figure 20-2. Example of a standard risk assessment

The quantified risk from the risk matrix can be accumulated by the risk criteria and also by the service or domain area. For example, notice in Figure 20-2 that the accumulated risk for data integrity is the highest risk area at a total of 17, whereas the accumulated risk for Availability is only 10 (the least amount of risk). The relative risk of each domain area can also be determined by the example risk assessment. Here, customer registration carries the highest area of risk, whereas order fulfillment carries the lowest risk. These relative numbers can then be tracked to demonstrate either improvements or degradation of risk within a particular risk category or domain area.

Although the risk assessment example in Figure 20-2 contains all the risk analysis results, rarely is it presented as such. Filtering is essential for visually indicating a particular message within a given context. For example, suppose an architect is in a meeting for the purpose of presenting areas of the system that are high risk. Rather than presenting the risk assessment as illustrated in Figure 20-2, filtering can be used to only show the high risk areas (shown in Figure 20-3), improving the overall signal-to-noise ratio and presenting a clear picture of the state of the system (good or bad).

RISK CRITERIA	Customer registration	Catalog checkout	Order fulfillment	Order shipment	TOTAL RISK
Scalability		(6)			6
Availability					0
Performance				(6)	6
Security	(6)				6
Data integrity	(9)	(6)			15
TOTAL RISK	15	12	0	6	

Figure 20-3. Filtering the risk assessment to only high risk

Another issue with Figure 20-2 is that this assessment report only shows a snapshot in time; it does not show whether things are improving or getting worse. In other words, Figure 20-2 does not show the direction of risk. Rendering the direction of risk presents somewhat of an issue. If an up or down arrow were to be used to indicate direction, what would an up arrow mean? Are things getting better or worse? We've spent years asking people if an up arrow meant things were getting better or worse, and almost 50% of people asked said that the up arrow meant things were progressively getting worse, whereas almost 50% said an up arrow indicated things were getting better. The same is true for left and right arrows. For this reason, when using arrows to indicate direction, a key must be used. However, we've also found this doesn't work either. Once the user scrolls beyond the key, confusion happens once again.

We usually use the universal direction symbol of a plus (+) and minus (-) sign next to the risk rating to indicate direction, as illustrated in Figure 20-4. Notice in Figure 20-4 that although performance for customer registration is medium (4), the direction is a minus sign (red), indicating that it is progressively getting worse and heading toward high risk. On the other hand, notice that scalability of catalog checkout is high (6) with a plus sign (green), showing that it is improving. Risk ratings without a plus or minus sign indicate that the risk is stable and neither getting better nor worse.

RISK CRITERIA	Customer registration	Catalog checkout	Order fulfillment	Order shipment	TOTAL RISK
Scalability	②	⑥ +	①	②	11
Availability	③	④	② −	①	10
Performance	④ −	② +	③ −	⑥ +	15
Security	⑥ −	③	①	①	11
Data integrity	⑨ +	⑥ −	① −	①	17
TOTAL RISK	24	21	8	11	

Figure 20-4. Showing direction of risk with plus and minus signs

Occasionally, even the plus and minus signs can be confusing to some people. Another technique for indicating direction is to leverage an arrow along with the risk rating number it is trending toward. This technique, as illustrated in Figure 20-5, does not require a key because the direction is clear. Furthermore, the use of colors (red arrow for worse, green arrow for better) makes it even more clear where the risk is heading.

RISK CRITERIA	Customer registration	Catalog checkout	Order fulfillment	Order shipment	TOTAL RISK
Scalability	②	⑥ ↑4	①	②	11
Availability	③	④	② ↓3	①	10
Performance	④ ↓6	② ↑1	③ ↓4	⑥ ↑4	15
Security	⑥ ↓9	③	①	①	11
Data integrity	⑨ ↑6	⑥ ↓9	① ↓2	①	17
TOTAL RISK	24	21	8	11	

Figure 20-5. Showing direction of risk with arrows and numbers

The direction of risk can be determined by using continuous measurements through fitness functions described earlier in the book. By objectively analyzing each risk criteria, trends can be observed, providing the direction of each risk criteria.

Risk Storming

No architect can single-handedly determine the overall risk of a system. The reason for this is two-fold. First, a single architect might miss or overlook a risk area, and very few architects have full knowledge of every part of the system. This is where *risk storming* can help.

Risk storming is a collaborative exercise used to determine architectural risk within a specific dimension. Common dimensions (areas of risk) include unproven technology, performance, scalability, availability (including transitive dependencies), data loss, single points of failure, and security. While most risk storming efforts involve multiple architects, it is wise to include senior developers and tech leads as well. Not only will they provide an implementation perspective to the architectural risk, but involving developers helps them gain a better understanding of the architecture.

The risk storming effort involves both an individual part and a collaborative part. In the individual part, all participants individually (without collaboration) assign risk to areas of the architecture using the risk matrix described in the previous section. This noncollaborative part of risk storming is essential so that participants don't influence or direct attention away from particular areas of the architecture. In the collaborative part of risk storming, all participants work together to gain consensus on risk areas, discuss risk, and form solutions for mitigating the risk.

An architecture diagram is used for both parts of the risk storming effort. For holistic risk assessments, usually a comprehensive architecture diagram is used, whereas risk storming within specific areas of the application would use a contextual architecture diagram. It is the responsibility of the architect conducting the risk storming effort to make sure these diagrams are up to date and available to all participants.

Figure 20-6 shows an example architecture we'll use to illustrate the risk storming process. In this architecture, an Elastic Load Balancer fronts each EC2 instance containing the web servers (Nginx) and application services. The application services make calls to a MySQL database, a Redis cache, and a MongoDB database for logging. They also make calls to the Push Expansion Servers. The expansion servers, in turn, all interface with the MySQL database, Redis cache, and MongoDB logging facility.

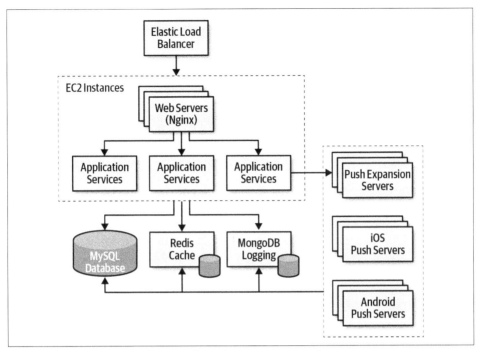

Figure 20-6. Architecture diagram for risk storming example

Risk storming is broken down into three primary activities:

1. Identification
2. Consensus
3. Mitigation

Identification is always an individual, noncollaborative activity, whereas consensus and mitigation are always collaborative and involve all participants working together in the same room (at least virtually). Each of these primary activities is discussed in detail in the following sections.

Identification

The *identification* activity of risk storming involves each participant individually identifying areas of risk within the architecture. The following steps describe the identification part of the risk storming effort:

1. The architect conducting the risk storming sends out an invitation to all participants one to two days prior to the collaborative part of the effort. The invitation
   contains the architecture diagram (or the location of where to find it), the risk

storming dimension (area of risk being analyzed for that particular risk storming effort), the date when the collaborative part of risk storming will take place, and the location.

2. Using the risk matrix described in the first section of this chapter, participants individually analyze the architecture and classify the risk as low (1-2), medium (3-4), or high (6-9).

3. Participants prepare small Post-it notes with corresponding colors (green, yellow, and red) and write down the corresponding risk number (found on the risk matrix).

Most risk storming efforts only involve analyzing one particular dimension (such as performance), but there might be times, due to the availability of staff or timing issues, when multiple dimensions are analyzed within a single risk storming effort (such as performance, scalability, and data loss). When multiple dimensions are analyzed within a single risk storming effort, the participants write the dimension next to the risk number on the Post-it notes so that everyone is aware of the specific dimension. For example, suppose three participants found risk within the central database. All three identified the risk as high (6), but one participant found risk with respect to availability, whereas two participants found risk with respect to performance. These two dimensions would be discussed separately.

 Whenever possible, restrict risk storming efforts to a single dimension. This allows participants to focus their attention to that specific dimension and avoids confusion about multiple risk areas being identified for the same area of the architecture.

Consensus

The *consensus* activity in the risk storming effort is highly collaborative with the goal of gaining consensus among all participants regarding the risk within the architecture. This activity is most effective when a large, printed version of the architecture diagram is available and posted on the wall. In lieu of a large printed version, an electronic version can be displayed on a large screen.

Upon arrival at the risk storming session, participants begin placing their Post-it notes on the architecture diagram in the area where they individually found risk. If an electronic version is used, the architect conducting the risk storming session queries every participant and electronically places the risk on the diagram in the area of the architecture where the risk was identified (see Figure 20-7).

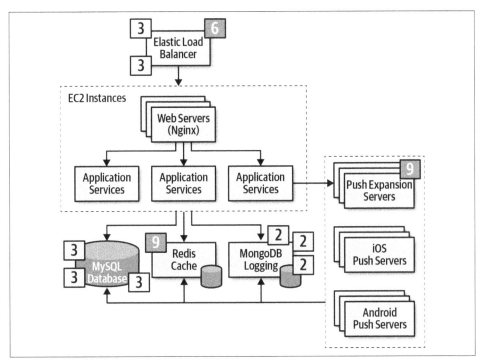

Figure 20-7. Initial identification of risk areas

Once all of the Post-it notes are in place, the collaborative part of risk storming can begin. The goal of this activity of risk storming is to analyze the risk areas as a team and gain consensus in terms of the risk qualification. Notice several areas of risk were identified in the architecture, illustrated in Figure 20-7:

1. Two participants individually identified the Elastic Load Balancer as medium risk (3), whereas one participant identified it as high risk (6).

2. One participant individually identified the Push Expansion Servers as high risk (9).

3. Three participants individually identified the MySQL database as medium risk (3).

4. One participant individually identified the Redis cache as high risk (9).

5. Three participants identified MongoDB logging as low risk (2).

6. All other areas of the architecture were not deemed to carry any risk, hence there are no Post-it notes on any other areas of the architecture.

Items 3 and 5 in the prior list do not need further discussion in this activity since all participants agreed on the level and qualification of risk. However, notice there was a difference of opinion in item 1 in the list, and items 2 and 4 only had a single participant identifying the risk. These items need to be discussed during this activity.

Item 1 in the list showed that two participants individually identified the Elastic Load Balancer as medium risk (3), whereas one participant identified it as high risk (6). In this case the other two participants ask the third participant why they identified the risk as high. Suppose the third participant says that they assigned the risk as high because if the Elastic Load Balancer goes down, the entire system cannot be accessed. While this is true and in fact does bring the overall impact rating to high, the other two participants convince the third participant that there is low risk of this happening. After much discussion, the third participant agrees, bringing that risk level down to a medium (3). However, the first and second participants might not have seen a particular aspect of risk in the Elastic Load Balancer that the third did, hence the need for collaboration within this activity of risk storming.

Case in point, consider item 2 in the prior list where one participant individually identified the Push Expansion Servers as high risk (9), whereas no other participant identified them as any risk at all. In this case, all other participants ask the participant who identified the risk why they rated it as high. That participant then says that they have had bad experiences with the Push Expansion Servers continually going down under high load, something this particular architecture has. This example shows the value of risk storming—without that participant's involvement, no one would have seen the high risk (until well into production of course!).

Item 4 in the list is an interesting case. One participant identified the Redis cache as high risk (9), whereas no other participant saw that cache as any risk in the architecture. The other participants ask what the rationale is for the high risk in that area, and the one participant responds with, "What is a Redis cache?" In this case, Redis was unknown to the participant, hence the high risk in that area.

 For unproven or unknown technologies, always assign the highest risk rating (9) since the risk matrix cannot be used for this dimension.

The example of item 4 in the list illustrates why it is wise (and important) to bring developers into risk storming sessions. Not only can developers learn more about the architecture, but the fact that one participant (who was in this case a developer on the team) didn't know a given technology provides the architect with valuable information regarding overall risk.

This process continues until all participants agree on the risk areas identified. Once all the Post-it notes are consolidated, this activity ends, and the next one can begin. The final outcome of this activity is shown in Figure 20-8.

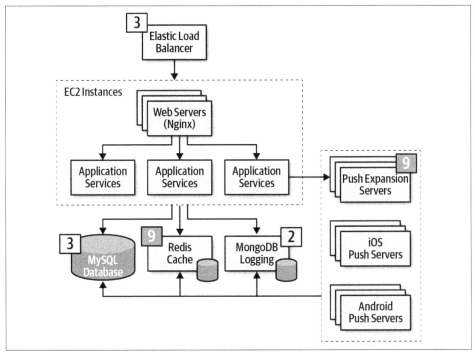

Figure 20-8. Consensus of risk areas

Mitigation

Once all participants agree on the qualification of the risk areas of the architecture, the final and most important activity occurs—*risk mitigation*. Mitigating risk within an architecture usually involves changes or enhancements to certain areas of the architecture that otherwise might have been deemed perfect the way they were.

This activity, which is also usually collaborative, seeks ways to reduce or eliminate the risk identified in the first activity. There may be cases where the original architecture needs to be completely changed based on the identification of risk, whereas others might be a straightforward architecture refactoring, such as adding a queue for back pressure to reduce a throughput bottleneck issue.

Regardless of the changes required in the architecture, this activity usually incurs additional cost. For that reason, key stakeholders typically decide whether the cost outweighs the risk. For example, suppose that through a risk storming session the central database was identified as being medium risk (4) with regard to overall system availability. In this case, the participants agreed that clustering the database, combined with breaking the single database into separate physical databases, would mitigate that risk. However, while risk would be significantly reduced, this solution would cost $20,000. The architect would then conduct a meeting with the key business stakeholder to discuss this trade-off. During this negotiation, the business owner decides that the price tag is too high and that the cost does not outweigh the risk. Rather than giving up, the architect then suggests a different approach—what about skipping the clustering and splitting the database into two parts? The cost in this case is reduced to $8,000 while still mitigating most of the risk. In this case, the stakeholder agrees to the solution.

The previous scenario shows the impact risk storming can have not only on the overall architecture, but also with regard to negotiations between architects and business stakeholders. Risk storming, combined with the risk assessments described at the start of this chapter, provide an excellent vehicle for identifying and tracking risk, improving the architecture, and handling negotiations between key stakeholders.

Agile Story Risk Analysis

Risk storming can be used for other aspects of software development besides just architecture. For example, we've leveraged risk storming for determining overall risk of user story completion within a given Agile iteration (and consequently the overall risk assessment of that iteration) during story grooming. Using the risk matrix, user story risk can be identified by the first dimension (the overall impact if the story is not completed within the iteration) and the second dimension (the likelihood that the story will not be completed). By utilizing the same architecture risk matrix for stories, teams can identify stories of high risk, track those carefully, and prioritize them.

Risk Storming Examples

To illustrate the power of risk storming and how it can improve the overall architecture of a system, consider the example of a call center system to support nurses advising patients on various health conditions. The requirements for such a system are as follows:

- The system will use a third-party diagnostics engine that serves up questions and guides the nurses or patients regarding their medical issues.

- Patients can either call in using the call center to speak to a nurse or choose to use a self-service website that accesses the diagnostic engine directly, bypassing the nurses.

- The system must support 250 concurrent nurses nationwide and up to hundreds of thousands of concurrent self-service patients nationwide.

- Nurses can access patients' medical records through a medical records exchange, but patients cannot access their own medical records.
- The system must be HIPAA compliant with regard to the medical records. This means that it is essential that no one but nurses have access to medical records.
- Outbreaks and high volume during cold and flu season need to be addressed in the system.
- Call routing to nurses is based on the nurse's profile (such as bilingual needs).
- The third-party diagnostic engine can handle about 500 requests a second.

The architect of the system created the high-level architecture illustrated in Figure 20-9. In this architecture there are three separate web-based user interfaces: one for self-service, one for nurses receiving calls, and one for administrative staff to add and maintain the nursing profile and configuration settings. The call center portion of the system consists of a call accepter which receives calls and the call router which routes calls to the next available nurse based on their profile (notice how the call router accesses the central database to get nurse profile information). Central to this architecture is a diagnostics system API gateway, which performs security checks and directs the request to the appropriate backend service.

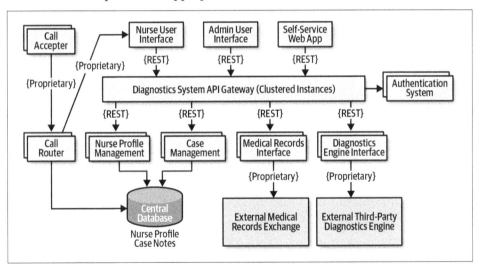

Figure 20-9. High-level architecture for nurse diagnostics system example

There are four main services in this system: a case management service, a nurse profile management service, an interface to the medical records exchange, and the external third-party diagnostics engine. All communications are using REST with the exception of proprietary protocols to the external systems and call center services.

The architect has reviewed this architecture numerous times and believes it is ready for implementation. As a self-assessment, study the requirements and the architecture diagram in Figure 20-9 and try to determine the level of risk within this architecture in terms of availability, elasticity, and security. After determining the level of risk, then determine what changes would be needed in the architecture to mitigate that risk. The sections that follow contain scenarios that can be used as a comparison.

Availability

During the first risk storming exercise, the architect chose to focus on availability first since system availability is critical for the success of this system. After the risk storming identification and collaboration activities, the participants came up with the following risk areas using the risk matrix (as illustrated in Figure 20-10):

- The use of a central database was identified as high risk (6) due to high impact (3) and medium likelihood (2).

- The diagnostics engine availability was identified as high risk (9) due to high impact (3) and unknown likelihood (3).

- The medical records exchange availability was identified as low risk (2) since it is not a required component for the system to run.

- Other parts of the system were not deemed as risk for availability due to multiple instances of each service and clustering of the API gateway.

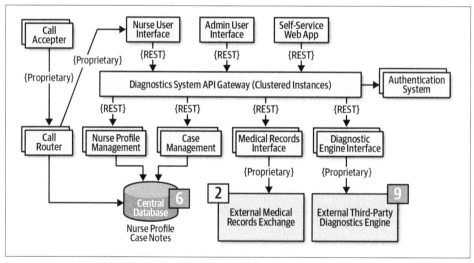

Figure 20-10. Availability risk areas

During the risk storming effort, all participants agreed that while nurses can manually write down case notes if the database went down, the call router could not function if the database were not available. To mitigate the database risk, participants chose to break apart the single physical database into two separate databases: one clustered database containing the nurse profile information, and one single instance database for the case notes. Not only did this architecture change address the concerns about availability of the database, but it also helped secure the case notes from admin access. Another option to mitigate this risk would have been to cache the nurse profile information in the call router. However, because the implementation of the call router was unknown and may be a third-party product, the participants went with the database approach.

Mitigating the risk of availability of the external systems (diagnostics engine and medical records exchange) is much harder to manage due to the lack of control of these systems. One way to mitigate this sort of availability risk is to research if there is a published service-level agreement (SLA) or service-level objective (SLO) for each of these systems. An SLA is usually a contractual agreement and is legally binding, whereas an SLO is usually not. Based on research, the architect found that the SLA for the diagnostics engine is guaranteed to be 99.99% available (that's 52.60 minutes of downtime per year), and the medical records exchange is guaranteed at 99.9% availability (that's 8.77 hours of downtime per year). Based on the relative risk, this information was enough to remove the identified risk.

The corresponding changes to the architecture after this risk storming session are illustrated in Figure 20-11. Notice that two databases are now used, and also the SLAs are published on the architecture diagram.

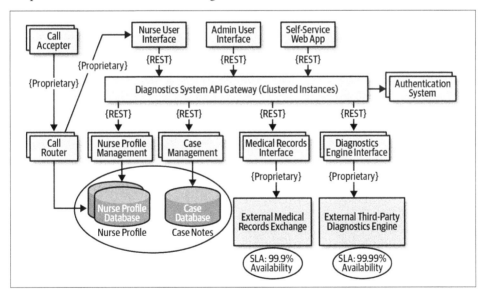

Figure 20-11. Architecture modifications to address availability risk

Elasticity

On the second risk storming exercise, the architect chose to focus on elasticity—spikes in user load (otherwise known as variable scalability). Although there are only 250 nurses (which provides an automatic governor for most of the services), the self-service portion of the system can access the diagnostics engine as well as nurses, significantly increasing the number of requests to the diagnostics interface. Participants were concerned about outbreaks and flu season, when anticipated load on the system would significantly increase.

During the risk storming session, the participants all identified the diagnostics engine interface as high risk (9). With only 500 requests per second, the participants calculated that there was no way the diagnostics engine interface could keep up with the anticipated throughput, particularly with the current architecture utilizing REST as the interface protocol.

One way to mitigate this risk is to leverage asynchronous queues (messaging) between the API gateway and the diagnostics engine interface to provide a back-pressure point if calls to the diagnostics engine get backed up. While this is a good practice, it still doesn't mitigate the risk, because nurses (as well as self-service patients) would be waiting too long for responses from the diagnostics engine, and those requests would likely time out. Leveraging what is known as the Ambulance Pattern (*https://oreil.ly/ZfLU0*) would give nurses a higher priority over self-service. Therefore two message channels would be needed. While this technique helps mitigate the risk, it still doesn't address the wait times. The participants decided that in addition to the queuing technique to provide back-pressure, caching the particular diagnostics questions related to an outbreak would remove outbreak and flu calls from ever having to reach the diagnostics engine interface.

The corresponding architecture changes are illustrated in Figure 20-12. Notice that in addition to two queue channels (one for the nurses and one for self-service patients), there is a new service called the *Diagnostics Outbreak Cache Server* that handles all requests related to a particular outbreak or flu-related question. With this architecture in place, the limiting factor was removed (calls to the diagnostics engine), allowing for tens of thousands of concurrent requests. Without a risk storming effort, this risk might not have been identified until an outbreak or flu season happened.

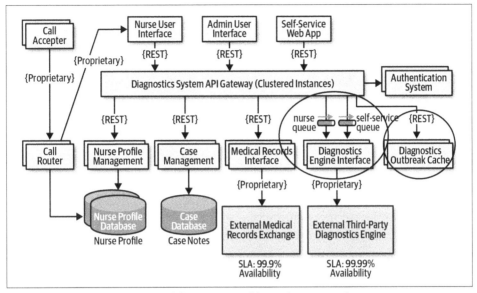

Figure 20-12. Architecture modifications to address elasticity risk

Security

Encouraged by the results and success of the first two risk storming efforts, the architect decides to hold a final risk storming session on another important architecture characteristic that must be supported in the system to ensure its success—security. Due to HIPAA regulatory requirements, access to medical records via the medical record exchange interface must be secure, allowing only nurses to access medical records if needed. The architect believes this is not a problem due to security checks in the API gateway (authentication and authorization) but is curious whether the participants find any other elements of security risk.

During the risk storming, the participants all identified the Diagnostics System API gateway as a high security risk (6). The rationale for this high rating was the high impact of admin staff or self-service patients accessing medical records (3) combined with medium likelihood (2). Likelihood of risk occurring was not rated high because of the security checks for each API call, but still rated medium because all calls (self-service, admin, and nurses) are going through the same API gateway. The architect, who only rated the risk as low (2), was convinced during the risk storming consensus activity that the risk was in fact high and needed mitigation.

The participants all agreed that having separate API gateways for each type of user (admin, self-service/diagnostics, and nurses) would prevent calls from either the admin web user interface or the self-service web user interface from ever reaching the medical records exchange interface. The architect agreed, creating the final architecture, as illustrated in Figure 20-13.

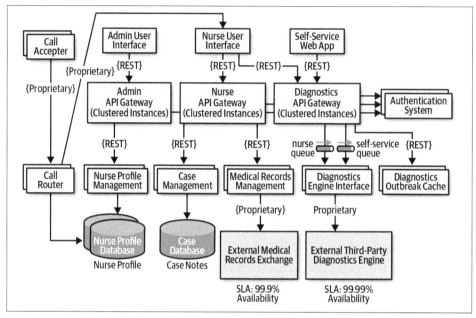

Figure 20-13. Final architecture modifications to address security risk

The prior scenario illustrates the power of risk storming. By collaborating with other architects, developers, and key stakeholders on dimensions of risk that are vital to the success of the system, risk areas are identified that would otherwise have gone unnoticed. Compare figures Figure 20-9 and Figure 20-13 and notice the significant difference in the architecture prior to risk storming and then after risk storming. Those significant changes address availability concerns, elasticity concerns, and security concerns within the architecture.

Risk storming is not a one-time process. Rather, it is a continuous process through the life of any system to catch and mitigate risk areas before they happen in production. How often the risk storming effort happens depends on many factors, including frequency of change, architecture refactoring efforts, and the incremental development of the architecture. It is typical to undergo a risk storming effort on some particular dimension after a major feature is added or at the end of every iteration.

CHAPTER 21

Diagramming and Presenting Architecture

Newly minted architects often comment on how surprised they are at how varied the job is outside of technical knowledge and experience, which enabled their move into the architect role to begin with. In particular, effective communication becomes critical to an architect's success. No matter how brilliant an architect's technical ideas, if they can't convince managers to fund them and developers to build them, their brilliance will never manifest.

Diagramming and presenting architectures are two critical soft skills for architects. While entire books exist about each topic, we'll hit some particular highlights for each.

These two topics appear together because they have a few similar characteristics: each forms an important visual representation of an architecture vision, presented using different media. However, representational consistency is a concept that ties both together.

When visually describing an architecture, the creator often must show different views of the architecture. For example, the architect will likely show an overview of the entire architecture topology, then drill into individual parts to delve into design details. However, if the architect shows a portion without indicating where it lies within the overall architecture, it confuses viewers. *Representational consistency* is the practice of always showing the relationship between parts of an architecture, either in diagrams or presentations, before changing views.

For example, if an architect wanted to describe the details of how the plug-ins relate to one another in the Silicon Sandwiches solution, the architecture would show the entire topology, then drill into the plug-in structure, showing the viewers the relationship between them; an example of this appears in Figure 21-1.

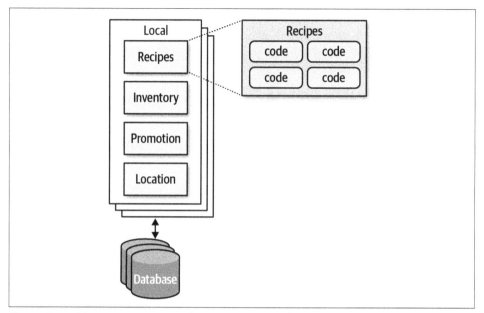

Figure 21-1. Using representational consistency to indicate context in a larger diagram

Careful use of representational consistency ensures that viewers understand the scope of items being presented, eliminating a common source of confusion.

Diagramming

The topology of architecture is always of interest to architects and developers because it captures how the structure fits together and forms a valuable shared understanding across the team. Therefore, architects should hone their diagramming skills to razor sharpness.

Tools

The current generation of diagramming tools for architects is extremely powerful, and an architect should learn their tool of choice deeply. However, before going to a nice tool, don't neglect low-fidelity artifacts, especially early in the design process. Building very ephemeral design artifacts early prevents architects from becoming overly attached to what they have created, an anti-pattern we named the *Irrational Artifact Attachment* anti-pattern.

Irrational Artifact Attachment

…is the proportional relationship between a person's irrational attachment to some artifact and how long it took to produce. If an architect creates a beautiful diagram using some tool like Visio that takes two hours, they have an irrational attachment to that artifact that's roughly proportional to the amount of time invested, which also means they will be more attached to a four-hour diagram than a two-hour one.

One of the benefits to the low-ritual approach used in Agile software development revolves around creating just-in-time artifacts, with as little ceremony as possible (this helps explain the dedication of lots of agilists to index cards and sticky notes). Using low-tech tools lets team members throw away what's not right, freeing them to experiment and allow the true nature of the artifact emerge through revision, collaboration, and discussion.

An architect's favorite variation on the cell phone photo of a whiteboard (along with the inevitable "Do Not Erase!" imperative) uses a tablet attached to an overhead projector rather than a whiteboard. This offers several advantages. First, the tablet has an unlimited canvas and can fit as many drawings that a team might need. Second, it allows copy/paste "what if" scenarios that obscure the original when done on a whiteboard. Third, images captured on a tablet are already digitized and don't have the inevitable glare associated with cell phone photos of whiteboards.

Eventually, an architect needs to create nice diagrams in a fancy tool, but make sure the team has iterated on the design sufficiently to invest time in capturing something.

Powerful tools exist to create diagrams on every platform. While we don't necessarily advocate one over another (we quite happily used OmniGraffle (*https://oreil.ly/fEoKR*) for all the diagrams in this book), architects should look for at least this baseline of features:

Layers

    Drawing tools often support layers, which architects should learn well. A layer allows the drawer to link a group of items together logically to enable hiding/showing individual layers. Using layers, an architect can build a comprehensive diagram but hide overwhelming details when they aren't necessary. Using layers also allows architects to incrementally build pictures for presentations later (see "Incremental Builds" on page 322).

Stencils/templates

    Stencils allow an architect to build up a library of common visual components, often composites of other basic shapes. For example, throughout this book, readers have seen standard pictures of things like microservices, which exist as a single item in the authors' stencil. Building a stencil for common patterns and artifacts within an organization creates consistency within architecture diagrams and allows the architect to build new diagrams quickly.

Magnets
Many drawing tools offer assistance when drawing lines between shapes. Magnets represent the places on those shapes where lines snap to connect automatically, providing automatic alignment and other visual niceties. Some tools allow the architect to add more magnets or create their own to customize how the connections look within their diagrams.

In addition to these specific helpful features, the tool should, of course, support lines, colors, and other visual artifacts, as well as the ability to export in a wide variety of formats.

Diagramming Standards: UML, C4, and ArchiMate

Several formal standards exist for technical diagrams in software.

UML

Unified Modeling Language (UML) was a standard that unified three competing design philosophies that coexisted in the 1980s. It was supposed to be the best of all worlds but, like many things designed by committee, failed to create much impact outside organizations that mandated its use.

Architects and developers still use UML class and sequence diagrams to communicate structure and workflow, but most of the other UML diagram types have fallen into disuse.

C4

C4 is a diagramming technique developed by Simon Brown to address deficiencies in UML and modernize its approach. The four C's in C4 are as follows:

Context
Represents the entire context of the system, including the roles of users and external dependencies.

Container
The physical (and often logical) deployment boundaries and containers within the architecture. This view forms a good meeting point for operations and architects.

Component
The component view of the system; this most neatly aligns with an architect's view of the system.

Class

C4 uses the same style of class diagrams from UML, which are effective, so there is no need to replace them.

If a company seeks to standardize on a diagramming technique, C4 offers a good alternative. However, like all technical diagramming tools, it suffers from an inability to express every kind of design an architecture might undertake. C4 is best suited for monolithic architectures where the container and component relationships may differ, and it's less suited to distributed architectures, such as microservices.

ArchiMate

ArchiMate (an amalgam of Arch*itecture-Ani*mate) is an open source enterprise architecture modeling language to support the description, analysis, and visualization of architecture within and across business domains. ArchiMate is a technical standard from The Open Group, and it offers a lighter-weight modeling language for enterprise ecosystems. The goal of ArchiMate is to be "as small as possible," not to cover every edge case scenario. As such, it has become a popular choice among many architects.

Diagram Guidelines

Regardless of whether an architect uses their own modeling language or one of the formal ones, they should build their own style when creating diagrams and should feel free to borrow from representations they think are particularly effective. Here are some general guidelines to use when creating technical diagrams.

Titles

Make sure all the elements of the diagram have titles or are well known to the audience. Use rotation and other effects to make titles "sticky" to the thing they associate with and to make efficient use of space.

Lines

Lines should be thick enough to see well. If lines indicate information flow, then use arrows to indicate directional or two-way traffic. Different types of arrowheads might suggest different semantics, but architects should be consistent.

Generally, one of the few standards that exists in architecture diagrams is that solid lines tend to indicate synchronous communication and dotted lines indicate asynchronous communication.

Shapes

While the formal modeling languages described all have standard shapes, no pervasive standard shapes exist across the software development world. Thus, each architect tends to make their own standard set of shapes, sometimes spreading those across an organization to create a standard language.

We tend to use three-dimensional boxes to indicate deployable artifacts and rectangles to indicate containership, but we don't have any particular key beyond that.

Labels

Architects should label each item in a diagram, especially if there is any chance of ambiguity for the readers.

Color

Architects often don't use color enough—for many years, books were out of necessity printed in black and white, so architects and developers became accustomed to monochrome drawings. While we still favor monochrome, we use color when it helps distinguish one artifact from another. For example, when discussing microservices communication strategies in "Communication" on page 254, we used color to indicate that two difference microservices participate in the coordination, not two instances of the same service, as reproduced in Figure 21-2.

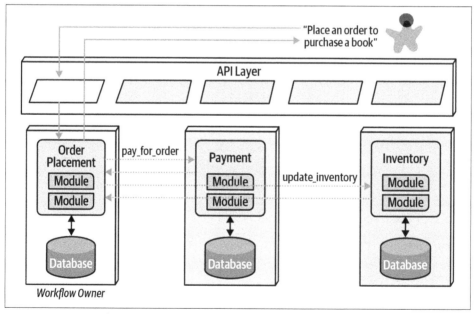

Figure 21-2. Reproduction of microservices communication example showing different services in unique colors

Keys

If shapes are ambiguous for any reason, include a key on the diagram clearly indicating what each shape represents. Nothing is worse than a diagram that leads to misinterpretation, which is worse than no diagram.

Presenting

The other soft skill required by modern architects is the ability to conduct effective presentations using tools like PowerPoint and Keynote. These tools are the lingua franca of modern organizations, and people throughout the organization expect competent use of these tools. Unfortunately, unlike word processors and spreadsheets, no one seems to spend much time studying how to use these tools well.

Neal, one of the coauthors of this book, wrote a book several years ago entitled *Presentation Patterns* (*https://presentationpatterns.com*) (Addison-Wesley Professional), about taking the patterns/anti-patterns approach common in the software world and applying it to technical presentations.

Presentation Patterns makes an important observation about the fundamental difference between creating a document versus a presentation to make a case for something—*time*. In a presentation, the presenter controls how quickly an idea is unfolding, whereas the reader of a document controls that. Thus, one of the most important skills an architect can learn in their presentation tool of choice is how to manipulate time.

Manipulating Time

Presentation tools offer two ways to manipulate time on slides: transitions and animations. Transitions move from slide to slide, and animations allow the designer to create movement within a slide. Typically, presentation tools allow just one transition per slide but a host of animations for each element: build in (appearance), build out (disappearance), and actions (such as movement, scale, and other dynamic behavior).

While tools offer a variety of splashy effects like dropping anvils, architects use transition and animations to hide the boundaries between slides. One common anti-pattern called out in *Presentation Patterns* named Cookie-Cutter (*https://oreil.ly/_Wldy*) states that ideas don't have a predetermined word count, and accordingly, designers shouldn't artificially pad content to make it appear to fill a slide. Similarly, many ideas are bigger than a single slide. Using subtle combinations of transitions and animations such as dissolve allows presenters to hide individual slide boundaries, stitching together a set of slides to tell a single story. To indicate the end of a thought, presenters should use a distinctly different transition (such as door or cube) to provide a visual clue that they are moving to a different topic.

Incremental Builds

The *Presentation Patterns* book calls out the Bullet-Riddled Corpse (*https://oreil.ly/ jS7DO*) as a common anti-pattern of corporate presentations, where every slide is essentially the speaker's notes, projected for all to see. Most readers have the excruciating experience of watching a slide full of text appear during a presentation, then reading the entire thing (because no one can resist reading it all as soon as it appears), only to sit for the next 10 minutes while the presenter slowly reads the bullets to the audience. No wonder so many corporate presentations are dull!

When presenting, the speaker has two information channels: verbal and visual. By placing too much text on the slides and then saying essentially the same words, the presenter is overloading one information channel and starving the other. The better solution to this problem is to use incremental builds for slides, building up (hopefully graphical) information as needed rather than all at once.

For example, say that an architect creates a presentation explaining the problems using feature branching and wants to talk about the negative consequences of keeping branches alive too long. Consider the graphical slide shown in Figure 21-3.

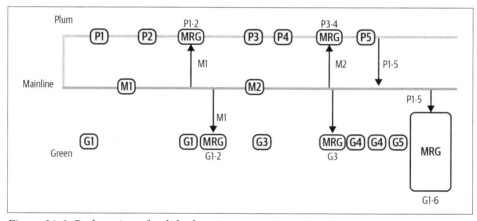

Figure 21-3. Bad version of a slide showing a negative anti-pattern

In Figure 21-3, if the presenter shows the entire slide right away, the audience can see that something bad happens toward the end, but they have to wait for the exposition to get to that point.

Instead, the architect should use the same image but obscure parts of it when showing the slide (using a borderless white box) and expose a portion at a time (by performing a build out on the covering box), as shown in Figure 21-4.

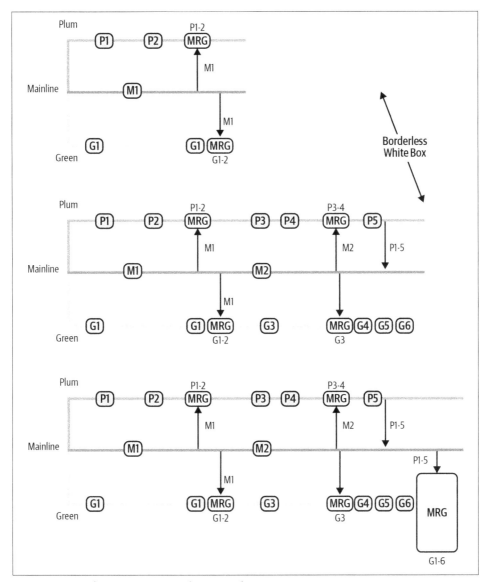

Figure 21-4. A better, incremental version that maintains suspense

In Figure 21-4, the presenter still has a fighting chance of keeping some suspense alive, making the talk inherently more interesting.

Using animations and transitions in conjunction with incremental builds allows the presenter to make more compelling, entertaining presentations.

Infodecks Versus Presentations

Some architects build slide decks in tools like PowerPoint and Keynote but never actually present them. Rather, they are emailed around like a magazine article, and each individual reads them at their own pace. *Infodecks* are slide decks that are not meant to be projected but rather summarize information graphically, essentially using a presentation tool as a desktop publishing package.

The difference between these two media is comprehensiveness of content and use of transitions and animations. If someone is going to flip through the deck like a magazine article, the author of the slides does not need to add any time elements. The other key difference between infodecks and presentations is the amount of material. Because infodecks are meant to be standalone, they contain all the information the creator wants to convey. When doing a presentation, the slides are (purposefully) meant to be half of the presentation, the other half being the person standing there talking!

Slides Are Half of the Story

A common mistake that presenters make is building the entire content of the presentation into the slides. However, if the slides are comprehensive, the presenter should spare everyone the time of sitting through a presentation and just email it to everyone as a deck! Presenters make the mistake of adding too much material to slides when they can make important points more powerfully. Remember, presenters have two information channels, so using them strategically can add more punch to the message. A great example of that is the strategic use of invisibility.

Invisibility

Invisibility is a simple pattern where the presenter inserts a blank black slide within a presentation to refocus attention solely on the speaker. If someone has two information channels (slides and speaker) and turns one of them off (the slides), it automatically adds more emphasis to the speaker. Thus, if a presenter wants to make a point, insert a blank slide—everyone in the room will focus their attention back on the speaker because they are now the only interesting thing in the room to look at.

Learning the basics of a presentation tool and a few techniques to make presentations better is a great addition to the skill set of architects. If an architect has a great idea but can't figure out a way to present it effectively, they will never get a chance to realize that vision. Architecture requires collaboration; to get collaborators, architects must convince people to sign on to their vision. The modern corporate soapboxes are presentation tools, so it's worth learning to use them well.

CHAPTER 22

Making Teams Effective

In addition to creating a technical architecture and making architecture decisions, a software architect is also responsible for guiding the development team through the implementation of the architecture. Software architects who do this well create effective development teams that work closely together to solve problems and create winning solutions. While this may sound obvious, too many times we've seen architects ignore development teams and work in siloed environments to create an architecture. This architecture then gets handed it off to a development team which then struggles to implement the architecture correctly. Being able to make teams productive is one of the ways effective and successful software architects differentiate themselves from other software architects. In this chapter we introduce some basic techniques an architect can leverage to make development teams effective.

Team Boundaries

It's been our experience that a software architect can significantly influence the success or failure of a development team. Teams that feel left out of the loop or estranged from software architects (and also the architecture) often do not have the right level of guidance and right level of knowledge about various constraints on the system, and consequently do not implement the architecture correctly.

One of the roles of a software architect is to create and communicate the constraints, or the box, in which developers can implement the architecture. Architects can create boundaries that are too tight, too loose, or just right. These boundaries are illustrated in Figure 22-1. The impact of having too tight or too loose of a boundary has a direct impact on the teams' ability to successfully implement the architecture.

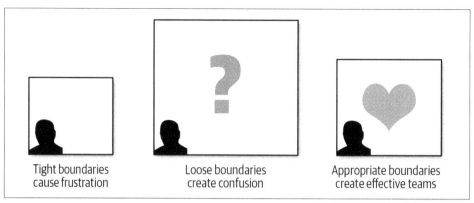

| Tight boundaries | Loose boundaries | Appropriate boundaries |
| cause frustration | create confusion | create effective teams |

Figure 22-1. Boundary types created by a software architect

Architects that create too many constraints form a tight box around the development teams, preventing access to many of the tools, libraries, and practices that are required to implement the system effectively. This causes frustration within the team, usually resulting in developers leaving the project for happier and healthier environments.

The opposite can also happen. A software architect can create constraints that are too loose (or no constraints at all), leaving all of the important architecture decisions to the development team. In this scenario, which is just as bad as tight constraints, the team essentially takes on the role of a software architect, performing proof of concepts and battling over design decisions without the proper level of guidance, resulting in unproductiveness, confusion, and frustration.

An effective software architect strives to provide the right level of guidance and constraints so that the team has the correct tools and libraries in place to effectively implement the architecture. The rest of this chapter is devoted to how to create these effective boundaries.

Architect Personalities

There are three basic types of architect personalities: a *control freak architect* (Figure 22-2), an *armchair architect* (Figure 22-3), and an *effective architect* (Figure 22-5). Each personality matches a particular boundary type discussed in the prior section on team boundaries: control freak architects produce tight boundaries, armchair architects produce loose boundaries, and effective architects produce just the right kinds of boundaries.

Control Freak

Figure 22-2. Control freak architect (iStockPhoto)

The control freak architect tries to control every detailed aspect of the software development process. Every decision a control freak architect makes is usually too fine-grained and too low-level, resulting in too many constraints on the development team.

Control freak architects produce the tight boundaries discussed in the prior section. A control freak architect might restrict the development team from downloading any useful open source or third-party libraries and instead insist that the teams write everything from scratch using the language API. Control freak architects might also place tight restrictions on naming conventions, class design, method length, and so on. They might even go so far as to write pseudocode for the development teams. Essentially, control freak architects steal the art of programming away from the developers, resulting in frustration and a lack of respect for the architect.

It is very easy to become a control freak architect, particularly when transitioning from developer to architect. An architect's role is to create the building blocks of the application (the components) and determine the interactions between those components. The developer's role in this effort is to then take those components and determine how they will be implemented using class diagrams and design patterns. However, in the transition from developer to architect, it is all too tempting to want to create the class diagrams and design patterns as well since that was the newly minted architect's prior role.

For example, suppose an architect creates a component (building block of the architecture) to manage reference data within the system. Reference data consists of static name-value pair data used on the website, as well as things like product codes and warehouse codes (static data used throughout the system). The architect's role is to identify the component (in this case, `Reference Manager`), determine the core set of operations for that component (for example, `GetData`, `SetData`, `ReloadCache`, `NotifyOnUpdate`, and so on), and which components need to interact with the `Reference Manager`. The control freak architect might think that the best way to *implement* this component is through a parallel loader pattern leveraging an internal cache, with a particular data structure for that cache. While this might be an effective design, it's not the only design. More importantly, it's no longer the architect's role to come up with this internal design for the `Reference Manager`—it's the role of the developer.

As we'll talk about in "How Much Control?" on page 331, sometimes an architect needs to play the role of a control freak, depending on the complexity of the project and the skill level on the team. However, in most cases a control freak architect disrupts the development team, doesn't provide the right level of guidance, gets in the way, and is ineffective at leading the team through the implementation of the architecture.

Armchair Architect

Figure 22-3. Armchair architect (iStockPhoto)

The armchair architect is the type of architect who hasn't coded in a very long time (if at all) and doesn't take the implementation details into account when creating an architecture. They are typically disconnected from the development teams, never around, or simply move from project to project once the initial architecture diagrams are completed.

In some cases the armchair architect is simply in way over their head in terms of the technology or business domain and therefore cannot possibly lead or guide teams from a technical or business problem standpoint. For example, what do developers do? Why, they code, of course. Writing program code is really hard to fake; either a developer writes software code, or they don't. However, what does an architect do? No one knows! Most architects draw lots of lines and boxes—but how detailed should an architect be in those diagrams? Here's a dirty little secret about architecture—it's really easy to fake it as an architect!

Suppose an armchair architect is in way over their head or doesn't have the time to architect an appropriate solution for a stock trading system. In that case the architecture diagram might look like the one illustrated in Figure 22-4. There's nothing wrong with this architecture—it's just too high level to be of any use to anyone.

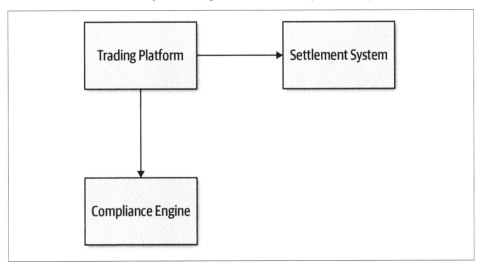

Figure 22-4. Trading system architecture created by an armchair architect

Armchair architects create loose boundaries around development teams, as discussed in the prior section. In this scenario, development teams end up taking on the role of architect, essentially doing the work an architect is supposed to be doing. Team velocity and productivity suffer as a result, and teams get confused about how the system should work.

Like the control freak architect, it is all too easy to become an armchair architect. The biggest indicator that an architect might be falling into the armchair architect personality is not having enough time to spend with the development teams implementing the architecture (or choosing not to spend time with the development teams). Development teams need an architect's support and guidance, and they need the architect available for answering technical or business-related questions when they arise. Other indicators of an armchair architect are following:

- Not fully understanding the business domain, business problem, or technology used
- Not enough hands-on experience developing software
- Not considering the implications associated with the implementation of the architecture solution

In some cases it is not the intention of an architect to become an armchair architect, but rather it just "happens" by being spread too thin between projects or development teams and loosing touch with technology or the business domain. An architect can avoid this personality by getting more involved in the technology being used on the project and understanding the business problem and business domain.

Effective Architect

Figure 22-5. Effective software architect (iStockPhoto)

An effective software architect produces the appropriate constraints and boundaries on the team, ensuring that the team members are working well together and have the right level of guidance on the team. The effective architect also ensures that the team has the correct and appropriate tools and technologies in place. In addition, they remove any roadblocks that may be in the way of the development teams reaching their goals.

While this sounds obvious and easy, it is not. There is an art to becoming an effective leader on the development team. Becoming an effective software architect requires working closely and collaborating with the team, and gaining the respect of the team as well. We'll be looking at other ways of becoming an effective software architect in later chapters in this part of the book. But for now, we'll introduce some guidelines for knowing how much control an effective architect should exert on a development team.

How Much Control?

Becoming an effective software architect is knowing how much control to exert on a given development team. This concept is known as Elastic Leadership (*https:// www.elasticleadership.com*) and is widely evangelized by author and consultant Roy Osherove. We're going to deviate a bit from the work Osherove has done in this area and focus on specific factors for software architecture.

Knowing how much an effective software architect should be a control freak and how much they should be an armchair architect involves five main factors. These factors also determine how many teams (or projects) a software architect can manage at once:

Team familiarity

> How well do the team members know each other? Have they worked together before on a project? Generally, the better team members know each other, the less control is needed because team members start to become self-organizing. Conversely, the newer the team members, the more control needed to help facilitate collaboration among team members and reduce cliques within the team.

Team size

> How big is the team? (We consider more than 12 developers on the same team to be a big team, and 4 or fewer to be a small team.) The larger the team, the more control is needed. The smaller the team, less control is needed. This is discussed in more detail in "Team Warning Signs" on page 335.

Overall experience

> How many team members are senior? How many are junior? Is it a mixed team of junior and senior developers? How well do they know the technology and business domain? Teams with lots of junior developers require more control and mentoring, whereas teams with more senior developers require less control. In the latter cases, the architect moves from the role of a mentor to that of a facilitator.

Project complexity

> Is the project highly complex or just a simple website? Highly complex projects require the architect to be more available to the team and to assist with issues

that arise, hence more control is needed on the team. Relatively simple projects are straightforward and hence do not require much control.

Project duration

Is the project short (two months), long (two years), or average duration (six months)? The shorter the duration, the less control is needed; conversely, the longer the project, the more control is needed.

While most of the factors make sense with regard to more or less control, the project duration factor may not appear to make sense. As indicated in the prior list, the shorter the project duration, the less control is needed; the longer the project duration, the more control is needed. Intuitively this might seem reversed, but that is not the case. Consider a quick two-month project. Two months is not a lot of time to qualify requirements, experiment, develop code, test every scenario, and release into production. In this case the architect should act more as an armchair architect, as the development team already has a keen sense of urgency. A control freak architect would just get in the way and likely delay the project. Conversely, think of a project duration of two years. In this scenario the developers are relaxed, not thinking in terms of urgency, and likely planning vacations and taking long lunches. More control is needed by the architect to ensure the project moves along in a timely fashion and that complex tasks are accomplished first.

It is typical within most projects that these factors are utilized to determine the level of control at the start of a project; but as the system continues to evolve, the level of control changes. Therefore, we advise that these factors continually be analyzed throughout the life cycle of a project to determine how much control to exert on the development team.

To illustrate how each of these factors can be used to determine the level of control an architect should have on a team, assume a fixed scale of 20 points for each factor. Minus values point more toward being an armchair architect (less control and involvement), whereas plus values point more toward being a control freak architect (more control and involvement). This scale is illustrated in Figure 22-6.

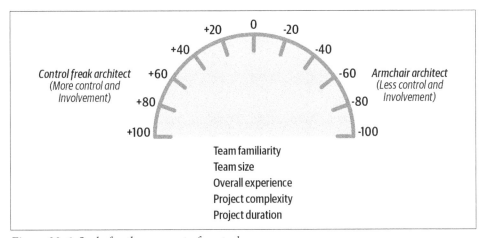

Figure 22-6. Scale for the amount of control

Applying this sort of scaling is not exact, of course, but it does help in determining the relative control to exert on a team. For example, consider the project scenario shown in Table 22-1 and Figure 22-7. As shown in the table, the factors point to either a control freak (+20) or an armchair architect (-20). These factors add up and to an accumulated score of -60, indicating that the architect should play more of an armchair architect role and not get in the team's way.

Table 22-1. Scenario 1 example for amount of control

Factor	Value	Rating	Personality
Team familiarity	New team members	+20	Control freak
Team size	Small (4 members)	-20	Armchair architect
Overall experience	All experienced	-20	Armchair architect
Project complexity	Relatively simple	-20	Armchair architect
Project duration	2 months	-20	Armchair architect
Accumulated score		-60	Armchair architect

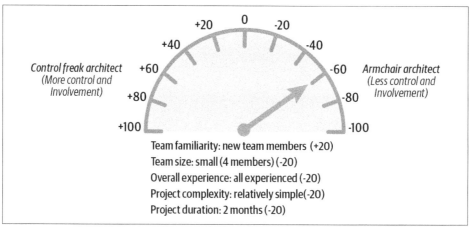

Team familiarity: new team members (+20)
Team size: small (4 members) (-20)
Overall experience: all experienced (-20)
Project complexity: relatively simple(-20)
Project duration: 2 months (-20)

Figure 22-7. Amount of control for scenario 1

In scenario 1, these factors are all taken into account to demonstrate that an effective software architect should initially play the role of facilitator and not get too involved in the day-to-day interactions with the team. The architect will be needed for answering questions and to make sure the team is on track, but for the most part the architect should be largely hands-off and let the experienced team do what they know best —develop software quickly.

Consider another type of scenario described in Table 22-2 and illustrated in Figure 22-8, where the team members know each other well, but the team is large (12 team members) and consists mostly of junior (inexperienced) developers. The project is relatively complex with a duration of six months. In this case, the accumulated score comes out to -20, indicating that the effective architect should be involved in the day-to-day activities within the team and take on a mentoring and coaching role, but not so much as to disrupt the team.

Table 22-2. Scenario 2 example for amount of control

Factor	Value	Rating	Personality
Team familiarity	Know each other well	-20	Armchair architect
Team size	Large (12 members)	+20	Control freak
Overall experience	Mostly junior	+20	Control freak
Project complexity	High complexity	+20	Control freak
Project duration	6 months	-20	Armchair architect
Accumulated score		-20	Control freak

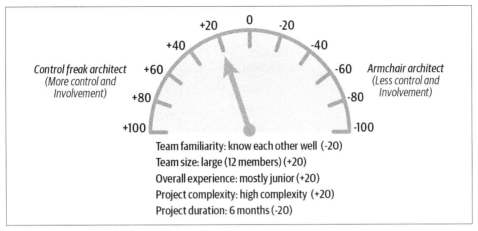

Figure 22-8. Amount of control for scenario 2

It is difficult to objectify these factors, as some of them (such as the overall team experience) might be more weighted than others. In these cases the metrics can easily be weighted or modified to suit any particular scenario or condition. Regardless, the primary message here is that the amount of control and involvement a software architect has on the team varies by these five main factors and that by taking these factors into account, an architect can gauge what sort of control to exert on the team and what the box in which development teams can work in should look like (tight boundaries and constraints or loose ones).

Team Warning Signs

As indicated in the prior section, team size is one of the factors that influence the amount of control an architect should exert on a development team. The larger a team, the more control needed; the smaller the team, the less control needed. Three factors come into play when considering the most effective development team size:

- Process loss
- Pluralistic ignorance
- Diffusion of responsibility

Process loss, otherwise known as Brook's law (*https://oreil.ly/rZt88*), was originally coined by Fred Brooks in his book *The Mythical Man Month* (Addison-Wesley). The basic idea of process loss is that the more people you add to a project, the more time the project will take. As illustrated in Figure 22-9, the *group potential* is defined by the collective efforts of everyone on the team. However, with any team, the *actual productivity* will always be less than the group potential, the difference being the *process loss* of the team.

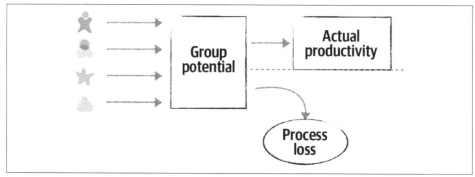

Figure 22-9. Team size impacts actual productivity (Brook's law)

An effective software architect will observe the development team and look for process loss. Process loss is a good factor in determining the correct team size for a particular project or effort. One indication of process loss is frequent merge conflicts when pushing code to a repository. This is an indication that team members are possibly stepping on each other's toes and working on the same code. Looking for areas of parallelism within the team and having team members working on separate services or areas of the application is one way to avoid process loss. Anytime a new team member comes on board a project, if there aren't areas for creating parallel work streams, an effective architect will question the reason why a new team member was added to the team and demonstrate to the project manager the negative impact that additional person will have on the team.

Pluralistic ignorance also occurs as the team size gets too big. Pluralistic ignorance is when everyone agrees to (but privately rejects) a norm because they think they are missing something obvious. For example, suppose on a large team the majority agree that using messaging between two remote services is the best solution. However, one person on the team thinks this is a silly idea because of a secure firewall between the two services. However, rather than speak up, that person also agrees to the use of messaging (but privately rejects the idea) because they are afraid that they are either missing something obvious or afraid they might be seen as a fool if they were to speak up. In this case, the person rejecting the norm was correct—messaging would not work because of a secure firewall between the two remote services. Had they spoken up (and had the team size been smaller), the original solution would have been challenged and another protocol (such as REST) used instead, which would be a better solution in this case.

The concept of pluralistic ignorance was made famous by the Danish children's story "The Emperor's New Clothes" (*https://oreil.ly/ROvce*), by Hans Christian Andersen. In the story, the king is convinced that his new clothes are invisible to anyone unworthy to actually see them. He struts around totally nude, asking all of his subjects how they like his new clothes. All the subjects, afraid of being considered stupid or unworthy, respond to the king that his new clothes are the best thing ever. This folly continues until a child finally calls out to the king that he isn't wearing any clothes at all.

An effective software architect should continually observe facial expressions and body language during any sort of collaborative meeting or discussion and act as a facilitator if they sense an occurrence of pluralistic ignorance. In this case, the effective architect might interrupt and ask the person what they think about the proposed solution and be on their side and support them when they speak up.

The third factor that indicates appropriate team size is called *diffusion of responsibility*. Diffusion of responsibility is based on the fact that as team size increases, it has a negative impact on communication. Confusion about who is responsible for what on the team and things getting dropped are good signs of a team that is too large.

Look at the picture in Figure 22-10. What do you observe?

Figure 22-10. Diffusion of responsibility

This picture shows someone standing next to a broken-down car on the side of a small country road. In this scenario, how many people might stop and ask the motorist if everything is OK? Because it's a small road in a small community, probably everyone who passes by. However, how many times have motorists been stuck on the side of a busy highway in the middle of a large city and had thousands of cars simply drive by without anyone stopping and asking if everything is OK? All the time. This is a good example of the diffusion of responsibility. As cities get busier and more crowded, people assume the motorist has already called or help is on the way due to the large number of people witnessing the event. However, in most of these cases help is not on the way, and the motorist is stuck with a dead or forgotten cell phone, unable to call for help.

An effective architect not only helps guide the development team through the implementation of the architecture, but also ensures that the team is healthy, happy, and working together to achieve a common goal. Looking for these three warning signs and consequently helping to correct them helps to ensure an effective development team.

Leveraging Checklists

Airline pilots use checklists on every flight—even the most experienced, seasoned veteran pilots. Pilots have checklists for takeoff, landing, and thousands of other situations, both common and unusual edge cases. They use checklists because one missed aircraft setting (such as setting the flaps to 10 degrees) or procedure (such as gaining clearance into a terminal control area) can mean the difference between a safe flight and a disastrous one.

Dr. Atul Gawande wrote an excellent book called *The Checklist Manifesto* (*https://oreil.ly/XNcV9*) (Picador), in which he describes the power of checklists for surgical procedures. Alarmed at the high rate of staph infections in hospitals, Dr. Gawande created surgical checklists to attempt to reduce this rate. In the book he demonstrates that staph infection rates in hospitals using the checklists went down to near zero, while staph infection rates in control hospitals not using the checklists continued to rise.

Checklists work. They provide an excellent vehicle for making sure everything is covered and addressed. If checklists work so well, then why doesn't the software development industry leverage them? We firmly believe through personal experience that checklists make a big difference in the effectiveness of development teams. However, there are caveats to this claim. First, most software developers are not flying airliners or performing open heart surgery. In other words, software developers don't require checklists for everything. The key to making teams effective is knowing when to leverage checklists and when not to.

Consider the checklist shown in Figure 22-11 for creating a new database table.

Done	Task description
☐	Determine database column field names and types
☐	Fill out database table request form
☐	Obtain permission for new database table
☐	Submit request form to database group
☐	Verify table once created

Figure 22-11. Example of a bad checklist

This is not a checklist, but a set of procedural steps, and as such should not be in a checklist. For example, the database table cannot be verified if the form has not yet been submitted! Any processes that have a procedural flow of dependent tasks should not be in a checklist. Simple, well-known processes that are executed frequently without error also do not need a checklist.

Processes that are good candidates for checklists are those that don't have any procedural order or dependent tasks, as well as those that tend to be error-prone or have steps that are frequently missed or skipped. The key to making checklists effective is to not go overboard making everything a checklist. Architects find that checklists do, in fact, make development teams more effective, and as such start to make everything a checklist, invoking what is known as the *law of diminishing returns*. The more checklists an architect creates, the less chance developers will use them. Another key success factor when creating checklists is to make them as small as possible while still capturing all the necessary steps within a process. Developers generally will not follow checklists that are too big. Seek items that can be performed through automation and remove those from the checklist.

 Don't worry about stating the obvious in a checklist. It's the obvious stuff that's usually skipped or missed.

Three key checklists that we've found to be most effective are a *developer code completion* checklist, a *unit and functional testing* checklist, and a *software release* checklist. Each checklist is discussed in the following sections.

> ## The Hawthorne Effect
>
> One of the issues associated with introducing checklists to a development team is making developers actually use them. It's all too common for some developers to run out of time and simply mark all the items in a particular checklist as completed without having actually performed the tasks.
>
> One of the ways of addressing this issue is by talking with the team about the importance of using checklists and how checklists can make a difference in the team. Have team members read *The Checklist Manifesto* by Atul Gawande to fully understand the power of a checklist, and make sure each team member understands the reasoning behind each checklist and why it is being used. Having developers collaborate on what should and shouldn't be on a checklist also helps.
>
> When all else fails, architects can invoke what is known as the Hawthorne effect (*https://oreil.ly/caGH_*). The Hawthorne effect essentially means that if people know they are being observed or monitored, their behavior changes, and generally they will do the right thing. Examples include highly visible cameras in and around buildings that actually don't work or aren't really recording anything (this is very common!) and website monitoring software (how many of those reports are actually viewed?).
>
> The Hawthorne effect can be used to govern the use of checklists as well. An architect can let the team know that the use of checklists is critical to the team's effectiveness, and as a result, all checklists will be verified to make sure the task was actually performed, when in fact the architect is only occasionally spot-checking the checklists for correctness. By leveraging the Hawthorne effect, developers will be much less likely to skip items or mark them as completed when in fact the task was not done.

Developer Code Completion Checklist

The developer code completion checklist is an effective tool to use, particularly when a software developer states that they are "done" with the code. It also is useful for defining what is known as the "definition of done." If everything in the checklist is completed, then the developer can claim they are actually done with the code.

Here are some of the things to include in a developer code completion checklist:

- Coding and formatting standards not included in automated tools
- Frequently overlooked items (such as absorbed exceptions)
- Project-specific standards
- Special team instructions or procedures

Figure 22-12 illustrates an example of a developer code completion checklist.

Done	Task description
☐	Run code cleanup and code formatting
☐	Execute custom source validation tool
☐	Verify the audit log is written for all updates
☐	Make sure there are no absorbed exceptions
☐	Check for hardcoded values and convert to constants
☐	Verify that only public methods are calling setFailure()
☐	Include @ServiceEntrypoint on service API class

Figure 22-12. Example of a developer code completion checklist

Notice the obvious tasks "Run code cleanup and code formatting" and "Make sure there are no absorbed exceptions" in the checklist. How may times has a developer been in a hurry either at the end of the day or at the end of an iteration and forgotten to run code cleanup and formatting from the IDE? Plenty of times. In *The Checklist Manifesto*, Gawande found this same phenomenon with respect to surgical procedures—the obvious ones were often the ones that were usually missed.

Notice also the project-specific tasks in items 2, 3, 6, and 7. While these are good items to have in a checklist, an architect should always review the checklist to see if any items can be automated or written as plug-in for a code validation checker. For example, while "Include @ServiceEntrypoint on service API class" might not be able to have an automated check, the "Verify that only public methods are calling setFailure()" certainly can (this is a straightforward automated check with any sort of code crawling tool). Checking for areas of automation helps reduce both the size and the noise within a checklist, making it more effective.

Unit and Functional Testing Checklist

Perhaps one of the most effective checklists is a unit and functional testing checklist. This checklist contains some of the more unusual and edge-case tests that software developers tend to forget to test. Whenever someone from QA finds an issue with the code based on a particular test case, that test case should be added to this checklist.

This particular checklist is usually one of the largest ones due to all the types of tests that can be run against code. The purpose of this checklist is to ensure the most complete coding possible so that when the developer is done with the checklist, the code is essentially production ready.

Here are some of the items found in a typical unit and functional testing checklist:

- Special characters in text and numeric fields
- Minimum and maximum value ranges
- Unusual and extreme test cases
- Missing fields

Like the developer code completion checklist, any items that can be written as automated tests should be removed from the checklist. For example, suppose there is an item in the checklist for a stock trading application to test for negative shares (such as a BUY for –1,000 shares of Apple [AAPL]). If this check is automated through a unit or functional test within the test suite, then the item should be removed from the checklist.

Developers sometimes don't know where to start when writing unit tests or how many unit tests to write. This checklist provides a way of making sure general or specific test scenarios are included in the process of developing the software. This checklist is also effective in bridging the gap between developers and testers in environments that have these activities performed by separate teams. The more development teams perform complete testing, the easier the job of the testing teams, allowing the testing teams to focus on certain business scenarios not covered in the checklists.

Software Release Checklist

Releasing software into production is perhaps one of the most error-prone aspects of the software development life cycle, and as such makes for a great checklist. This checklist helps avoid failed builds and failed deployments, and it significantly reduces the amount of risk associated with releasing software.

The software release checklist is usually the most volatile of the checklists in that it continually changes to address new errors and circumstances each time a deployment fails or has issues.

Here are some of the items typically included within the software release checklist:

- Configuration changes in servers or external configuration servers
- Third-party libraries added to the project (JAR, DLL, etc.)
- Database updates and corresponding database migration scripts

Anytime a build or deployment fails, the architect should analyze the root cause of the failure and add a corresponding entry to the software release checklist. This way the item will be verified on the next build or deployment, preventing that issue from happening again.

Providing Guidance

A software architect can also make teams effective by providing guidance through the use of design principles. This also helps form the box (constraints), as described in the first section of this chapter, that developers can work in to implement the architecture. Effectively communicating these design principles is one of the keys to creating a successful team.

To illustrate this point, consider providing guidance to a development team regarding the use of what is typically called the *layered stack*—the collection of third-party libraries (such as JAR files, and DLLs) that make up the application. Development teams usually have lots of questions regarding the layered stack, including whether they can make their own decisions about various libraries, which ones are OK, and which ones are not.

Using this example, an effective software architect can provide guidance to the development team by first having the developer answer the following questions:

1. Are there any overlaps between the proposed library and existing functionality within the system?

2. What is the justification for the proposed library?

The first question guides developers to looking at the existing libraries to see if the functionality provided by the new library can be satisfied through an existing library or existing functionality. It has been our experience that developers sometimes ignore this activity, creating lots of duplicate functionality, particularly in large projects with large teams.

The second question prompts the developer into questioning why the new library or functionality is truly needed. Here, an effective software architect will ask for both a technical justification as well as a business justification as to why the additional library is needed. This can be a powerful technique to create awareness within the development team of the need for business justifications.

The Impact of Business Justifications

One of your authors (Mark) was the lead architect on a particularly complex Java-based project with a large development team. One of the team members was particularly obsessed with the Scala programming language and desperately wanted to use it on the project. This desire for the use of Scala ended up becoming so disruptive that several key team members informed Mark that they were planning on leaving the project and moving on to other, "less toxic," environments. Mark convinced the two key team members to hold off on their decision for a bit and had a discussion with the Scala enthusiast. Mark told the Scala enthusiast that he would support the use of Scala within the project, but the Scala enthusiast would have to provide a business justification for the use of Scala because of the training costs and rewriting effort involved. The Scala enthusiast was ecstatic and said he would get right on it, and he left the meeting yelling, "Thank you—you're the best!"

The next day the Scala enthusiast came into the office completely transformed. He immediately approached Mark and asked to speak with him. They both went into the conference room, and the Scala enthusiast immediately (and humbly) said, "Thank you." The Scala enthusiast explained to Mark that he could come up with all the technical reasons in the world to use Scala, but none of those technical advantages had any sort of business value in terms of the architecture characteristics needed ("-ilities"): cost, budget, and timeline. In fact, the Scala enthusiast realized that the increase in cost, budget, and timeline would provide no benefit whatsoever.

Realizing what a disruption he was, the Scala enthusiast quickly transformed himself into one of the best and most helpful members on the team, all because of being asked to provide a business justification for something he wanted on the project. This increased awareness of justifications not only made him a better software developer, but also made for a stronger and healthier team.

As a postscript, the two key developers stayed on the project until the very end.

Continuing with the example of governing the layered stack, another effective technique of communicating design principles is through graphical explanations about what the development team can make decisions on and what they can't. The illustration in Figure 22-13 is an example of what this graphic (as well as the guidance) might look like for controlling the layered stack.

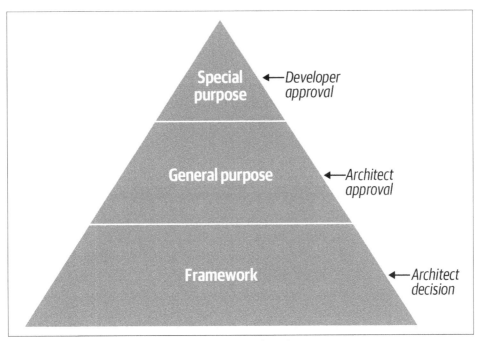

Figure 22-13. Providing guidance for the layered stack

In Figure 22-13, an architect would provide examples of what each category of the third-party library would contain and then what the guidance is (the design principle) in terms of what the developers can and can't do (the box described in the first section of the chapter). For example, here are the three categories defined for any third-party library:

Special purpose
> These are specific libraries used for things like PDF rendering, bar code scanning, and circumstances that do not warrant writing custom software.

General purpose
> These libraries are wrappers on top of the language API, and they include things like Apache Commons, and Guava for Java.

Framework
> These libraries are used for things like persistence (such as Hibernate) and inversion of control (such as Spring). In other words, these libraries make up an entire layer or structure of the application and are highly invasive.

Once categorized (the preceding categories are only an example—there can be many more defined), the architect then creates the box around this design principle. Notice in the example illustrated in Figure 22-13 that for this particular application or project, the architect has specified that for special-purpose libraries, the developer can make the decision and does not need to consult the architect for that library. However, notice that for general purpose, the architect has indicated that the developer can undergo overlap analysis and justification to make the recommendation, but that category of library requires architect approval. Finally, for framework libraries, that is an architect decision—in other words, the development teams shouldn't even undergo analysis for these types of libraries; the architect has decided to take on that responsibility for those types of libraries.

Summary

Making development teams effective is hard work. It requires lots of experience and practice, as well as strong people skills (which we will discuss in subsequent chapters in this book). That said, the simple techniques described in this chapter about elastic leadership, leveraging checklists, and providing guidance through effectively communicating design principles do, in fact, work, and have proven effective in making development teams work smarter and more effectively.

One might question the role of an architect for such activities, instead assigning the effort of making teams effective to the development manager or project manager. We strongly disagree with this premise. A software architect not only provides technical guidance to the team, but also leads the team through the implementation of the architecture. The close collaborative relationship between a software architect and a development team allows the architect to observe the team dynamics and hence facilitate changes to make the team more effective. This is exactly what differentiates a technical architect from an effective software architect.

CHAPTER 23

Negotiation and Leadership Skills

Negotiation and leadership skills are hard skills to obtain. It takes many years of learning, practice, and "lessons learned" experiences to gain the necessary skills to become an effective software architect. Knowing that this book cannot make an architect an expert in negotiation and leadership overnight, the techniques introduced in this chapter provide a good starting point for gaining these important skills.

Negotiation and Facilitation

In the beginning of this book, we listed the core expectations of an architect, the last being the expectation that a software architect must understand the political climate of the enterprise and be able to navigate the politics. The reason for this key expectation is that almost every decision a software architect makes will be challenged. Decisions will be challenged by developers who think they know more than the architect and hence have a better approach. Decisions will be challenged by other architects within the organization who think they have a better idea or way of approaching the problem. Finally, decisions will be challenged by stakeholders who will argue that the decision is too expensive or will take too much time.

Consider the decision of an architect to use database clustering and federation (using separate physical domain-scoped database instances) to mitigate risk with regard to overall availability within a system. While this is a sound solution to the issue of database availability, it is also a costly decision. In this example, the architect must negotiate with key business stakeholders (those paying for the system) to come to an agreement about the trade-off between availability and cost.

Negotiation is one of the most important skills a software architect can have. Effective software architects understand the politics of the organization, have strong negotiation and facilitation skills, and can overcome disagreements when they occur to create solutions that all stakeholders agree on.

Negotiating with Business Stakeholders

Consider the following real-world scenario (scenario 1) involving a key business stakeholder and lead architect:

Scenario 1

The senior vice president project sponsor is insistent that the new trading system must support five nines of availability (99.999%). However, the lead architect is convinced, based on research, calculations, and knowledge of the business domain and technology, that three nines of availability (99.9%) would be sufficient. The problem is, the project sponsor does not like to be wrong or corrected and really hates people who are condescending. The sponsor isn't overly technical (but thinks they are) and as a result tends to get involved in the nonfunctional aspects of projects. The architect must convince the project sponsor through negotiation that three nines (99.9%) of availability would be enough.

In this sort of negotiation, the software architect must be careful to not be too egotistical and forceful in their analysis, but also make sure they are not missing anything that might prove them wrong during the negotiation. There are several key negotiation techniques an architect can use to help with this sort of stakeholder negotiation.

 Leverage the use of grammar and buzzwords to better understand the situation.

Phrases such as "we must have zero downtime" and "I needed those features yesterday" are generally meaningless but nevertheless provide valuable information to the architect about to enter into a negotiation. For example, when the project sponsor is asked when a particular feature is needed and responds, "I needed it yesterday," that is an indication to the software architect that time to market is important to that stakeholder. Similarly, the phrase "this system must be lightning fast" means performance is a big concern. The phase "zero downtime" means that availability is critical in the application. An effective software architect will leverage this sort of nonsense grammar to better understand the real concerns and consequently leverage that use of grammar during a negotiation.

Consider scenario 1 described previously. Here, the key project sponsor wants five nines of availability. Leveraging this technique tells the architect that availability is very important. This leads to a second negotiation technique:

Gather as much information as possible *before* entering into a negotiation.

The phrase "five nines" is grammar that indicates high availability. However, what exactly is five nines of availability? Researching this ahead of time and gathering knowledge prior to the negotiation yields the information shown in Table 23-1.

Table 23-1. Nines of availability

Percentage uptime	Downtime per year (per day)
90.0% (one nine)	36 days 12 hrs (2.4 hrs)
99.0% (two nines)	87 hrs 46 min (14 min)
99.9% (three nines)	8 hrs 46 min (86 sec)
99.99% (four nines)	52 min 33 sec (7 sec)
99.999% (five nines)	5 min 35 sec (1 sec)
99.9999% (six nines)	31.5 sec (86 ms)

"Five nines" of availability is 5 minutes and 35 seconds of downtime per year, or 1 second a day of unplanned downtime. Quite ambitious, but also quite costly and unnecessary for the prior example. Putting things in hours and minutes (or in this case, seconds) is a much better way to have the conversation than sticking with the nines vernacular.

Negotiating scenario 1 would include validating the stakeholder's concerns ("I understand that availability is very important for this system") and then bringing the negotiation from the nines vernacular to one of reasonable hours and minutes of unplanned downtime. Three nines (which the architect deemed good enough) averages 86 seconds of unplanned downtime per day—certainly a reasonable number given the context of the global trading system described in the scenario. The architect can always resort to this tip:

When all else fails, state things in terms of cost and time.

We recommend saving this negotiation tactic for last. We've seen too many negotiations start off on the wrong foot due to opening statements such as, "That's going to cost a lot of money" or "We don't have time for that." Money and time (effort involved) are certainly key factors in any negotiation but should be used as a last resort so that other justifications and rationalizations that matter more be tried first. Once an agreement is reached, then cost and time can be considered if they are important attributes to the negotiation.

Another important negotiation technique to always remember is the following, particularly in situations as described in scenario 1:

Leverage the "divide and conquer" rule to qualify demands or requirements.

The ancient Chinese warrior Sun Tzu wrote in *The Art of War*, "If his forces are united, separate them." This same divide-and-conquer tactic can be applied by an architect during negotiations as well. Consider scenario 1 previously described. In this case, the project sponsor is insisting on five nines (99.999%) of availability for the new trading system. However, does the *entire system* need five nines of availability? Qualifying the requirement to the specific area of the system actually requiring five nines of availability reduces the scope of difficult (and costly) requirements and the scope of the negotiation as well.

Negotiating with Other Architects

Consider the following actual scenario (scenario 2) between a lead architect and another architect on the same project:

Scenario 2

The lead architect on a project believes that asynchronous messaging would be the right approach for communication between a group of services to increase both performance and scalability. However, the other architect on the project once again strongly disagrees and insists that REST would be a better choice, because REST is always faster than messaging and can scale just as well ("see for yourself by Googling it!"). This is not the first heated debate between the two architects, nor will it be the last. The lead architect must convince the other architect that messaging is the right solution.

In this scenario, the lead architect can certainly tell the other architect that their opinion doesn't matter and ignore it based on the lead architect's seniority on the project. However, this will only lead to further animosity between the two architects and create an unhealthy and noncollaborative relationship, and consequently will end up having a negative impact on the development team. The following technique will help in these types of situations:

Always remember that *demonstration defeats discussion.*

Rather than arguing with another architect over the use of REST versus messaging, the lead architect should demonstrate to the other architect how messaging would be a better choice in their specific environment. Every environment is different, which is why simply Googling it will never yield the correct answer. By running a comparison between the two options in a production-like environment and showing the other architect the results, the argument would likely be avoided.

Another key negotiation technique that works in these situations is as follows:

 Avoid being too argumentative or letting things get too personal in a negotiation—calm leadership combined with clear and concise reasoning will always win a negotiation.

This technique is a very powerful tool when dealing with adversarial relationships like the one described in scenario 2. Once things get too personal or argumentative, the best thing to do is stop the negotiation and reengage at a later time when both parties have calmed down. Arguments will happen between architects; however, approaching these situations with calm leadership will usually force the other person to back down when things get too heated.

Negotiating with Developers

Effective software architects don't leverage their title as architect to tell developers what to do. Rather, they work with development teams to gain respect so that when a request is made of the development team, it doesn't end up in an argument or resentment. Working with development teams can be difficult at times. In many cases development teams feel disconnected from the architecture (and also the architect), and as a result feel left out of the loop with regard to decisions the architect makes. This is a classic example of the *Ivory Tower* architecture anti-pattern. Ivory tower architects are ones who simply dictate from on high, telling development teams what to do without regard to their opinion or concerns. This usually leads to a loss of respect for the architect and an eventual breakdown of the team dynamics. One negotiation technique that can help address this situation is to always provide a justification:

When convincing developers to adopt an architecture decision or to do a specific task, provide a justification rather than "dictating from on high."

By providing a reason why something needs to be done, developers will more likely agree with the request. For example, consider the following conversation between an architect and a developer with regard to making a simple query within a traditional n-tiered layered architecture:

Architect: "You must go through the business layer to make that call."
Developer: "No. It's much faster just to call the database directly."

There are several things wrong with this conversation. First, notice the use of the words "you must." This type of commanding voice is not only demeaning, but is one of the worst ways to begin a negotiation or conversation. Also notice that the developer responded to the architect's demand with a reason to counter the demand (going through the business layer will be slower and take more time). Now consider an alternative approach to this demand:

Architect: "Since change control is most important to us, we have formed a closed-layered architecture. This means all calls to the database need to come from the business layer."
Developer: "OK, I get it, but in that case, how am I going to deal with the performance issues for simple queries?"

Notice here the architect is providing the justification for the demand that all requests need to go through the business layer of the application. Providing the justification or reason first is always a good approach. Most of the time, once a person hears something they disagree with, they stop listening. By stating the reason first, the architect is sure that the justification will be heard. Also notice the architect removed the personal nature of this demand. By not saying "you must" or "you need to," the architect effectively turned the demand into a simple statement of fact ("this means…"). Now take a look at the developer's response. Notice the conversation shifted from disagreeing with the layered architecture restrictions to a question about increasing performance for simple calls. Now the architect and developer can engage in a collaborative conversation to find ways to make simple queries faster while still preserving the closed layers in the architecture.

Another effective negotiation tactic when negotiating with a developer or trying to convince them to accept a particular design or architecture decision they disagree with is to have the developer arrive at the solution on their own. This creates a win-win situation where the architect cannot lose. For example, suppose an architect is choosing between two frameworks, Framework X and Framework Y. The architect sees that Framework Y doesn't satisfy the security requirements for the system and so naturally chooses Framework X. A developer on the team strongly disagrees and insists that Framework Y would still be the better choice. Rather than argue the matter, the architect tells the developer that the team will use Framework Y if the developer can show how to address the security requirements if Framework Y is used. One of two things will happen:

1. The developer will fail trying to demonstrate that Framework Y will satisfy the security requirements and will understand firsthand that the framework cannot be used. By having the developer arrive at the solution on their own, the architect automatically gets buy-in and agreement for the decision to use Framework X by essentially making it the developer's decision. This is a win.

2. The developer finds a way to address the security requirements with Framework Y and demonstrates this to the architect. This is a win as well. In this case the architect missed something in Framework Y, and it also ended up being a better framework over the other one.

 If a developer disagrees with a decision, have them arrive at the solution on their own.

It's really through collaboration with the development team that the architect is able to gain the respect of the team and form better solutions. The more developers respect an architect, the easier it will be for the architect to negotiate with those developers.

The Software Architect as a Leader

A software architect is also a leader, one who can guide a development team through the implementation of the architecture. We maintain that about 50% of being an effective software architect is having good people skills, facilitation skills, and leadership skills. In this section we discuss several key leadership techniques that an effective software architect can leverage to lead development teams.

The 4 C's of Architecture

Each day things seem to be getting more and more complex, whether it be increased complexity in business processes or increased complexity of systems and even architecture. Complexity exists within architecture as well as software development, and always will. Some architectures are very complex, such as ones supporting six nines of availability (99.9999%)—that's equivalent to unplanned downtime of about 86 milliseconds a day, or 31.5 seconds of downtime per year. This sort of complexity is known as *essential complexity*—in other words, "we have a hard problem."

One of the traps many architects fall into is adding unnecessary complexity to solutions, diagrams, and documentation. Architects (as well as developers) seem to love complexity. To quote Neal:

> Developers are drawn to complexity like moths to a flame—frequently with the same result.

Consider the diagram in Figure 23-1 illustrating the major information flows for the backend processing systems at a very large global bank. Is this necessarily complex? No one knows the answer to this question because the architect has made it complex. This sort of complexity is called *accidental complexity*—in other words, "we have made a problem hard." Architects sometimes do this to prove their worth when things seem too simple or to guarantee that they are always kept in the loop on discussions and decisions that are made regarding the business or architecture. Other architects do this to maintain job security. Whatever the reason, introducing accidental complexity into something that is not complex is one of the best ways to become an ineffective leader as an architect.

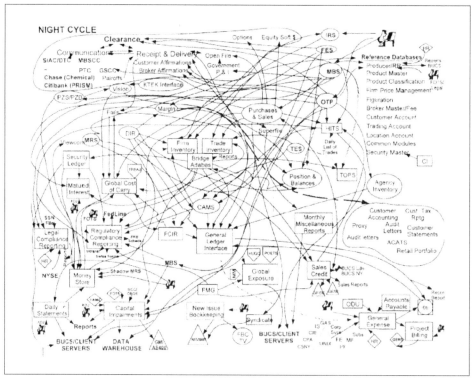

Figure 23-1. Introducing accidental complexity into a problem

An effective way of avoiding accidental complexity is what we call the *4 C's* of architecture: *communication, collaboration, clarity*, and *conciseness*. These factors (illustrated in Figure 23-2) all work together to create an effective communicator and collaborator on the team.

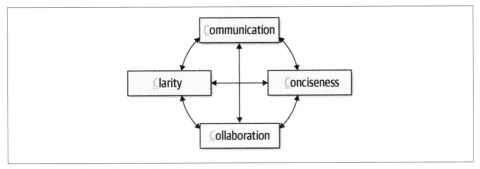

Figure 23-2. The 4 C's of architecture

As a leader, facilitator, and negotiator, is it vital that a software architect be able to effectively communicate in a clear and concise manner. It is equally important that an architect also be able to collaborate with developers, business stakeholders, and other architects to discuss and form solutions together. Focusing on the 4 C's of architecture helps an architect gain the respect of the team and become the go-to person on the project that everyone comes to not only for questions, but also for advice, mentoring, coaching, and leadership.

Be Pragmatic, Yet Visionary

An effective software architect must be pragmatic, yet visionary. Doing this is not as easy as it sounds and takes a fairly high level of maturity and significant practice to accomplish. To better understand this statement, consider the definition of a visionary:

Visionary
> Thinking about or planning the future with imagination or wisdom.

Being a visionary means applying strategic thinking to a problem, which is exactly what an architect is supposed to do. Architecture is about planning for the future and making sure the architectural vitality (how valid an architecture is) remains that way for a long time. However, too many times, architects become too theoretical in their planning and designs, creating solutions that become too difficult to understand or even implement. Now consider the definition of being pragmatic:

Pragmatic
> Dealing with things sensibly and realistically in a way that is based on practical rather than theoretical considerations.

While architects need to be visionaries, they also need to apply practical and realistic solutions. Being pragmatic is taking all of the following factors and constraints into account when creating an architectural solution:

- Budget constraints and other cost-based factors
- Time constraints and other time-based factors
- Skill set and skill level of the development team
- Trade-offs and implications associated with an architecture decision
- Technical limitations of a proposed architectural design or solution

A good software architect is one that strives to find an appropriate balance between being pragmatic while still applying imagination and wisdom to solving problems (see Figure 23-3). For example, consider the situation where an architect is faced with a difficult problem dealing with elasticity (unknown sudden and significant increases in concurrent user load). A visionary might come up with an elaborate way to deal with this through the use of a complex data mesh (*https://oreil.ly/6HmSp*), which is a collection of distributed, domain-based databases. In theory this might be a good approach, but being pragmatic means applying reason and practicality to the solution. For example, has the company ever used a data mesh before? What are the trade-offs of using a data mesh? Would this really solve the problem?

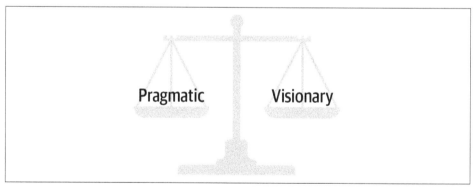

Figure 23-3. Good architects find the balance between being pragmatic, yet visionary

Maintaining a good balance between being pragmatic, yet visionary, is an excellent way of gaining respect as an architect. Business stakeholders will appreciate visionary solutions that fit within a set of constraints, and developers will appreciate having a practical (rather then theoretical) solution to implement.

A pragmatic architect would first look at what the limiting factor is when needing high levels of elasticity. Is it the database that's the bottleneck? Maybe it's a bottleneck with respect to some of the services invoked or other external sources needed. Finding and isolating the bottleneck would be a first practical approach to the problem. In fact, even if it is the database, could some of the data needed be cached so that the database need not be accessed at all?

Leading Teams by Example

Bad software architects leverage their title to get people to do what they want them to do. Effective software architects get people to do things by not leveraging their title as architect, but rather by leading through example, not by title. This is all about gaining the respect of development teams, business stakeholders, and other people throughout the organization (such as the head of operations, development managers, and product owners).

The classic "lead by example, not by title" story involves a captain and a sergeant during a military battle. The high-ranking captain, who is largely removed from the troops, commands all of the troops to move forward during the battle to take a particularly difficult hill. However, rather than listen to the high-ranking captain, the soldiers, full of doubt, look over to the lower-ranking sergeant for whether they should take the hill or not. The sergeant looks at the situation, nods his head slightly, and the soldiers immediately move forward with confidence to take the hill.

The moral of this story is that rank and title mean very little when it comes to leading people. The computer scientist Gerald Weinberg (*https://oreil.ly/6fI2m*) is famous for saying, "No matter what the problem is, it's a people problem." Most people think that solving technical issues has nothing to do with people skills—it has to do with *technical knowledge*. While having technical knowledge is certainly necessary for solving a problem, it's only a part of the overall equation for solving any problem. Suppose, for example, an architect is holding a meeting with a team of developers to solve an issue that's come up in production. One of the developers makes a suggestion, and the architect responds with, "Well, *that's* a dumb idea." Not only will that developer not make any more suggestions, but none of the other developers will dare say anything. The architect in this case has effectively shut down the entire team from collaborating on the solution.

Gaining respect and leading teams is about basic people skills. Consider the following dialogue between an architect and a customer, client, or development team with regard to a performance issue in the application:

> **Developer**: "So how are we going to solve this performance problem?"
> **Architect**: "What you need to do is use a cache. That would fix the problem."
> **Developer**: "Don't tell me what to do."
> **Architect**: "What I'm telling you is that it would fix the problem."

By using the words "what you need to do is…" or "you must," the architect is forcing their opinion onto the developer and essentially shutting down collaboration. This is a good example of using communication, not collaboration. Now consider the revised dialogue:

Developer: "So how are we going to solve this performance problem?"
Architect: "Have you considered using a cache? That might fix the problem."
Developer: "Hmmm, no we didn't think about that. What are your thoughts?"
Architect: "Well, if we put a cache here…"

Notice the use of the words "have you considered…" or "what about…" in the dialogue. By asking the question, it puts control back on the developer or client, creating a collaborative conversation where both the architect and developer are working together to form a solution. The use of grammar is vitally important when trying to build a collaborative environment. Being a leader as an architect is not only being able to collaborate with others to create an architecture, but also to help promote collaboration among the team by acting as a facilitator. As an architect, try to observe team dynamics and notice when situations like the first dialogue occurs. By taking team members aside and coaching them on the use of grammar as a means of collaboration, not only will this create better team dynamics, but it will also help create respect among the team members.

Another basic people skills technique that can help build respect and healthy relationships between an architect and the development team is to always try to use the person's name during a conversation or negotiation. Not only do people like hearing their name during a conversation, it also helps breed familiarity. Practice remembering people's names, and use them frequently. Given that names are sometimes hard to pronounce, make sure to get the pronunciation correct, then practice that pronunciation until it is perfect. Whenever we ask someone's name, we repeat it to the person and ask if that's the correct way to pronounce it. If it's not correct, we repeat this process until we get it right.

If an architect meets someone for the first time or only occasionally, always shake the person's hand and make eye contact. A handshake is an important people skill that goes back to medieval times. The physical bond that occurs during a simple handshake lets both people know they are friends, not foes, and forms a bond between them. However, it is sometimes hard to get a simple handshake right.

When shaking someone's hand, give a firm (but not overpowering) handshake while looking the person in the eye. Looking away while shaking someone's hand is a sign of disrespect, and most people will notice that. Also, don't hold on to the handshake too long. A simple two- to three-second, firm handshake is all that is needed to start off a conversation or to greet someone. There is also the issue of going overboard with the handshake technique and making the other person uncomfortable enough to not want to communicate or collaborate with you. For example, imagine a software architect who comes in every morning and starts shaking everyone's hand. Not only is this a little weird, it creates an uncomfortable situation. However, imagine a software architect who must meet with the head of operations monthly. This is the perfect opportunity to stand up, say "Hello Ruth, nice seeing you again," and give a quick, firm handshake. Knowing when to do a handshake and when not to is part of the complex art of people skills.

A software architect as a leader, facilitator, and negotiator should be careful to preserve the boundaries that exist between people at all levels. The handshake, as described previously, is an effective and professional technique of forming a physical bond with the person you are communicating or collaborating with. However, while a handshake is good, a hug in a professional setting, regardless of the environment, is not. An architect might think that it exemplifies more physical connection and bonding, but all it does is sometimes make the other person at work more uncomfortable and, more importantly, can lead to potential harassment issues within the workplace. Skip the hugs all together, regardless of the professional environment, and stick with the handshake instead (unless of course everyone in the company hugs each other, which would just be…weird).

Sometimes it's best to turn a request into a favor as a way of getting someone to do something they otherwise might not want to do. In general, people do not like to be told what to do, but for the most part, people want to help others. This is basic human nature. Consider the following conversation between an architect and developer regarding an architecture refactoring effort during a busy iteration:

> **Architect**: "I'm going to need you to split the payment service into five different services, with each service containing the functionality for each type of payment we accept, such as store credit, credit card, PayPal, gift card, and reward points, to provide better fault tolerance and scalability in the website. It shouldn't take too long."
> **Developer**: "No way, man. Way too busy this iteration for that. Sorry, can't do it."
> **Architect**: "Listen, this is important and needs to be done this iteration."
> **Developer**: "Sorry, no can do. Maybe one of the other developers can do it. I'm just too busy."

Notice the developer's response. It is an immediate rejection of the task, even though the architect justified it through better fault tolerance and scalability. In this case, notice that the architect is *telling* the developer to do something they are simply too busy to do. Also notice the demand doesn't even include the person's name! Now consider the technique of turning the request into a favor:

> **Architect**: "Hi, Sridhar. Listen, I'm in a real bind. I really need to have the payment service split into separate services for each payment type to get better fault tolerance and scalability, and I waited too long to do it. Is there any way you can squeeze this into this iteration? It would really help me out."
> **Developer**: "(Pause)…I'm really busy this iteration, but I guess so. I'll see what I can do."
> **Architect**: "Thanks, Sridhar, I really appreciate the help. I owe you one."
> **Developer**: "No worries, I'll see that it gets done this iteration."

First, notice the use of the person's name repeatedly throughout the conversation. Using the person's name makes the conversation more of a personal, familiar nature rather than an impersonal professional demand. Second, notice the architect admits they are in a "real bind" and that splitting the services would really "help them out a lot." This technique does not always work, but playing off of basic human nature of helping each other has a better probability of success over the first conversation. Try this technique the next time you face this sort of situation and see the results. In most cases, the results will be much more positive than telling someone what to do.

To lead a team and become an effective leader, a software architect should try to become the go-to person on the team—the person developers go to for their questions and problems. An effective software architect will seize the opportunity and take the initiative to lead the team, regardless of their title or role on the team. When a software architect observes someone struggling with a technical issue, they should step in and offer help or guidance. The same is true for nontechnical situations as well. Suppose an architect observes a team member that comes into work looking sort of depressed and bothered—clearly something is up. In this circumstance, an effective software architect would notice the situation and offer to talk—something like, "Hey, Antonio, I'm heading over to get some coffee. Why don't we head over together?" and then during the walk ask if everything is OK. This at least provides an opening for more of a personal discussion; and at it's best, a chance to mentor and coach at a more personal level. However, an effective leader will also recognize times to not be too pushy and will back off by reading various verbal signs and facial expressions.

Another technique to start gaining respect as a leader and become the go-to person on the team is to host periodic brown-bag lunches to talk about a specific technique or technology. Everyone reading this book has a particular skill or knowledge that others don't have. By hosting a periodic brown-bag lunch session, the architect not only is able to exhibit their technical prowess, but also practice speaking skills and mentoring skills. For example, host a lunch session on a review of design patterns or the latest features of the programming language release. Not only does this provide valuable information to developers, but it also starts identifying you as a leader and mentor on the team.

Integrating with the Development Team

An architect's calendar is usually filled with meetings, with most of those meetings overlapping with other meetings, such as the calendar shown in Figure 23-4. If this is what a software architect's calendar looks like, then when does the architect have the time to integrate with the development team, help guide and mentor them, and be available for questions or concerns when they come up? Unfortunately, meetings are a necessary evil within the information technology world. They happen frequently, and will always happen.

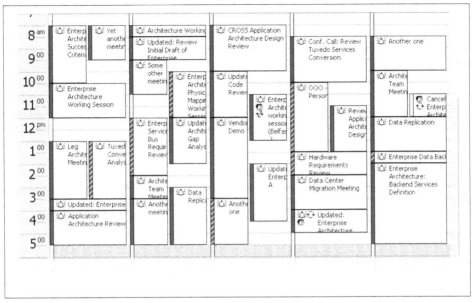

Figure 23-4. A typical calendar of a software architect

The key to being an effective software architect is making more time for the development team, and this means controlling meetings. There are two types of meetings an architect can be involved in: those imposed upon (the architect is invited to a meeting), and those imposed by (the architect is calling the meeting). These meeting types are illustrated in Figure 23-5.

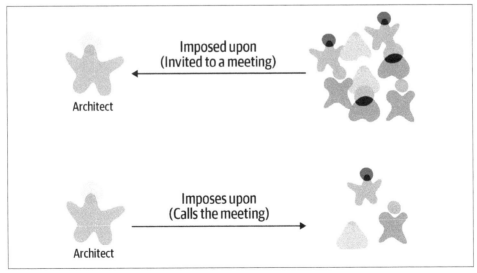

Figure 23-5. Meeting types

Imposed upon meetings are the hardest to control. Due to the number of stakeholders a software architect must communicate and collaborate with, architects are invited to almost every meeting that gets scheduled. When invited to a meeting, an effective software architect should always ask the meeting organizer why they are needed in that meeting. Many times architects get invited to meetings simply to keep them in the loop on the information being discussed. That's what meeting notes are for. By asking why, an architect can start to qualify which meetings they should attend and which ones they can skip. Another related technique to help reduce the number of meetings an architect is involved in is to ask for the meeting agenda before accepting a meeting invite. The meeting organizer may feel that the architect is necessary, but by looking at the agenda, the architect can qualify whether they really need to be in the meeting or not. Also, many times it is not necessary to attend the entire meeting. By reviewing the agenda, an architect can optimize their time by either showing up when relevant information is being discussed or leaving after the relevant discussion is over. Don't waste time in a meeting if you can be spending that time working with the development team.

 Ask for the meeting agenda ahead of time to help qualify if you are really needed at the meeting or not.

Another effective technique to keep a development team on track and to gain their respect is to take one for the team when developers are invited to a meeting as well. Rather than having the tech lead attend the meeting, go in their place, particularly if both the tech lead and architect are invited to a meeting. This keeps a development team focused on the task at hand rather than continually attending meetings as well. While deflecting meetings away from useful team members increases the time an architect is in meetings, it does increase the development team's productivity.

Meetings that an architect imposes upon others (the architect calls the meeting) are also a necessity at times but should be kept to an absolute minimum. These are the kinds of meetings an architect has control over. An effective software architect will always ask whether the meeting they are calling is more important than the work they are pulling their team members away from. Many times an email is all that is required to communicate some important information, which saves everyone tons of wasted time. When calling a meeting as an architect, always set an agenda and stick to it. Too often, meetings an architect calls get derailed due to some other issue, and that other issue may not be relevant to everyone else in the meeting. Also, as an architect, pay close attention to developer flow and be sure not to disrupt it by calling a meeting. Flow is a state of mind developers frequently get into where the brain gets 100% engaged in a particular problem, allowing full attention and maximum creativity. For example, a developer might be working on a particularly difficult algorithm or piece of code, and literally hours go by while it seems only minutes have passed. When calling a meeting, an architect should always try to schedule meetings either first thing in the morning, right after lunch, or toward the end of the day, but not during the day when most developers experience flow state.

Aside from managing meetings, another thing an effective software architect can do to integrate better with the development team is to sit with that team. Sitting in a cubicle away from the team sends the message that the architect is special, and those physical walls surrounding the cubicle are a distinct message that the architect is not to be bothered or disturbed. Sitting alongside a development team sends the message that the architect is an integral part of the team and is available for questions or concerns as they arise. By physically showing that they are part of the development team, the architect gains more respect and is better able to help guide and mentor the team.

Sometimes it is not possible for an architect to sit with a development team. In these cases the best thing an architect can do is continually walk around and be seen. Architects that are stuck on a different floor or always in their offices or cubicles and never seen cannot possibly help guide the development team through the implementation of the architecture. Block off time in the morning, after lunch, or late in the day and make the time to converse with the development team, help with issues, answer questions, and do basic coaching and mentoring. Development teams appreciate this type of communication and will respect you for making time for them during the day. The same holds true for other stakeholders. Stopping in to say hi to the head of operations while on the way to get more coffee is an excellent way of keeping communication open and available with business and other key stakeholders.

Summary

The negotiation and leadership tips presented and discussed in this chapter are meant to help the software architect form a better collaborative relationship with the development team and other stakeholders. These are necessary skills an architect must have in order to become an effective software architect. While the tips we presented in this chapter are good tips for starting the journey into becoming more of an effective leader, perhaps the best tip of all is from a quote from Theodore Roosevelt (*https://oreil.ly/dCN_t*), the 26th US president:

> The most important single ingredient in the formula of success is knowing how to get along with people.
>
> —Theodore Roosevelt

CHAPTER 24

Developing a Career Path

Becoming an architect takes time and effort, but based on the many reasons we've outlined throughout this book, managing a career path after becoming an architect is equally tricky. While we can't chart a specific career path for you, we can point you to some practices that we have seen work well.

An architect must continue to learn throughout their career. The technology world changes at a dizzying pace. One of Neal's former coworkers was a world-renowned expert in Clipper. He lamented that he couldn't take the enormous body of (now useless) Clipper knowledge and replace it with something else. He also speculated (and this is still an open question): has any group in history learned and thrown away so much detailed knowledge within their lifetimes as software developers?

Each architect should keep an eye out for relevant resources, both technology and business, and add them to their personal stockpile. Unfortunately, resources come and go all too quickly, which is why we don't list any in this book. Talking to colleagues or experts about what resources they use to keep current is one good way of seeking out the latest newsfeeds, websites, and groups that are active in a particular area of interest. Architects should also build into their day some time to maintain breadth utilizing those resources.

The 20-Minute Rule

As illustrated in Figure 2-6, technology breadth is more important to architects than depth. However, maintaining breadth takes time and effort, something architects should build into their day. But how in the world does anyone have the time to actually go to various websites to read articles, watch presentations, and listen to podcasts? The answer is…not many do. Developers and architects alike struggle with the balance of working a regular job, spending time with the family, being available for our children, carving out personal time for interests and hobbies, and trying to develop careers, while at the same time trying to keep up with the latest trends and buzzwords.

One technique we use to maintain this balance is something we call the *20-minute rule*. The idea of this technique, as illustrated in Figure 24-1, is to devote *at least* 20 minutes a day to your career as an architect by learning something new or diving deeper into a specific topic. Figure 24-1 illustrates examples of some of the types of resources to spend 20 minutes a day on, such as InfoQ (*https://www.infoq.com*), DZone Refcardz (*https://dzone.com/refcardz*), and the ThoughtWorks Technology Radar (*https://www.thoughtworks.com/radar*). Spend that minimum of 20 minutes to Google some unfamiliar buzzwords ("the things you don't know you don't know" from Chapter 2) to learn a little about them, promoting that knowledge into the "things you know you don't know." Or maybe spend the 20 minutes going deeper into a particular topic to gain a little more knowledge about it. The point of this technique is to be able to carve out some time for developing a career as an architect and continuously gaining technical breadth.

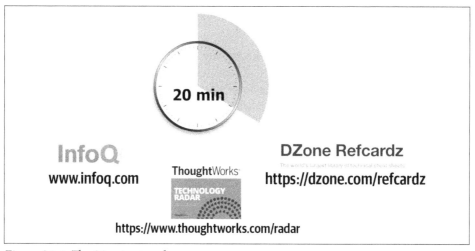

Figure 24-1. The 20-minute rule

Many architects embrace this concept and plan to spend 20 minutes at lunch or in the evening after work to do this. What we have experienced is that this rarely works. Lunchtime gets shorter and shorter, becoming more of a catch-up time at work rather than a time to take a break and eat. Evenings are even worse—situations change, plans get made, family time becomes more important, and the 20-minute rule never happens.

We strongly recommend leveraging the 20-minute rule first thing in the morning, as the day is starting. However, there is a caveat to this advice as well. For example, what is the first thing an architect does after getting to work in the morning? Well, the very first thing the architect does is to get that wonderful cup of coffee or tea. OK, in that case, what is the second thing every architect does after getting that necessary coffee or tea—check email. Once an architect checks email, diversion happens, email responses are written, and the day is over. Therefore, our strong recommendation is to invoke the 20-minute rule first thing in the morning, right after grabbing that cup of coffee or tea and before checking email. Go in to work a little early. Doing this will increase an architect's technical breadth and help develop the knowledge required to become an effective software architect.

Developing a Personal Radar

For most of the '90s and the beginning of the '00s, Neal was the CTO of a small training and consulting company. When he started there, the primary platform was Clipper, which was a rapid-application development tool for building DOS applications atop dBASE files. Until one day it vanished. The company had noticed the rise of Windows, but the business market was still DOS…until it abruptly wasn't. That lesson left a lasting impression: ignore the march of technology at your peril.

It also taught an important lesson about technology bubbles. When heavily invested in a technology, a developer lives in a memetic bubble, which also serves as an echo chamber. Bubbles created by vendors are particularly dangerous, because developers never hear honest appraisals from within the bubble. But the biggest danger of Bubble Living comes when it starts collapsing, which developers never notice from the inside until it's too late.

What they lacked was a technology radar: a living document to assess the risks and rewards of existing and nascent technologies. The radar concept comes from ThoughtWorks; first, we'll describe how this concept came to be and then how to use it to create a personal radar.

The ThoughtWorks Technology Radar

The ThoughtWorks Technology Advisory Board (TAB) is a group of senior technology leaders within ThoughtWorks, created to assist the CTO, Dr. Rebecca Parsons, in deciding technology directions and strategies for the company and its clients. This group meets face-to-face twice a year. One of the outcomes of the face to face meeting was the Technology Radar. Over time, it gradually grew into the biannual Technology Radar (*https://www.thoughtworks.com/radar*).

The TAB gradually settled into a twice-a-year rhythm of Radar production. Then, as often happens, unexpected side effects occurred. At some of the conferences Neal spoke at, attendees sought him out and thanked him for helping produce the Radar and said that their company had started producing their own version of it.

Neal also realized that this was the answer to a pervasive question at conference speaker panels everywhere: "How do you (the speakers) keep up with technology? How do you figure out what things to pursue next?" The answer, of course, is that they all have some form of internal radar.

Parts

The ThoughtWorks Radar consists of four quadrants that attempt to cover most of the software development landscape:

Tools
> Tools in the software development space, everything from developers tools like IDEs to enterprise-grade integration tools

Languages and frameworks
> Computer languages, libraries, and frameworks, typically open source

Techniques
> Any practice that assists software development overall; this may include software development processes, engineering practices, and advice

Platforms
> Technology platforms, including databases, cloud vendors, and operating systems

Rings

The Radar has four rings, listed here from outer to inner:

Hold
> The original intent of the hold ring was "hold off for now," to represent technologies that were too new to reasonably assess yet—technologies that were getting lots of buzz but weren't yet proven. The hold ring has evolved into indicating "don't start anything new with this technology." There's no harm in using it on existing projects, but developers should think twice about using it for new development.

Assess
> The assess ring indicates that a technology is worth exploring with the goal of understanding how it will affect an organization. Architects should invest some effort (such as development spikes, research projects, and conference sessions) to see if it will have an impact on the organization. For example, many large companies visibly went through this phase when formulating a mobile strategy.

Trial

The trial ring is for technologies worth pursuing; it is important to understand how to build up this capability. Now is the time to pilot a low-risk project so that architects and developers can really understand the technology.

Adopt

For technologies in the adopt ring, ThoughtWorks feels strongly that the industry should adopt those items.

An example view of the Radar appears in Figure 24-2.

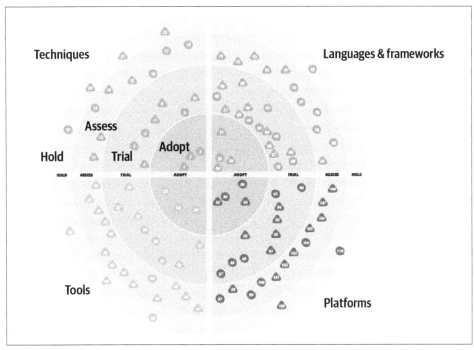

Figure 24-2. A sample ThoughtWorks Technology Radar

In Figure 24-2, each blip represents a different technology or technique, with associated short write-ups. While ThoughtWorks uses the radar to broadcast their opinions about the software world, many developers and architects also use it as a way of structuring their technology assessment process. Architects can use the tool described in "Open Source Visualization Bits" on page 371 to build the same visuals used by ThoughtWorks as a way to organize their thinking about what to invest time in.

When using the radar for personal use, we suggest altering the meanings of the quadrants to the following:

Hold

An architect can include not only technologies and techniques to avoid, but also habits they are trying to break. For example, an architect from the .NET world may be accustomed to reading the latest news/gossip on forums about team internals. While entertaining, it may be a low-value information stream. Placing that in hold forms a reminder for an architect to avoid problematic things.

Assess

Architects should use *assess* for promising technologies that they have heard good things about but haven't had time to assess for themselves yet—see "Using Social Media" on page 371. This ring forms a staging area for more serious research at some time in the future.

Trial

The *trial* ring indicates active research and development, such as an architect performing spike experiments within a larger code base. This ring represents technologies worth spending time on to understand more deeply so that an architect can perform an effective trade-off analysis.

Adopt

The *adopt* ring represents the new things an architect is most excited about and best practices for solving particular problems.

It is dangerous to adopt a laissez-faire attitude toward a technology portfolio. Most technologists pick technologies on a more or less ad hoc basis, based on what's cool or what your employer is driving. Creating a technology radar helps an architect formalize their thinking about technology and balance opposing decision criteria (such as the "more cool" technology factor and being less likely to get a new job versus a huge job market but with less interesting work). Architects should treat their technology portfolio like a financial portfolio: in many ways, they are the same thing. What does a financial planner tell people about their portfolio? Diversify!

Architects should choose some technologies and/or skills that are widely in demand and track that demand. But they might also want to try some technology gambits, like open source or mobile development. Anecdotes abound about developers who freed themselves from cubicle-dwelling servitude by working late at night on open source projects that became popular, purchasable, and eventually, career destinations. This is yet another reason to focus on breadth rather than depth.

Architects should set aside time to broaden their technology portfolio, and building a radar provides a good scaffolding. However, the exercise is more important than the outcome. Creating the visualization provides an excuse to think about these things, and, for busy architects, finding an excuse to carve out time in a busy schedule is the only way this kind of thinking can occur.

Open Source Visualization Bits

By popular demand, ThoughtWorks released a tool in November 2016 to assist technologists in building their own radar visualization. When ThoughtWorks does this exercise for companies, they capture the output of the meeting in a spreadsheet, with a page for each quadrant. The ThoughtWorks Build Your Own Radar tool uses a Google spreadsheet as input and generates the radar visualization using an HTML 5 canvas. Thus, while the important part of the exercise is the conversations it generates, it also generates useful visualizations.

Using Social Media

Where can an architect find new technologies and techniques to put in the assess ring of their radar? In Andrew McAfee's book *Enterprise 2.0* (Harvard Business Review Press), he makes an interesting observation about social media and social networks in general. When thinking about a person's network of contact between people, three categories exist, as illustrated in Figure 24-3.

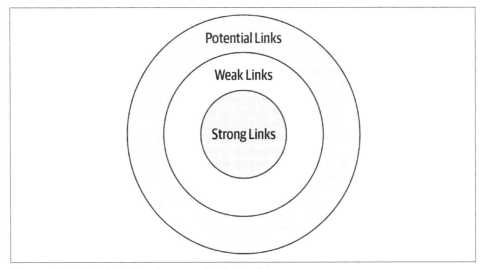

Figure 24-3. Social circles of a person's relationships

In Figure 24-3, *strong links* represent family members, coworkers, and other people whom a person regularly contacts. One litmus test for how close these connections are: they can tell you what a person in their strong links had for lunch at least one day last week. *Weak links* are casual acquaintances, distant relatives, and other people seen only a few times a year. Before social media, it was difficult to keep up with this circle of people. Finally, *potential links* represent people you haven't met yet.

McAfee's most interesting observation about these connections was that someone's next job is more likely to come from a weak link than a strong one. Strongly linked people know everything within the strongly linked group—these are people who see each other all the time. Weak links, on the other hand, offer advice from outside someone's normal experience, including new job offers.

Using the characteristics of social networks, architects can utilize social media to enhance their technical breadth. Using social media like Twitter professionally, architects should find technologists whose advice they respect and follow them on social media. This allows an architect to build a network on new, interesting technologies to assess and keep up with the rapid changes in the technology world.

Parting Words of Advice

> How do we get great designers? Great designers design, of course.
>
> > —Fred Brooks

> So how are we supposed to get great architects, if they only get the chance to architect fewer than a half-dozen times in their career?
>
> > —Ted Neward

Practice is the proven way to build skills and become better at anything in life… including architecture. We encourage new and existing architects to keep honing their skills, both for individual technology breadth but also for the craft of designing architecture. To that end, check out the architecture katas (*https://oreil.ly/EPop7*) on the companion website for the book. Modeled after the katas used as examples here, we encourage architects to use these to practice building skills in architecture.

A common question we get about katas: is there an answer guide somewhere? Unfortunately such an answer key does not exist. To quote your author, Neal:

> There are not right or wrong answers in architecture—only *trade-offs*.

When we started using the architecture katas exercise during live training classes, we initially kept the drawings the students produced with the goal of creating an answer repository. We quickly gave up, though, because we realized that we had incomplete artifacts. In other words, the teams had captured the topology and explained their decisions in class but didn't have the time to create architecture decision records. While how they implemented their solutions was interesting, the why was much more interesting because it contains the trade-offs they considered in making that decision. Keeping just the how was only half of the story. So, our last parting words of advice: always learn, always practice, and *go do some architecture*!

Self-Assessment Questions

Chapter 1: Introduction

1. What are the four dimensions that define software architecture?

2. What is the difference between an architecture decision and a design principle?

3. List the eight core expectations of a software architect.

4. What is the First Law of Software Architecture?

Chapter 2: Architectural Thinking

1. Describe the traditional approach of architecture versus development and explain why that approach no longer works.

2. List the three levels of knowledge in the knowledge triangle and provide an example of each.

3. Why is it more important for an architect to focus on technical breadth rather than technical depth?

4. What are some of the ways of maintaining your technical depth and remaining hands-on as an architect?

Chapter 3: Modularity

1. What is meant by the term *connascence*?
2. What is the difference between static and dynamic connascence?
3. What does *connascence of type* mean? Is it static or dynamic connascence?
4. What is the strongest form of connascence?
5. What is the weakest form of connascence?
6. Which is preferred within a code base—static or dynamic connascence?

Chapter 4: Architecture Characteristics Defined

1. What three criteria must an attribute meet to be considered an architecture characteristic?
2. What is the difference between an implicit characteristic and an explicit one? Provide an example of each.
3. Provide an example of an operational characteristic.
4. Provide an example of a structural characteristic.
5. Provide an example of a cross-cutting characteristic.
6. Which architecture characteristic is more important to strive for—availability or performance?

Chapter 5: Identifying Architecture Characteristics

1. Give a reason why it is a good practice to limit the number of characteristics ("-ilities") an architecture should support.
2. True or false: most architecture characteristics come from business requirements and user stories.
3. If a business stakeholder states that time-to-market (i.e., getting new features and bug fixes pushed out to users as fast as possible) is the most important business concern, which architecture characteristics would the architecture need to support?
4. What is the difference between scalability and elasticity?
5. You find out that your company is about to undergo several major acquisitions to significantly increase its customer base. Which architectural characteristics should you be worried about?

Chapter 6: Measuring and Governing Architecture Characteristics

1. Why is cyclomatic complexity such an important metric to analyze for architecture?

2. What is an architecture fitness function? How can they be used to analyze an architecture?

3. Provide an example of an architecture fitness function to measure the scalability of an architecture.

4. What is the most important criteria for an architecture characteristic to allow architects and developers to create fitness functions?

Chapter 7: Scope of Architecture Characteristics

1. What is an architectural quantum, and why is it important to architecture?

2. Assume a system consisting of a single user interface with four independently deployed services, each containing its own separate database. Would this system have a single quantum or four quanta? Why?

3. Assume a system with an administration portion managing static reference data (such as the product catalog, and warehouse information) and a customer-facing portion managing the placement of orders. How many quanta should this system be and why? If you envision multiple quanta, could the admin quantum and customer-facing quantum share a database? If so, in which quantum would the database need to reside?

Chapter 8: Component-Based Thinking

1. We define the term *component* as a building block of an application—something the application does. A component usually consist of a group of classes or source files. How are components typically manifested within an application or service?

2. What is the difference between technical partitioning and domain partitioning? Provide an example of each.

3. What is the advantage of domain partitioning?

4. Under what circumstances would technical partitioning be a better choice over domain partitioning?

5. What is the entity trap? Why is it not a good approach for component identification?

6. When might you choose the workflow approach over the Actor/Actions approach when identifying core components?

Chapter 9: Architecture Styles

1. List the eight fallacies of distributed computing.

2. Name three challenges that distributed architectures have that monolithic architectures don't.

3. What is stamp coupling?

4. What are some ways of addressing stamp coupling?

Chapter 10: Layered Architecture Style

1. What is the difference between an open layer and a closed layer?

2. Describe the layers of isolation concept and what the benefits are of this concept.

3. What is the architecture sinkhole anti-pattern?

4. What are some of the main architecture characteristics that would drive you to use a layered architecture?

5. Why isn't testability well supported in the layered architecture style?

6. Why isn't agility well supported in the layered architecture style?

Chapter 11: Pipeline Architecture

1. Can pipes be bidirectional in a pipeline architecture?

2. Name the four types of filters and their purpose.

3. Can a filter send data out through multiple pipes?

4. Is the pipeline architecture style technically partitioned or domain partitioned?

5. In what way does the pipeline architecture support modularity?

6. Provide two examples of the pipeline architecture style.

Chapter 12: Microkernel Architecture

1. What is another name for the microkernel architecture style?

2. Under what situations is it OK for plug-in components to be dependent on other plug-in components?

3. What are some of the tools and frameworks that can be used to manage plug-ins?

4. What would you do if you had a third-party plug-in that didn't conform to the standard plug-in contract in the core system?

5. Provide two examples of the microkernel architecture style.

6. Is the microkernel architecture style technically partitioned or domain partitioned?

7. Why is the microkernel architecture always a single architecture quantum?

8. What is domain/architecture isomorphism?

Chapter 13: Service-Based Architecture

1. How many services are there in a typical service-based architecture?

2. Do you have to break apart a database in service-based architecture?

3. Under what circumstances might you want to break apart a database?

4. What technique can you use to manage database changes within a service-based architecture?

5. Do domain services require a container (such as Docker) to run?

6. Which architecture characteristics are well supported by the service-based architecture style?

7. Why isn't elasticity well supported in a service-based architecture?

8. How can you increase the number of architecture quanta in a service-based architecture?

Chapter 14: Event-Driven Architecture Style

1. What are the primary differences between the broker and mediator topologies?

2. For better workflow control, would you use the mediator or broker topology?

3. Does the broker topology usually leverage a publish-and-subscribe model with topics or a point-to-point model with queues?

4. Name two primary advantage of asynchronous communications.

5. Give an example of a typical request within the request-based model.

6. Give an example of a typical request in an event-based model.

7. What is the difference between an initiating event and a processing event in event-driven architecture?

8. What are some of the techniques for preventing data loss when sending and receiving messages from a queue?

9. What are three main driving architecture characteristics for using event-driven architecture?

10. What are some of the architecture characteristics that are not well supported in event-driven architecture?

Chapter 15: Space-Based Architecture

1. Where does space-based architecture get its name from?

2. What is a primary aspect of space-based architecture that differentiates it from other architecture styles?

3. Name the four components that make up the virtualized middleware within a space-based architecture.

4. What is the role of the messaging grid?

5. What is the role of a data writer in space-based architecture?

6. Under what conditions would a service need to access data through the data reader?

7. Does a small cache size increase or decrease the chances for a data collision?

8. What is the difference between a replicated cache and a distributed cache? Which one is typically used in space-based architecture?

9. List three of the most strongly supported architecture characteristics in space-based architecture.

10. Why does testability rate so low for space-based architecture?

Chapter 16: Orchestration-Driven Service-Oriented Architecture

1. What was the main driving force behind service-oriented architecture?

2. What are the four primary service types within a service-oriented architecture?

3. List some of the factors that led to the downfall of service-oriented architecture.

4. Is service-oriented architecture technically partitioned or domain partitioned?

5. How is domain reuse addressed in SOA? How is operational reuse addressed?

Chapter 17: Microservices Architecture

1. Why is the bounded context concept so critical for microservices architecture?

2. What are three ways of determining if you have the right level of granularity in a microservice?

3. What functionality might be contained within a sidecar?

4. What is the difference between orchestration and choreography? Which does microservices support? Is one communication style easier in microservices?

5. What is a saga in microservices?

6. Why are agility, testability, and deployability so well supported in microservices?

7. What are two reasons performance is usually an issue in microservices?

8. Is microservices a domain-partitioned architecture or a technically partitioned one?

9. Describe a topology where a microservices ecosystem might be only a single quantum.

10. How was domain reuse addressed in microservices? How was operational reuse addressed?

Chapter 18: Choosing the Appropriate Architecture Style

1. In what way does the data architecture (structure of the logical and physical data models) influence the choice of architecture style?

2. How does it influence your choice of architecture style to use?

3. Delineate the steps an architect uses to determine style of architecture, data partitioning, and communication styles.

4. What factor leads an architect toward a distributed architecture?

Chapter 19: Architecture Decisions

1. What is the covering your assets anti-pattern?

2. What are some techniques for avoiding the email-driven architecture anti-pattern?

3. What are the five factors Michael Nygard defines for identifying something as architecturally significant?

4. What are the five basic sections of an architecture decision record?

5. In which section of an ADR do you typically add the justification for an architecture decision?

6. Assuming you don't need a separate Alternatives section, in which section of an ADR would you list the alternatives to your proposed solution?

7. What are three basic criteria in which you would mark the status of an ADR as Proposed?

Chapter 20: Analyzing Architecture Risk

1. What are the two dimensions of the risk assessment matrix?

2. What are some ways to show direction of particular risk within a risk assessment? Can you think of other ways to indicate whether risk is getting better or worse?

3. Why is it necessary for risk storming to be a collaborative exercise?

4. Why is it necessary for the identification activity within risk storming to be an individual activity and not a collaborative one?

5. What would you do if three participants identified risk as high (6) for a particular area of the architecture, but another participant identified it as only medium (3)?

6. What risk rating (1-9) would you assign to unproven or unknown technologies?

Chapter 21: Diagramming and Presenting Architecture

1. What is irrational artifact attachment, and why is it significant with respect to documenting and diagramming architecture?

2. What do the 4 C's refer to in the C4 modeling technique?

3. When diagramming architecture, what do dotted lines between components mean?

4. What is the bullet-riddled corpse anti-pattern? How can you avoid this anti-pattern when creating presentations?

5. What are the two primary information channels a presenter has when giving a presentation?

Chapter 22: Making Teams Effective

1. What are three types of architecture personalities? What type of boundary does each personality create?

2. What are the five factors that go into determining the level of control you should exhibit on the team?

3. What are three warning signs you can look at to determine if your team is getting too big?

4. List three basic checklists that would be good for a development team.

Chapter 23: Negotiation and Leadership Skills

1. Why is negotiation so important as an architect?

2. Name some negotiation techniques when a business stakeholder insists on five nines of availability, but only three nines are really needed.

3. What can you derive from a business stakeholder telling you "I needed it yesterday"?

4. Why is it important to save a discussion about time and cost for last in a negotiation?

5. What is the divide-and-conquer rule? How can it be applied when negotiating architecture characteristics with a business stakeholder? Provide an example.

6. List the 4 C's of architecture.

7. Explain why it is important for an architect to be both pragmatic and visionary.

8. What are some techniques for managing and reducing the number of meetings you are invited to?

Chapter 24: Developing a Career Path

1. What is the 20-minute rule, and when is it best to apply it?

2. What are the four rings in the ThoughtWorks technology radar, and what do they mean? How can they be applied to your radar?

3. Describe the difference between depth and breadth of knowledge as it applies to software architects. Which should architects aspire to maximize?

Index

A

acceleration of rate of change in software development ecosystem, 268
accessibility, 59
accidental architecture anti-pattern, 133
accidental complexity, 354
accountability, 61
achievability, 60
ACID transactions, 132
    in service-based architecture, 177
    in services of service-based architecture, 168
actions provided by presention tools, 321
actor/actions approach to designing components, 111
    in Going, Going, Gone case study, 112
actual productivity (of development teams), 335
adaptability, 62
administrators (network), 129
ADR-tools, 285
ADRs (architecture decision records), 285-295
    as documentation, 293
    auction system example, 294
    basic structure of, 285
    compliance section, 290
    context section, 288
    decision section, 288
    draft ADR, request for comments on, 287
    notes section, 291
    status, 286
    storing, 291
    title, 286
    using for standards, 293
Agile development

Agile Story risk analysis, 308
    creation of just-in-time artifacts, 317
    extreme programming and, 15
    software architecture and, 18, 101
agility
    process measures of, 81
    rating in service-based architecture, 176
    versus time to market, 67
Ambulance pattern, 312
analyzability, 62
animations provided by presentation tools, 321
anti-patterns
    Big Ball of Mud, 85, 120
    Bullet-Riddled Corpse in corporate presentations, 322
    Cookie-Cutter, 321
    Covering Your Assets, 282
    Email-Driven Architecture, 283
    Entity Trap, 110
    Frozen Caveman, 30
    Generic Architecture, 65
    Groundhog Day, 282
    Irrational Artifact Attachment, 316
    Ivory Tower Architect, 74, 351
anvils dropping effects, 321
Apache Camel, 186
Apache Ignite, 213
Apache Kafka, 146
Apache ODE, 187
Apache Zookeeper, 157
API layer
    in microservices architecture, 249
    in service-based architecture, 167

calculating, 79
good value for, 81
removal from core system of microkernel architecture, 150

D

data
deciding where it should live, 270
preventing data loss in event-driven architecture, 201-203
software architecture and, 19
data abstraction layer, 223
data access layer, 223
data collisions, 224-226
cache size and, 226
formula to calculate probable number of, 224
number of processing unit instances and, 226
data grid, 215
data isolation in microservices, 249
data meshes, 356
"Data Monolith to Data Mesh" article (Fowler), 356
data pumps, 213, 219
data reader with reverse data pump, 223
in domain-based data writers, 221
data readers, 213, 222
data writers, 213, 221
database entities, user interface frontend built on, 111
Database Output transformer filter, 146
database server, desktop and, 122
databases
ACID transactions in services of service-based architecture, 168
component-relational mapping of framework to, 111
data pump sending data to in space-based architecture, 220
licensing of database servers, problems with, 235
in microkernel architecture core system, 151
in microkernel architecture plug-ins, 156
in orchestration-driven service-oriented architecture, 242
partitioning in service-based architecture, 169-171

removing as synchronous constraint in space-based architecture, 212
scaling database server, problems with, 211
in service-based architecture, 164
transactions in service-based architecture, 177
variants in service-based architecture, 166
DDD (see domain-driven design)
demonstration defeats discussion, 350
dependencies
architecturally significant decisions impacting, 284
cyclic, modularity and, 84-86
timing, modules and, 41
deployability
low rating in layered architecture, 140
process measures of, 81
rating in microkernel architecture, 161
rating in orchestration-driven service-oriented architecture, 242
rating in pipeline architecture, 147
rating in service-based architecture, 176
deployment
automated deployment in microservices architecture, 263
deployment manager in space-based architecture, 219
physical topology variants in layered architecture, 134
design
architecture versus, 23
versus architecture and trade-offs, 74
understanding long-term implication of decisions on, 123
design principles in software architecture, 7
developer code completion checklist, 340
developer flow, 362
developers
drawn to complexity, 354
negotiating with, 351
role in components, 108
roles in layered architecture, 133
development process, separation from software architecture, 14, 101
development teams, making effective, 325-346
amount of control exerted by sotware architect, 331-335
leveraging checklists, 338-343
developer code completion checklist, 340

door or cube transitions, 321
driving characteristics, focus on, 65
duplication, favoring over reuse, 246
Duration Calculator transformer filter, 146
Duration filter, 146
dynamic connascence, 92
DZone Refcardz, 366

About the Authors

Mark Richards is an experienced hands-on software architect involved in the architecture, design, and implementation of microservices and other distributed architectures. He is the founder of *DeveloperToArchitect.com*, a website devoted to assisting developers in the journey from developer to a software architect.

Neal Ford is director, software architect, and meme wrangler at ThoughtWorks, a global IT consultancy with an exclusive focus on end-to-end software development and delivery. Before joining ThoughtWorks, Neal was the chief technology officer at The DSW Group, Ltd., a nationally recognized training and development firm.

Colophon

The animal on the cover of *Fundamentals of Software Engineering* is the red-fan parrot (*Deroptyus accipitrinus*), a native to South America where it is known by several names such as *loro cacique* in Spanish, or *anacã*, *papagaio-de-coleira*, and *vanaquiá* in Portugese. This New World bird makes its home up in the canopies and tree holes of the Amazon rainforest, where it feeds on the fruits of the *Cecropia* tree, aptly known as "snake fingers," as well as the hard fruits of various palm trees.

As the only member of the genus *Deroptyus*, the red-fan parrot is distinguished by the deep red feathers that cover its nape. Its name comes from the fact that those feathers will "fan" out when it feels excited or threatened and reveal the brilliant blue that highlights each tip. The head is topped by a white crown and yellow eyes, with brown cheeks that are streaked in white. The parrot's breast and belly are covered in the same red feathers dipped in blue, in contrast with the layered bright green feathers on its back.

Between December and January, the red-fan parrot will find its lifelong mate and then begin laying 2-4 eggs a year. During the 28 days in which the female is incubating the eggs, the male will provide her with care and support. After about 10 weeks, the young are ready to start fledging in the wild and begin their 40-year life span in the world's largest tropical rainforest.

While the red-fan parrot's current conservation status is designated as of Least Concern, many of the animals on O'Reilly covers are endangered; all of them are important to the world.

The cover illustration is by Karen Montgomery, based on a black and white engraving from *Lydekker's Royal Natural History*. The cover fonts are Gilroy Semibold and Guardian Sans. The text font is Adobe Minion Pro; the heading font is Adobe Myriad Condensed; and the code font is Dalton Maag's Ubuntu Mono.

O'REILLY®

There's much more where this came from.

Experience books, videos, live online training courses, and more from O'Reilly and our 200+ partners—all in one place.

Learn more at oreilly.com/online-learning

O'REILLY®

There's much more
where this came from.

Experience books, videos, live online
training courses, and more from O'Reilly
and our 200+ partners—all in one place.

Learn more at oreilly.com/online-learning

Milton Keynes UK
Ingram Content Group UK Ltd.
UKHW030044240823
427375UK00003B/5